John Stanley

GIVING LIFE TO LITTLE LULU

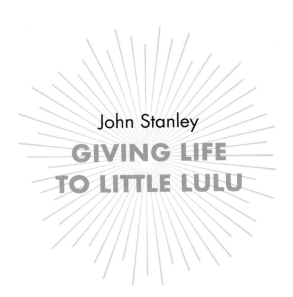

Executive Editor: Gary Groth
Editor: Kristy Valenti
Designer: Keeli McCarthy
Production: Preston White
Editorial assistance: RJ Casey, Reed Draper,
Sharon Frijlich, Mackenzie Pitcock
Associate Publisher: Eric Reynolds
Publisher: Gary Groth

Cover photo by E. B. Boatner

For the sake of simplicity, the comic book series officially titled *Marge's Little Lulu* and *Marge's Tubby* will generally be referred to as *Little Lulu* and *Tubby*. Another comic book title is officially Dell's *Single Series*, but fans and collectors refer to it as Dell's *Four Color*, which will be used throughout this book. *New Funnies*, which was retitled *Walter Lantz New Funnies* with issue #109, dated March 1946, is referred to as *New Funnies* throughout. Also, to avoid confusion among the three people named "James Stanley," John Stanley's father will consistently be referred to as James, his brother will be referred to as Jimmy, and his son will be referred to as Jim.

Fantagraphics Books
7563 Lake City Way NE
Seattle, Washington 98115

Fantagraphics.com

ISBN: 978-1-60699-990-5
Library of Congress Control Number: 2016947686
First Fantagraphics printing: March 2017

Printed in China

John Stanley

GIVING LIFE TO

Little Lulu

A BIOGRAPHY BY BILL SCHELLY

FANTAGRAPHICS BOOKS

Special thanks to Jim Stanley for permission to reprint or publish work by his father for the first time. I dedicate this book to him and to his children, Isabel and Adam.

Contents

"LITTLE LULU WAS ME. AND SO WAS TUBBY, AND SO WAS EVERYONE ELSE. EVERYTHING COMES FROM INSIDE YOURSELF. NOTHING COMES FROM OUTSIDE. NOTHING IMAGINATIVE. YOU DON'T LEARN ANYTHING BY OBSERVING PEOPLE. YOU HAVE TO KNOW YOURSELF."

—JOHN STANLEY

Author's Preface

MARJORIE HENDERSON BUELL ("Marge") created Little Lulu in a weekly, one-panel cartoon in the *Saturday Evening Post*, but John Stanley was the creative genius who gave Lulu a life in comic books that made her one of the best-selling, best-loved characters of all time.

Stanley's work on *Little Lulu*, from 1945 to 1959—he wrote more than 6,000 Lulu pages—ensured the moppet's immortality as an iconic figure in American popular culture. He developed or created all of Lulu's memorable supporting cast: Tubby, Alvin, Gloria, Witch Hazel, the Boys' Club and more.

Stanley is an important figure because of his ability to tell the truth about children in some of the funniest stories ever to appear in comics. His work is comparable to Charles Schulz's *Peanuts* in terms of quality, but is almost the exact opposite in its formulation. Schulz's comic strip grafts adult thoughts and behavior onto children. Stanley reveals children as they really are. That truth gives his work its great appeal, evoking a shock of recognition among readers as soon as they start reading.

His work made a big impression on some people who grew up to become giants of comics in their own right. Robert Crumb enthused, "*Little Lulu* had incredible stories. I still read those *Little Lulu* comics from the late '40s, early '50s, and they're great." Art

Spiegelman is also a fan. In his book *The TOON Treasury of Classic Children's Comics* (2009), which reprinted several stories by Stanley, he wrote, "John Stanley's character-driven tales of Little Lulu and Tubby . . . are at least as sophisticated as the Dark Knight and the X-Men—and a lot funnier."

Little Lulu can accurately be described as a feminist (or pro-to-feminist) figure in American popular culture. She was created by a woman, and her assertive, take-no-prisoners attitude in the panels by Marjorie Buell is enough to make that claim. However, Stanley, not Buell, is the one chiefly responsible for Lulu's reputation as a feminist. In his stories, her mission in life is to prove that a girl can do anything a boy can do; and, that girls are often a lot smarter than boys. He explicitly stated this during his fourteen years as the author of *Little Lulu*. For more than a decade, Stanley worked for a company, Dell Comics, that was run by a woman, Helen Meyer (for whom he had a great deal of respect), on a character created by a woman.

Unlike Charles Schulz, John Stanley isn't a household name. In all those issues of *Little Lulu*, his name appears just once, in 1952—and even then, he's listed in a group of people responsible for the stories, when he was actually the prime creative force behind the entire endeavor. Stanley was singled out only as "the cover artist,"

Opposite: Commissioned John Stanley painting (ca. late 1980s), based on the cover of *Marge's Lulu and Tubby Halloween Fun #6* (1957).

which was true enough. He did the art on all 145 Lulu comic book covers, plus most annual and "giant" issues. Yet, his name is known by a relatively small number of devoted fans of Lulu, who have made it a point to look behind the scenes.

Who was John Patrick Stanley? That is the challenge for the biographer because he's one of the most enigmatic major figures in the history of comics. He was a native New Yorker of Irish extraction, but almost nothing beyond that has been known about his family of origin, his youth or his dreams and aspirations. Few details about his experiences working for Dell Comics had emerged, nor had his reasons for leaving comic books at the age of fifty-six been well understood. This is because Stanley was a reticent, reclusive man who shunned the spotlight. In the latter part of his life, he had no interest in digging up the past, largely due to a self-deprecating attitude toward his work. Most who wanted to interview him were turned away; they didn't realize their subject was coping with the twin demons of alcoholism and clinical depression. Thus, Stanley has remained a "man of mystery"— until now.

Evidence of his talent as a cartoonist, cover artist and storyteller is displayed in the pages of this book, and speaks for itself. The earliest piece is from 1932; the latest is from 1993, the year of his passing. But these wonderful, intriguing examples raise the question: how did Stanley's life inform his art, and

how did his art inform his life? The challenge in answering these questions was enormous—at times, seemingly insurmountable.

As a biographer, I've learned that virtually everyone leaves footprints. The hard part is finding them, when the subject in question is no longer living, and, when his last work in comic books appeared in 1970. Nearly all of Stanley's colleagues and collaborators in his active years in that medium are also gone. Nevertheless, in the fall of 2014, I started digging, and am happy to report that, although my journey of discovery met with many obstacles and frustrations, it ended up yielding results that exceeded my expectations.

In addition to answering many of the key questions about his life and work, this book sheds light on his creative process on Little Lulu and other comics as never before. Through interviews with his son Jim Stanley and his niece Barbara Stanley Steggles, unknown aspects of his family life are revealed. Equally important, Stanley speaks for himself in these pages, quoted from recordings of the only extensive "interviews" that he gave about his life and work, one this writer transcribed for the first time. He is also extensively quoted from the substantial number of his letters to fans and colleagues, that have come to light. Readers will "meet John Stanley" in a way that was not possible before.

One clarification is needed: this isn't meant to be the definitive book on Little Lulu, whose comic book exploits continued

for twenty-five years after Stanley had moved on; who appeared in a magazine panel, a newspaper comic strip and various animated cartoon series that Stanley never touched. This is a book about the life and work of John Patrick Stanley, one of the supreme artists and writers to work in American comic books. *Little Lulu* represents the zenith of his career, but was by no means his only work of enduring value. His comic book career stretched from 1942 to 1970, writing and drawing other people's characters (as he did with Lulu), as well as characters of his own. His creations *Dunc and Loo*, *Melvin Monster* and *Thirteen* have their own special charms. None reached the heights of Little Lulu, but neither did Orson Welles's films after *Citizen Kane*, although his other movies are worthy in their own ways. Indeed, Stanley had his own *Touch of Evil* in the 1962 comic book *Tales from the Tomb*, which created a genuine uproar, much to his delight.

A relentless modesty caused Stanley to downplay the value of his work. Had they known this, millions of his readers would have strongly disagreed—as does this writer. Therefore, although I quote his self-deprecating statements in this regard, make no mistake about it: John Stanley belongs alongside Carl Barks, Harvey Kurtzman, Will Eisner and Jack Kirby, men who can rightly be called "the gods of comic books." His induction into the Will Eisner Comic Book Hall of Fame in 2004 was richly deserved.

—Bill Schelly

Top: John Stanley sketch, courtesy of Barbara Steggles. **Opposite:** *Marge's Little Lulu* #16, from Dell file copy, courtesy of Alan Hutchinson.

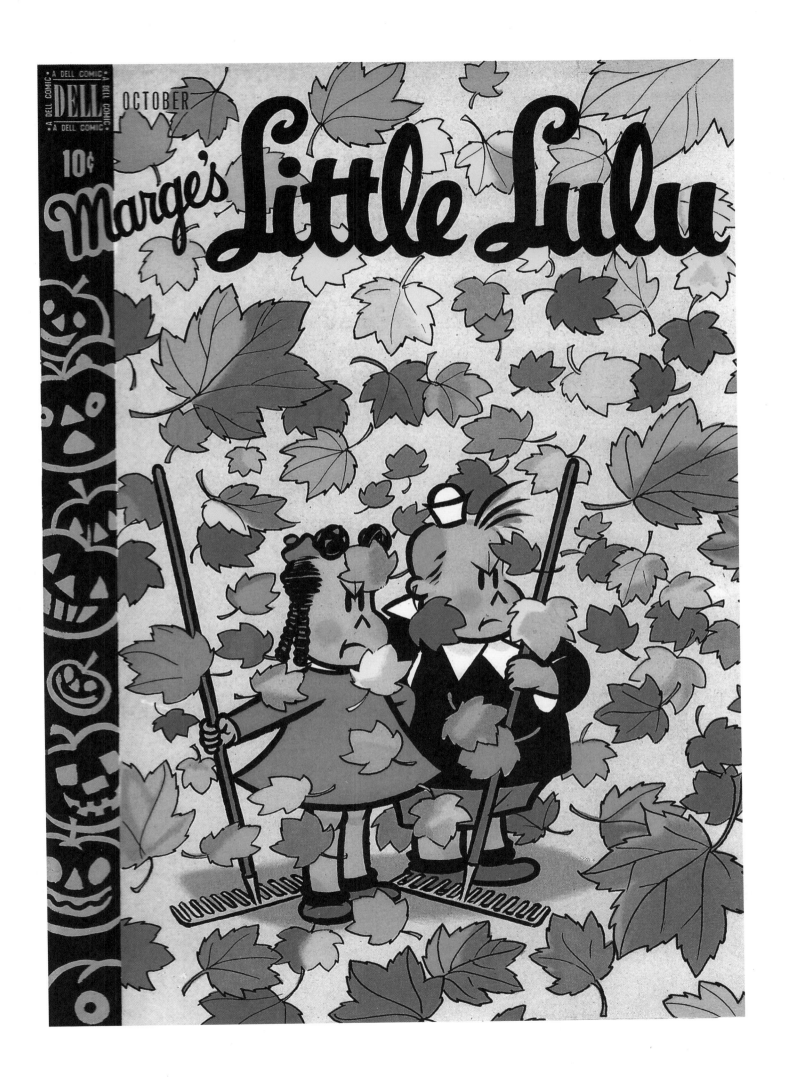

The Stanley family ca. 1934. *Top row:* James (Jimmy), John, Marian. *Bottom row:* Johanna (Anna), Marguerite and James. **Opposite:** Young Anna Stanley, posing for a photograph with John. (Standing woman is unidentified.) All family photographs are courtesy of Jim Stanley (John's son).

City Boy

JOHN PATRICK STANLEY was born March 22, 1914. His father, James Stanley, came to America from Ireland in 1905 at the age of twenty-three, seeking economic opportunity. John Stanley's mother, Johanna ("Anna") Ahearn, arrived in New York City in 1907. She hailed from the town of Adare in County Limerick, Ireland, and was two years younger than her future spouse.[1] James and Anna wed in 1911, and had their first child, a daughter named Marian, a year later. John was second born. Two more brothers followed: Thomas (Tom) in 1916, and James (Jimmy) in 1919. There would be one more addition: a second daughter, Marguerite, who arrived in 1925.

The Stanleys' earliest known address was 277 West 134th Street in Harlem.[2] They lived in a tenement apartment in the hardscrabble neighborhood alongside German, English and Irish neighbors. The Irish, the third largest immigrant group in the city, were widely considered an inferior ethnic group, and were discriminated against. By the end of World War I, their lot was improving because the Tammany Hall political machine gave them access to city jobs. James Stanley worked for New York Transit as a subway conductor.

Although James was the breadwinner, and almost a foot taller than his wife, Anna Stanley had the more forceful personality. Two words are said to best describe John's mother: "Catholic" and "stern." Her granddaughter, Barbara Steggles (b. Stanley, 1940), remembers her as "very severe, very religious, the kind that went to Mass every morning."[3] Anna was a strict disciplinarian.[4] Each of the children had his or her own way of dealing with the demanding, devout matriarch. Soft-spoken Marian, who suffered from vision problems, lived entirely under Anna's wing. Tommy, the "bad boy," defied her. Jimmy, the baby of the family (until Marguerite came along) was the sweet, cooperative child. Anna's eldest son, John, did his best to toe the line. He was more temperamental and

moody than the others. Although his relationship with his mother was stormy, the attachment between the two was strong.

Part of being "a good Catholic family" meant sending the children to parochial schools. While providing religious instruction, and preventing Catholic children from being "infected" by children brought up in other Christian denominations (not to mention other religions), parochial schools, at this time, generally offered inferior educations than publicly funded schools. The teachers were mostly nuns who often received little or no special training as teachers or in the subjects they taught. The emphasis was on piety and classroom discipline. John's son, Jim Stanley, recently recalled, "[My father] would go on and on about how brutal the nuns were, smacking the kids around."[5] The most frequent punishment was

a slap to a student's outstretched hand with a ruler. For an even more emphatic sting, boys were spanked, usually with a paddle. Given how prominently "good spankings" are featured (or at least mentioned) in John Stanley's Little Lulu stories, it's not much of a stretch to presume that he received his share of them as a boy, both at school and at home. Corporal punishment was common in the 1920s (indeed, up through the 1950s), accepted and not considered abusive. A photograph of John with his second grade class shows a boy who is open of face and seemingly the typical "boy next door." But growing up Catholic meant that he grew up aware that he was a sinner, surrounded by temptation.

At some point in his youth, John Stanley contracted tuberculosis. It seems to have been a relatively minor case.[6] One of the dangers of high-density tenement living is that infectious diseases spread rapidly. In the 1910s and 1920s, a TB epidemic hit denizens of the tenements especially hard. Symptoms are chronic cough, fevers, night sweats and weight loss.

A TB diagnosis meant bed rest and isolation from others, surely a difficult proposition in a small apartment. It also meant missing school. Perhaps his lifelong propensity for immersing himself in books began as a way of filling the empty hours. His was the last generation of children who grew up before radio became a major source of popular entertainment. Thus, books were a much more important entertainment vehicle than they would be just a decade hence. One of his favorite childhood books, which Stanley spoke of with great warmth in later years, was *Treasure Island*, Robert Louis Stevenson's adventure tale of buccaneers, pirates and buried gold. Stanley was a precocious reader and went on to read other books by Stevenson, such as *Kidnapped* and *The Strange*

Case of Dr. Jekyll and Mr. Hyde, as well as the works of Jack London, Daniel Defoe, Charles Dickens and Mark Twain.

Young *John* Stanley also loved the newspaper comic strips. The Hearst newspapers the *New York Journal* and the *New York American* were the papers of choice in Irish households. They ran comics from the Hearst-owned King Features syndicate. In 1922, the *New York Sunday American* ballyhooed its new eight pages of comics ("Twice as Many Laughs as You Ever Got Before!"), which included *Bringing up Father*, *Down on the Farm*, *The Katzenjammer Kids*, *Boob McNutt*, *Barney Google*, *Toots and Casper*, *Little Jimmy*, and *Tillie the Toiler*. Stanley grew up on humorous comic strips. The adventure strips that influenced many who went on to write and draw comic books—*Flash Gordon* and *Terry and the Pirates* chief among them—wouldn't come along for another decade. Signs of nascent artistic talent in the eldest Stanley boy were apparent when he drew his own versions of his favorite comic strip characters. The arrival of the Sunday papers was an exciting weekly event in his life.

As with other first generation immigrants whose head of household had a good job, James Stanley was able, midway through the 1920s, to escape tenement life. After the birth of the fifth Stanley sibling in 1925, when they needed more room, they moved to the Bronx. The neighborhood was known as Kingsbridge. It had a large Irish population, and a high concentration of Catholic churches. Around that time, James Stanley went from being a conductor to a ticket agent.[7] The Stanleys lived in an ordinary row house at 2907 Heath Avenue in Kingsbridge for more than two decades. They lived mostly downstairs in an exposed basement, which went out to a garden. The whole house was always very

John Stanley with his second-grade class.

clean.[8] Typical of such houses, there's no front yard, just a stoop, with five steps down to a wide sidewalk. A stairway down from the sidewalk provides access to the basement from the street. It has a small backyard. Of his life as a boy in Kingsbridge, Stanley said, "I grew up in the Bronx, New York City, in a middle class neighborhood. It was pretty rural at that time. I had a lot of friends . . . and we did have huts. There's nothing original about that. A hut where there's 'no girls allowed.'"[9]

BY THE TIME HE was in the eighth grade, John Stanley had demonstrated a talent for caricature, cartooning and artwork in general.[10] Therefore, his parents allowed him to apply to Textile High School, a public school, rather than complete his education in a parochial high school in Kingsbridge. Given Anna Stanley's strict religious beliefs, this could not have been an easy decision, and showed commendable parental support for her son's dream of a career in the arts. It was a move that would have many ramifications.

Textile High School stood at 351 Eighteenth Street between Eighth and Ninth Avenues in Chelsea. The New York City Board of Education established the technical high school to provide vocational training in the textiles industry, recognizing that the future of one of the city's major industries depended on new generations of trained workers. The school opened its doors in the fall of 1919, offering a complete academic curriculum along with classes in textile design, manufacturing and marketing. It also offered a number of classes in commercial art. Before the High School of Music and Art was established in the city in 1936, Textile High was the place where young people hoping for a career in the arts wanted to go.

In the fall of 1928, Stanley entered Textile High as a freshman. He was fourteen when he began taking the daily subway ride from the Bronx to Chelsea, to the rundown building that originally housed the school. There he met Eugene Zion, a Jewish boy who aspired to be a writer, and they were soon best friends. In the 1950s, Zion became known as the author of the book *Harry the Dirty Dog* and other popular children's books (mostly illustrated by his wife Margaret Bloy Graham). Stanley and Zion both turned out to be prominent members of their high school class, although their years at Textile High occurred during a period of disruption. The school had no trouble attracting students, but for it to really flower, a modern facility was needed. After spending their freshman year in "the old building," Stanley and Zion were relocated to a school annex on West Fortieth Street, one of five locations around the city, while a massive, lavish school building was built on Eighteenth Street.[11]

Top: The Stanley home at 2907 Heath Avenue in the Bronx, as the row house looks today. Photo: Ben Asen. **Middle:** Young John Stanley with friend standing on those same steps ca. 1927. **Bottom:** According to Jim Stanley, "My dad was an avid hunter, but gave that up because my mom was very much an animal lover."

Full spread: The earliest known examples of John Stanley's artwork are these two pages and p. 19. He did them for the *Loom*, his senior yearbook at Textile High School. Note his self-caricature and signature.

Escaping from the nuns into a secular educational environment was an exciting time for the weedy youth, who was rapidly attaining what would be his adult height of six feet, two inches. Now he was out of the Bronx for much of his day, mingling with a more diverse student body. Parochial schools were segregated by gender, the better to avoid "distractions." THS school was co-educational, with distractions a-plenty. As he progressed through high school, Stanley only became taller and more handsome. (His weight, which didn't vary much for the rest of his life, was 170 pounds.) He received a lot of attention from his female classmates, and they from him.

As a "Spinner" or a "Textilite" (both nicknames were used), John Stanley blossomed. The teachers were well qualified, coming from colleges such as Hunter, Wellesley, Mt. Holyoke, Columbia and Fordham. The art faculty was educated at Pratt Institute, the New York School of Applied Design, Columbia, New York University, Hunter and the Art Students league. After a freshman year mostly dedicated to academic subjects, he was able to take several art classes as a sophomore. Future comic book artist Gill Fox, also attending THS, later told interviewer Jim Amash, "Textile High School . . . had some excellent art courses including

a course in advertising, and under that was a course in cartooning. Around me were some very good guys like John Stanley, who [was] a year ahead of me."[12] They both had the same art teacher, Mrs. Johnson, who Fox credits as a genius at developing early talent.

As much as he enjoyed the art- and design-related classes, it seems Stanley the bookworm began directing his reading into more literary directions at this time. He already read and enjoyed Robert Benchley's satirical essays in the *New Yorker* and other magazines. Now, under the sway of Max Horwitz, the chairman and dominant personality in the English department, he began reading literary classics. One of them may have been James Boswell's *The Life of Samuel Johnson*, which, in later life, he cited as possibly his favorite book. From there, Stanley branched out to Boswell's *London Diaries*, and *The Diary of Samuel Pepys*, a revised edition having been published in 1926. John Stanley would be an Anglophile for the rest of his life (not the most common avocation for one of Irish descent), and his taste would lean toward the highbrow and literary, although he never lost his love of the works of Dickens, Twain and Stevenson.

The new school building was finished in time for John Stanley's senior year (1931–1932). He had emerged as one of the best artists in the school. Gill Fox watched him work. "You wouldn't believe

MYLES GLYNN
Barrymore—watch your position,
For here come lots of competition.
Arista Leader, Dramatics.

JOHN STANLEY
Johnnie is real famous for,
The swell cartoons that he can draw.
Art Editor, Spinning Wheel.

EUGENE ZION
Little but smart is Eugene,
One of the best we've ever seen.
Treas. Senior Class, Secy. Treas. Arista, Dramatic Society, Pres. Pen & Brush Club.

Above: In June 1932, when he graduated, John Stanley received the Saint-Gaudens Medal for his art class work at Textile High. His name is engraved on the back. **Below:** In the *Loom*, John Stanley and Eugene Zion are pictured together in a section designated for outstanding seniors. Zion was his best friend.

IZOOXXNARIES

Koncieved and Konkokted by Prof. Stanley

DEAN BARTLEY

MR. COUGHLIN

MR. ROSENFELD

MISS GUILFOY

how good his work was at sixteen—as good as most professionals today," he recalled.[13] His only surviving artwork are three exceptional pages of cartoons that appeared in *The Loom*, the senior yearbook. These "Facultoons" offer mildly comic caricatures of teachers (including his art teacher Mrs. Johnson), and some students, including one of himself. In a page titled "Loominaries," signed "Koncieved and Konkokted by Prof. Stanley," he included his version of Mickey Mouse, who had made his debut just four years earlier in the silent cartoon *Steamboat Willie*.

Despite the promise of this teenage work, Stanley hit a personal low in 1931. He began suffering from what would now be diagnosed as clinical depression. "Throughout my life, at various times, I've experienced serious bouts of depression—ever since I was 17," he later told a friend.[14] One way it presented was in the form of panic attacks; other times, it was simply that he was unable to engage with the people and obligations in his life. In the 1930s, depression wasn't well understood. People affected by the disorder were urged to "cheer up," "count your blessings" and "get more exercise." There were no medical treatments, short of the barbaric: lobotomy (surgery to remove parts of the brain) was considered an easy, permanent fix to most mental illnesses. Later in the decade, Electroconvulsive therapy (ECT)—administered without anesthesia—was available as a more "enlightened" approach. Antidepressant drugs were thirty years away. Those who suffered from depression often tried to conceal the condition, out of shame or fear of institutionalization. In his case, we have no details, except that, like many others who suffered from depression and mood swings, he self-medicated with alcohol, caffeine and nicotine. He had started smoking non-filtered Camels when he was in high school. This was especially inadvisable for Stanley who, as a result of his TB, had a collapsed lung.

In addition, he lost his religion as high school graduation approached. He said, "I was brought up Catholic but I departed from that faith when I was eighteen. I became a skeptic."[15] It isn't known if this was a major "crisis of the soul," or a reaction to what he felt was his parents' religious strictness or to things that happened to him in parochial school. When John stopped going to Mass, it must have led to tension at home.

In the *Loom*, the senior yearbook, the photographs of John Stanley and Eugene Zion are together in a section for outstanding seniors. Under Stanley's photo, it says, "Johnnie is real famous for the swell cartoons that he can draw." While he's cited as "Art editor, *Spinning Wheel*," he doesn't appear in the photo of the school newspaper's staff. It's his only listed extracurricular activity, save for his participation in the yearbook itself (being on its "Art Board"). Stanley's name appears in one other place in the yearbook. In the "Hall of Fame," consisting of sixteen categories pertaining to both teachers and students (Best Athlete, Most Popular Girl, Favorite Teacher), he is dubbed "Handsomest Boy."

A disparity between Stanley's outer and inner worlds developed. On the one hand, he was the handsome "good son" who his Textile High School class recognized as an outstanding artist. On the other, he was a lapsed Catholic suffering from depression who escaped from the world's demands into the pages of books. His friends and his dates had to come to terms with the fact that he was hard to get to know. He was "complicated." Photographs give no hint of anything disturbing or disturbed about the young man. Those female classmates and other young women who received his attentions found his charm enormous, and the kind of sharp sense of humor that only a person of exceptional intelligence could possess. At the same time, they also discovered unsettling traits: a constant self-deprecation, a gloominess that alternated with flashes of anger and a sense that he was tied to the apron strings of his steely, strict mother.

Upon his graduation from Textile High in June 1932, John Stanley received the Saint Gaudens Medal for outstanding achievement in art by a high school student in the New York City school system.[16] The award was presented to him at a ceremony held at the Metropolitan Museum of Art. It was more than a form of recognition. It came with a two-year scholarship to art school, which would have otherwise been too expensive. Unexpectedly, at the height of the Great Depression, he was going to college.

THE NEW YORK SCHOOL of Fine and Applied Arts (Parsons), today known as The New York School of Design, was one of the top three art colleges in the United States in 1932. It was founded in 1904, when William M. Chase hired Frank Alva Parsons to establish the school's curriculum. Four years later, Parsons assumed management of the institution, located in a five-story building at 2239 Broadway. Its four professional courses of study were Interior Architecture and Decoration, Costume Design, Graphic Advertising and Illustration and Teacher Training. Each was a three-year course.

Stanley chose the Graphic Advertising and Illustration course. He registered on September 2, 1932, and began attending classes four days later. According to the school catalog, "In the first year, special emphasis is given to the fundamentals necessary to pictorial expression of ideas such as layout making, life drawing, object drawing, mechanical and freehand, perspective, museum research, color, lettering, and technique of rendering in different mediums."[17] The second year was particularly dedicated to developing the students' painting skills.

Stanley never said what he thought of the instruction at Parsons. The only thing he talked about was feeling like an outsider there. In high school, despite whatever behavior arose from his emerging mental health issues, he seems to have been almost a quintessential insider. But Textile High School was a public school,

NEW YORK SCHOOL OF

FINE AND APPLIED ART

Opposite: Portrait of Frank Alva Parsons ca. 1920. **Left:** The 1932 catalog for Parsons, then known as the New York School of Fine and Applied Art. **Right:** A Graphic Advertising and Illustration student art sample.

with a more or less typical cross section of economic and ethnic types. The tuition at Parsons, $300 a year (or, a little over $5,000 in 2015 dollars), meant that few students from lower and working class families could attend. Don Phelps, a fan who befriended Stanley in the 1970s, reported that "[John] felt very uncomfortable there as most of his classmates were well-to-do and, being a city kid, he did not really blend in."[18] In another context, Stanley confirmed his feelings of being a "poor kid at a rich kid's school."[19] (Anti-Irish and anti-Catholic sentiment may also have been a factor.) This hyperawareness of social status and dislike of the upper classes was something in Stanley that ran deep. Matters of social status would become a major theme in his future work.

The other known fact of his experience at Parsons was that he left after completing just two years of the three-year course, most

likely because his scholarship ran out. Although he didn't receive a diploma, he didn't walk away with nothing to show for it. The school gave special certificates for those who completed two years satisfactorily.

Now it was time to find a job. The economy of the United States was in freefall, but the world of magazines and publishing—which was centered in New York City—continued, as did the world of commercial advertising. Therefore, when twenty-year-old John Stanley hit the streets with his portfolio in the summer of 1934, it's probable that he was initially thinking in terms of those two types of artistic endeavor. Instead, his life took a different turn. John Stanley found a job as an animator-in-training.

The Kay Kamen crew in 1937. *Top row, left to right:* Lou Cunette, Fritz Mockow, Clarence Allen, Mike Pike, John Stanley. *Bottom row:* Henry Bausili, Lou Lispi. **Opposite:** *Fleischer's Animated News #6 (May 1935). Cover: Dave Tendlar. Courtesy of Jerry Beck.

2

Animator and Commercial Artist

LESS IS KNOWN about John Stanley's career from 1934 to 1942 than of any other period in his creative life. Documented statements about those nine years are few. As for his artwork, only two published pieces from this span can definitively be attributed to him, not unusual in animation and commercial art, which are known more as team or committee efforts than avenues of individual expression. The frustrated biographer can only add to what little is known by discussing the people for whom he worked during that period, and what he did for them.

Stanley said, "I worked for Max Fleischer [starting] out as an opaquer, and worked from opaques to inks to being an in-betweener."[1] In 1934, Fleischer Studios was riding high. It was founded in 1921 as Inkwell Studios (or Out of the Inkwell Films) by brothers Max and Dave Fleischer, and renamed Fleischer Studios in 1929, the year it produced its first talking cartoon. The first significant competitor to Walt Disney Productions, its *Betty Boop* series was at the peak of its popularity, and the *Popeye* cartoons were getting better with each new release. By the time Stanley showed up looking for work, Max and Dave Fleischer were presiding over a staff of some 150 animators, and always on the lookout for more talent. Most likely, he was hired by Dave Fleischer, who supervised production and handled most of the day-to-day management of the operation, located at 1600 Broadway in midtown Manhattan.

We know that Stanley was there by the end of 1934 because he contributed a small piece of artwork to the first issue of the firm's internal newsletter, *Fleischer's Animated News*, in December. The Fleischer brothers attempted to foster camaraderie and a sense of "family" in their studio (even though Max and Dave were barely on speaking terms) by instituting the in-house newsletter, an unpretentious mimeographed publication of several pages that carried news of developments at the studio, policies of various kinds and write-ups of employees' family news, accompanied by occasional drawings. The first issue included brief individual biographies ("Tintypes") of each Fleischer brother. As someone wrote in that issue, "Thanks to Tex Hastings and John Stanley for the swell caricatures of Dave and Max." His small drawing of Max is very much like the elegant caricatures he had done for *The Loom* yearbook in high school.

Stanley began at Fleischer Studios working at a desk in a room full of artists performing the lowest task on the animation totem pole: opaquing. An opaquer painted the back of the clear animation cel, following the outline on it, filling in the appropriate colors. Even in black-and-white cartoons, such as most of the cartoons produced by Fleischer at this time, there were at least two dozen different shades of gray from which inkers could choose. For this work, he was probably paid $17.50 a week.[2] He must have been appalled by the lack of creativity in opaquing, but this was the height of the Great Depression, and jobs were scarce. Besides, it would have been made clear from the beginning that he could advance quickly, if he did well, and work on the movement of the cartoon figures in less than a year.

Before then, there was an interim step: outlining the animator's original drawing in ink. Inking requires greater skill than opaquing. The cel is placed over the animator's pencil drawing and is traced in ink onto the front of the cel. One has to be careful to get the same line weight (thickness) so that it matches the next cel and the next (which may be being done by another inker). John Stanley was able to move to this step after a few months. That

Above left: Stanley's staff caricature page, from issue #6 (May 1935), is reminiscent of his work in the *Loom*. Courtesy of Jerry Beck. **Above right:** John Stanley drew a Max Fleischer caricature for *Fleischer's Animated News #1* (December 1934). **Below:** He worked as an "in-betweener" (uncredited) on several *Popeye* and *Betty Boop* cartoons during his stint with Fleischer Studios: perhaps, those depicted here.

seems to have roughly coincided with his second artistic contribution to the company newsletter, one much more elaborate than the first. The May 1935 issue (#6) of the *Fleischer's Animated News* featured a full page of Stanley caricatures titled, "But for the Grace of God (What They Might Have Been)." Again, it was much like the pages he did for *The Loom*, four years earlier.[3]

Stanley made good as an inker, and was promoted to an "in-betweener" in the summer of 1935. His raise in status was announced in the August 1935 issue of the *Animated News*. That was fast progress, although not singular at the time. The in-betweener filled in the gaps between the drawings of the animator and the assistant animator. By the time the drawings get to the in-betweener, the gaps are so small, often just one or two drawings, that it's easy to go from one pose to the next. This was considered preparation for becoming an animator (to understand movement and learn

how to match line quality).[4] Stanley would probably have moved up to assistant animator before the end of 1935.

There is perhaps a maximum of five months of animated cartoons John Stanley may have worked on as an in-betweener. The cartoons produced during that period include three in the Color Classics series, four Popeye cartoons, and five Betty Boop cartoons.[5] There's no way to determine precisely which cartoons John Stanley actually worked on, but it doesn't really matter since his work was just part of the amalgamated whole. (In-betweeners didn't work on every cartoon, and received no screen credit.)

Seventeen-year-old Jack Kirby, who co-created most of the Marvel super heroes in the 1960s, was also an in-betweener at the Fleischer Studio in 1935 on some Popeye cartoons.[6] Since all the in-betweeners worked in the same room, it's probable that Stanley and Kirby met—maybe worked side by side. There was

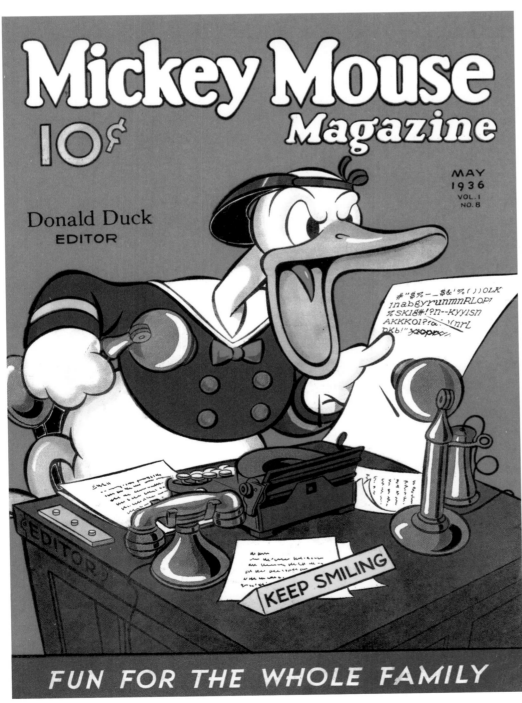

Stanley later claimed that he did at least one cover of *Mickey Mouse Magazine*. Was it for V1 #8 (May 1936, *left*), or V1 #6 (March, *right, top*) or V1 #10 (July *right, bottom*)? All three date from his tenure with Hal Horne. Courtesy of Michael Barrier.

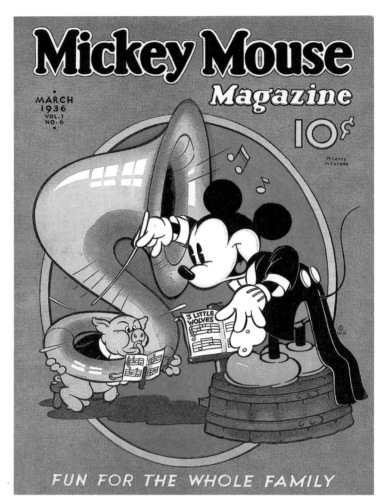

Pages 3, 13 and 25 from *Mickey Mouse Magazine* (V1. #6), which John Stanley may have worked on. (It was the sort of cartooning he did for the magazine.) None of the art in the publication was credited, except perhaps to Walt Disney. Courtesy of Michael Barrier.

constant flux, people coming in and people leaving for other work. In-betweeners were considered low on the food chain and easily replaceable. A lot of people burned out quickly and left because the job was so tedious. Others who worked there around the same time as John Stanley were Sheldon Mayer, Harry Lampert and Gill Fox, all who ended up working in comic books.

Stanley said that he worked for Fleischer Studios for about a year. "Then," he said, "I went to Hal Horne when I was around twenty-two or twenty-three. He turned out this big Walt Disney magazine."[7] He didn't say why he left animation, only the fact of it. It was most likely due to both the non-creative nature of the work, and low pay. The animators of Fleischer Studios went on strike in 1937. Kirby left about the same time as Stanley.

HAL HORNE ESTABLISHED his connection with Walt Disney Productions when he was the director of advertising and publicity for United Artists, who began distributing the Disney cartoons in 1932. When he decided to form his own company, one of the first items on the agenda was producing and publishing *Mickey Mouse Magazine*, a publication for children that was the direct precursor to the comic book *Walt Disney's Comics and Stories*. Even though the magazine struggled, always on the brink of failure, Horne hired John Stanley to work on it.

Stanley said that he did some interior art for *Mickey Mouse Magazine*, and also at least one of its covers.[8] Assuming he began working for Horne at the end of 1935, the first issue that could have

carried his work was Vol. 1, #6, dated March 1936. Its cover depicts Mickey as an orchestra conductor. Like all cartoons published under the aegis of Walt Disney at the time, it's unsigned, merely carrying a "© W. D." notation. It's impossible to know if this, or the covers of the next four monthly issues, were by Stanley, or which of the cartoons and illustrations on the inside pages he did.

The magazine's sales struggles are easy to understand when one examines what it really offered children for their precious dime. It was an entirely tepid, uninspired affair that slimmed from forty-four pages to thirty-six pages with #6. Sales were so dismal that Roy Disney took pity on Hal Horne, and waived royalty payments so that Horne could more easily recoup his losses. Working for Horne may be when John Stanley shook hands with Roy Disney. "That's my claim to fame," he later joked. "I never met Walt."[9] Hal Horne gave up on *Mickey Mouse Magazine* with its tenth issue (July 1936), letting it pass to a new publisher. Stanley went to work for that new publisher, Kay Kamen, whose office was at 1270 Sixth Avenue in Manhattan.

HERMAN "KAY" KAMEN was an advertising man when he approached the Walt Disney Company about licensing its characters to clothing, toy and other types of manufacturers. This arrangement began in June 1932. Comics and animation historian Michael Barrier wrote, "Kamen was an extraordinarily energetic and resourceful businessman who had talked himself into a deal in which he and Disney split the proceeds from licensing the Disney

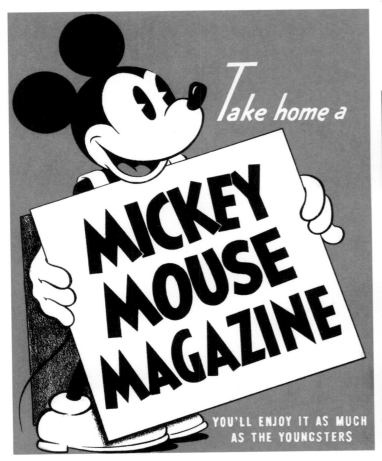

Above left: Store sign ca. 1936. **Above right:** Compare the black-and-white Mickey figure, by Stanley's hand (from a 1932 *Loom*), to the Ingersoll Mickey Mouse wristwatch box and watch face. Stanley stated that he drew Mickey for at least one version of this watch. Images courtesy Heritage Auction.

The Art Students League Building at 215 West Fifty-Sixth Street, between Seventh Avenue and Broadway in Midtown Manhattan, New York City, where John Stanley studied lithography, as it appeared on May 2009. Photo: Jim Henderson. **Opposite:** John Stanley in the mid-1930s.

cartoon characters. Kamen had delivered on that deal, spectacularly, by traveling incessantly and licensing Mickey Mouse and other characters to hundreds of manufacturers."[10] He set up a new entity called K. K. Publications, Inc., to take over the publication of *Mickey Mouse Magazine*.

Energetic though he was, Kay Kamen also failed to make the magazine a success, although he published a dozen more issues. Alice Nielson Cobb, the editor Kamen assigned to the project, ran items much like those in the Horne issues, a mix of poems, puzzles, short stories and cartoon drawings. The quality of those features continued to be uninspired.

Kamen had *Mickey Mouse Magazine* printed by Western Printing and Lithographing Company in its plant in Poughkeepsie, New York. The contents of the magazine were created in Kamen's New York office, but when sales did not pick up, the production of its editorial material was taken over by Western Printing. At that point, K. K. Publications became wholly owned by Western. They published the magazine until 1940, when it was converted to comic book form. As *Walt Disney's Comics and Stories*, it became the flagship title of all the Disney comic books for the next two decades, and their best seller for years. This time, John Stanley didn't move with the magazine. He stayed with Kay Kamen.

From the time he had entered Kamen's doors in July 1936, John Stanley had worked not only on the magazine, but was a member of a staff that did the artwork for a panoply of Disney licensed products. He described himself as "a commercial artist

and a letterer."[11] Kamen had arranged for the creation of the first Mickey Mouse watch by Ingersoll Waterbury, which was an enormous hit: so successful that it was followed by numerous styles of watches and other timepieces. According to Stanley, he drew the Mickey character on the face of one of those watches.[12] After the release of *Snow White and the Seven Dwarfs* in 1937, the merchandising market exploded, with the likenesses of Snow White and her friends appearing on all manner of toys and household items. With so many licensed products, it would seem there was plenty to keep Stanley (and the others of Kamen's small art staff) busy.

While the timing is uncertain, it seems that Stanley began to aspire to do work that could be considered "fine art" while working for Kamen. He was never a painter and didn't appreciate the abstract art of the time. In later years, he would mock the work of Picasso, Mondrian and Klee. He chose to study lithography (a medium for making art prints) at the Art Students League in the city. From September to December 1937, he attended evening classes in the League's building on West Fifty-Seventh Street. Nevertheless, a key question remains: if John Stanley had his druthers, what sort of work did he most want to do? Given his potential as a storyteller, did he dream of becoming a writer? Jim Stanley doesn't think so: "My father wanted to be an artist from the get-go. He never told me that he wanted to be a novelist or anything like that."[13] Perhaps even Stanley didn't know what sort of work would best suit him.

John Stanley admitted to partying and drinking heavily at this time. As Don Phelps wrote, "By his own admission, he didn't learn much about lithography but he did meet a group of 'good time guys' who believed in revelry and a whole lot of [bending] the elbow. It was a more personally satisfying experience than his stint at the New York School of Art had been."[14] Apparently, his consumption of alcohol increased substantially at this time.

Alcoholism, not thought to be a disease in the 1930s, was a pervasive problem in Irish society. Irish writer (and admitted alcoholic) Dr. Garrett O'Connor (somewhat harshly) attributes it to an "inferiority complex in Irish Catholics which [is] characterized by chronic fear, suppressed rage, self-loathing, procrastination, low self-esteem [and] false pride."[15] Yet neither of Stanley's parents were alcoholics. According to Barbara Steggles, "They were very straight-laced. They did not drink to excess, although they weren't teetotalers."[16] Even so, Stanley was living in a predominantly Irish neighborhood that winked at heavy drinking. He became what has come to be known as a "high functioning alcoholic."

Stanley continued to live at home on Heath Avenue with his family, although it was difficult because of his refusal to practice the Catholic faith. This would always be a sore point with his mother, but she ultimately moderated her objections in order to keep him close. His sister Marian would never break away from her mother, because she was blind (as a result of having two detached retinas). His brother Jimmy, an engineering student at New York University, turned twenty-one in 1940. The "baby" Marguerite was in high school.

Tommy, who had left home in the mid-1930s, married Margaret Santo in early 1940. Their first child, Barbara, was born at year's end. This is the Barbara Steggles cited in this book, who recently recalled, "My father [Tom] didn't get along with his mother, and I don't think John really got along with her either. She was very controlling, I believe. John didn't get married until much later. This is terrible to say, but I think his mother was very destructive. There are a lot of European women who act this way. They cling on to the son. And then the son can't break away. My father left as soon as he could. She was close to her daughters. But I don't know what this meant in terms of [John's] work or life. [John] had a lot of girlfriends. I don't know if he was allowed to bring them into the house. He probably would have been much healthier mentally if he had gotten away from his mother."[17]

Because World War II was already raging in Europe, Congress passed the first peacetime draft in September of 1940. John registered on October 16, 1940, in the Bronx.[18] However, he was classified 4-F because of his collapsed lung and history of tuberculosis.[19][20] Tommy was exempted because New York Transit was declared essential to the war effort. Jimmy was the only Stanley sibling to be classified I-A. When war came, he would be in it.

Eventually, John Stanley left Kay Kamen and went freelance. Little is known about this phase of his career. According to what he told Don Phelps, Stanley may have worked for Kamen as late as mid–1941.[21] If he left the firm voluntarily, it was apparently to become a graphic artist, but the going was tough. Stanley said, "Those were hard times and I couldn't find the kind of work I wanted as a graphic artist."[22] It's not clear exactly what Stanley meant by the term "graphic artist," although he may have been referring to pursuing his interest in lithography.

What type of work, then, did Stanley actually do after leaving Kamen? Phelps paraphrased Stanley as saying he "[sold] cartoons to various magazines, before going to work for Western Publishing [doing comic books]."[23] If so, it was with a certain ambivalence, considering that Stanley definitively stated, when entering the comic book business, "I didn't want to become a cartoonist." (See Chapter 3.) Or, perhaps he differentiated between creating gag cartoons for magazines and drawing comic books, two very different forms. We don't have enough information to sort out these matters with certainty, because Stanley never provided specifics about this freelance period. According to Jim Stanley, "He wouldn't have thought this work was worth mentioning."[24]

Whatever Stanley was doing in 1941, we know that his freelance career took a turn in the summer of 1942. Of his entry into comic art and comic books, which would prove to be his métier, he later told reporter Dorothy Krumeich of the *Peekskill Evening Star*, "I just drifted in. A friend who was in the comic book business asked for some help."[25]

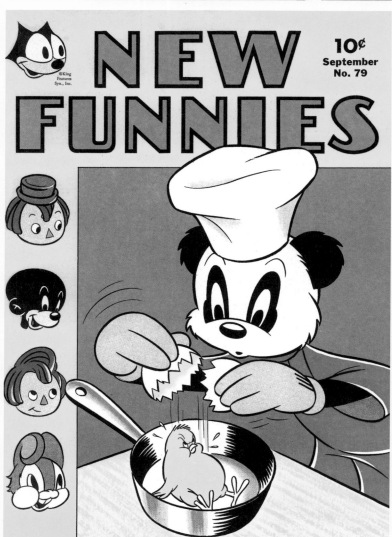

John Stanley cover art. *Top row: New Funnies #102 (August 1945) and #108. Bottom row: New Funnies #79 (September 1943) and #82 (December 1943).* **Opposite:** *Dell Four Color #9 (October 1942), with the classic story "Donald Duck Finds Pirate Gold," was on the stands about the time John Stanley applied for work at Western Publishing.*

3

His True Calling

IN 1938, DELL PUBLISHING, a large publisher of magazines, contracted with Western Printing and Lithographing Company to produce their line of comic books. Dell would handle the financing and distribution. The printing, the licensing of properties, and the creation of the stories and artwork for the comic books, would be handled by Western, who gave the job of editing the line to Oskar Lebeck. Lebeck, a German immigrant with an affinity for creating children's books, began working in 1935 on those sorts of projects for Whitman, Western's consumer division.[1] He was an artist capable of imaginative and subtle work, although when he wrote in English, his second language, the result could be heavy and plodding. Nevertheless, he was a cultured man with good taste who had the ability to recognize talent in others, and gave them the freedom to do their best work. He was supervising the production of comic books with not just Disney characters, but those licensed from other animation and movie studios. The titles included *Our Gang Comics*, *New Funnies* and *Animal Comics*. In 1942, he had a problem: his roster of freelancers was shrinking.

With the entry of the United States into World War II, many cartoonists in the city had enlisted or been drafted into the armed forces. In late 1942, an increasing number of comic books were written and drawn by teenagers, the middle aged and 4-Fs. Editors found quality difficult to maintain.[2] Exceptions were Walt Kelly, who was diabetic and therefore judged unsuitable for the armed forces, and Carl Barks, who was forty years old by the time he was drawing comic books.

John Stanley, who was 4-F, had been employed as a commercial artist, a higher echelon than working in comic books. But, after leaving Kay Kamen, John Stanley's efforts as a freelance artist seem to have met with indifferent, or intermittent, success. Therefore, when an opportunity to work for the most well-heeled, financially sound publisher in the comic book business presented itself, he looked into it, recalling, "I didn't want to be a cartoonist or writer.

I sort of backed into it. [A friend] put me on to Western. They were looking for a cartoonist."[3] If this anonymous friend explained that comic books produced by Western Printing were published and distributed by Dell, then Stanley may have bought a couple of Dell comics to check them out before his meeting with Lebeck. They could have been Dell *Four Color* #9 (October 1942) with "Donald Duck Finds Pirate Gold," Carl Barks' first comic book work, and *Walt Disney Comics and Stories* #25 (October 1942), sporting

a Walt Kelly cover. Both were on sale by mid-August, about the time of John Stanley's first meeting with Oskar Lebeck.[4] Western's offices were in the Fifth Avenue Building, located where Broadway, Fifth Avenue and 23rd Street came together (opposite the Flatiron Building) in New York City.

Sizing up Lebeck when they first shook hands, Stanley found him to be "an impressive, imposing man who could sell himself anywhere."[5] Lebeck liked what he saw of Stanley's samples, which would have been heavy with images of Disney characters. He also would have reacted favorably to Stanley's background in animation. "I went up there and they threw a couple of scripts at me," he recalled.[6] When he walked out of the interview that day, John Stanley had his first assignments for Western: two stories written by Gaylord DuBois for the *Tom and Jerry* series in *Our Gang Comics*.

Tom and Jerry, the stars of a popular series of animated cartoons, were created in 1940 by William Hanna and Joseph Barbera. A dozen or so Tom and Jerry cartoons had appeared by the time

Western secured the license to publish comic book stories of the pair, which began in *Our Gang Comics* #1, also on the stands when Stanley met with Lebeck. The *Our Gang* lead feature was written and drawn by Walt Kelly.[7] In that first issue, DuBois invented a friend for Jerry, a younger mouse (who wears a diaper) named Tuffy.[8]

John Stanley's handling of the art on *Tom and Jerry*, starting in *Our Gang Comics* #3 (January–February 1943), marks the beginning of his career in comic books.[9] The art is remarkably assured, and a distinct improvement over the work in the first two issues. *Tom and Jerry* was a good starting point for Stanley. The stories were uncomplicated, and it was fun drawing everyday objects to look giant-sized, in comparison to the mice who gamboled among and around them. The story in *Our Gang Comics* #3 has Jerry and Tuffy attempting to steal a cookie, and eluding Tom Cat, who discovers their efforts. The art is lively; the story is merely serviceable. Gaylord DuBois had a background in writing Western pulps, and had written the newspaper comics *Red Ryder* in 1938, and *King of the Royal Mounted* in 1939. He was in his element as a writer of Westerns; less so, the adventures of anthropomorphic animals.

Lebeck was pleased with the initial *Tom and Jerry* stories, which appeared in *Our Gang* #3 through #5 (a total of twenty-four pages). Stanley was not, in one important respect. He later stated, "I did the artwork, but was unhappy with the story and suggested I write my own."[10] On another occasion, he put it this way: "I was given an assignment, and I hated the story. It was so bad. And I told [Oskar Lebeck], 'I can do better than this. If I'm going to go to the trouble of illustrating this thing, I have to write it, too.'"[11]

Another editor might not have responded well to such a demand from a neophyte, but Oskar Lebeck wasn't a typical editor. Dan Noonan, who worked at Western for Lebeck after World War II, recalled, "Lebeck was a wonderful man to work for, and he was really the only comic book impresario that, in my opinion, ever deserved the name. He was a German who'd come

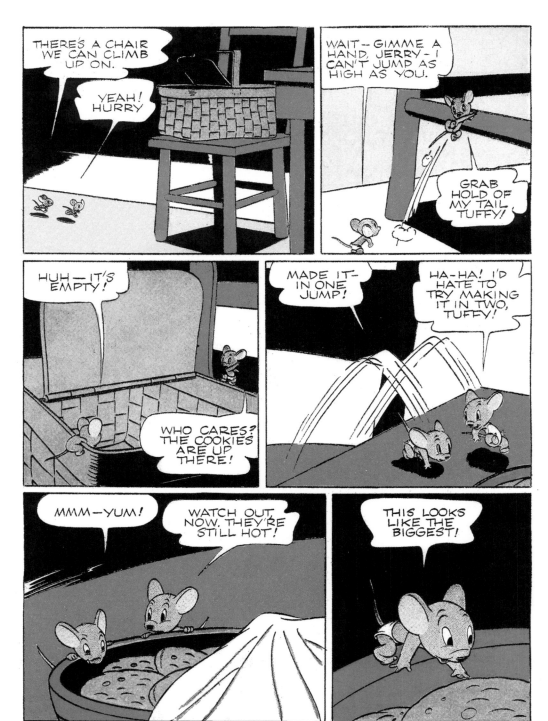

Header illustration and complete page 2 of the Tom and Jerry story in *Our Gang* #3, John Stanley's first comic book art. It was published December 1, 1942, according to the copyright records at the Library of Congress. The script is by Gaylord DuBois.

Left: *Our Gang* #3 (January–February 1943), cover by Walt Kelly. **Right:** The Dell title *The Funnies* was renamed *New Funnies* with #65 (June–July 1942) when it went to an all-comedy lineup.

here from Berlin and had worked with Max Reinhardt and with a number of stage people. He had also done a good deal of design work in New York. He had a wide-open mind for ideas. He initiated *Animal Comics*, a fairy story comic book, and these Raggedy Ann comics at the end of the war. And many other titles that were one-shots. Just about everything he did turned out rather well. He insisted on good stories. He'd buy a good story, and then he'd try to pick the best artist for it. But if an artist wrote a story himself, and he liked it, you could go right ahead and illustrate it, if he felt you were capable of doing so. With Oskar, the story was the thing. It didn't make too much difference to him who did the writing. Just so it was good."[12] According to Stanley, when he said, "I can do better than that," Lebeck said, "All right . . . try your hand at it." Stanley added, "At Western, they would let you do anything in those days."[13]

This was a major turning point in Stanley's life. Had Lebeck put him off, the artist might have soured on comic book work. Able cartoonists were hard to find, but not as scarce as first-rate writers for the medium. As the story of his life would show, Stanley's ability as a storyteller matched or exceeded his talent as an artist/cartoonist. As a writer, he could express new dimensions of his intelligence and sense of humor. He didn't know it at the time, but writing and drawing comic book stories would prove to be his true calling.

On a spring day in 1943, Stanley began writing his first comic book script. Coming up with an eight-page *Tom and Jerry* story wasn't the most difficult assignment. The MGM animated cartoons provided a kind of template. What he generated on his first try was better in every respect than the stories by the "experienced" DuBois.[14] The story in *Our Gang* #6 (July–August 1943) has Jerry and Tuffy exploring the bathroom in the "big folks'" house. They try to figure out the uses of the giant objects and fixtures—the bathtub, sink and contents of the medicine cabinet. Someone working on the toilet has left the top off its water tank. When Tuffy fears he's been poisoned by some shaving soap, he cries "Water!"

and dives into the tank. Jerry jumps down too, landing on the lever, causing the toilet to flush. As the waterline lowers, Tuffy clambers onto a bar of soap ("it floats!") and, finally, escapes from the strange swimming pool. This may be the first appearance of a toilet in an American comic book story. While indelicate at the time, this "toilet tank jeopardy" gives the story a bit of an edge, but what matters more is how he as writer-artist was able to create action that cascades from panel to panel with a cleverness and alacrity that had formerly been lacking.

Lebeck approved. Of John Stanley, a colleague at Western observed, "He's got a very fine mind, and I think he could have been a serious writer had he chosen to be one. Stanley's natural ability came through, and Lebeck was quick to recognize it."[15] He was given the ongoing *Tom and Jerry* feature, which continued as one of the several backup features to Walt Kelly's *Our Gang* stories. The rest of the fifty-two pages in *Our Gang* #6 (down from sixty-eight in the previous issues) was made up of stories starring Flip and Dip, Billy Dollar, Benny Burro, Barney Bear and Walt Kelly's Bumbazine and Albert, the former of whom would be replaced by Pogo. Over time, some were replaced by new, more promising features, but for the book's entire six-year run, Tom, Jerry and Tuffy were on hand. Stanley's last finished (penciled and inked) artwork on the series ended in *Our Gang* #22 (March 1946), although he did return as the writer and layout artist in issues #43 to #50, after the book was retitled *Our Gang with Tom and Jerry.*

WHEN OSKAR LEBECK was given the job of editing comic books for Western, he inherited the ongoing Dell anthology title *The Funnies*, which began in 1936. From 1938 to 1942, it offered original content featuring such characters as Mr. District Attorney (based on the radio series) and John Carter of Mars (adapted from the novels of Edgar Rice Burroughs). The book was revamped as *New Funnies* with issue #65 (July 1942) to exclusively consist of humorous stories for younger readers, such as Andy Panda, Raggedy Ann, Peter Rabbit, Oswald the Rabbit and Lil' Eightball, among others.

Walter Lantz's *Andy Panda* was the second series entrusted to Stanley, after he had shown his ability with *Tom and Jerry*. The Walter Lantz Studio began producing theatrical cartoons starring the character in 1939, which were distributed by Universal Studios. Eight appeared from 1939 to 1941, at which time Western licensed the character. The problem facing Stanley was that Andy Panda's personality had been ill-defined in his animated cartoons, and, again, Gaylord DuBois's writing fell short. He hadn't found a way to make the character interesting, and artist George Kerr's art suffered from terminal cuteness.

The first thing Stanley did was introduce a friend and regular costar for Andy named Charlie Chicken. He may have been inspired by the appearance of a feisty rooster in the animated cartoon *Andy Panda's Victory Garden*, released on September 7, 1942. In Charlie Chicken's origin story in *New Funnies* #79 (September 1943), he is a newly hatched, unnamed chick. In the next issue, he's

Full spread: Pages 1 (*left*) and 4 (*right*) are from the first comic book story John Stanley wrote and drew, for *Our Gang* #6 (July–August 1943). Note the highly unusual toilet imagery on page 4.

an "adolescent" chicken, with his assertive personality emerging. Then, in *New Funnies* #80, Charlie assumes his familiar form as Andy's best friend (some would say "life partner" since they sleep in the same bed). Charlie is an instigator who often provides the impetus for the story. Monitoring the self-centered, impulsive behavior of his flawed friend gives Andy something to do: a *raison d'être*.

Since Charlie Chicken was given his name, personality and story function (as a friend, rather than a nemesis) by John

Stanley, who also did the finished art on the initial stories, he qualifies as Stanley's first ongoing, original character. Charlie is the first of a series of troublesome friends in Stanley's work, such as Lulu Moppet's best friend, Tubby Tompkins. Charlie is a true eccentric; the tale in *New Funnies* #121 begins with him obsessively counting the number of pennies in his collection.

Stanley did the finished art for many of the *New Funnies* covers. His first appeared on *New Funnies* #79, the issue that ran his initial

Andy Panda story. Although his interior art is deft and fully professional, Stanley's covers are even better. They are bold, zestful and inviting, and have a stripped down, streamlined appearance that fits the no-nonsense tenor of wartime America. Charlie Chicken was added to the covers as of #81, as befitting his status as *de facto* costar. He would remain at Andy's side through the rest of the bear's run in comic books, which ended in 1978. That means Charlie was John Stanley's longest-lived original character in comics.[16]

NINETEEN-FORTY-THREE SHOULD have been his apprentice period in comic books, but he was an unusually quick study. Stanley seems to have instantly understood the requirements of the medium: establishing characters through action, and staging the action to build the story to a satisfying conclusion. He was an innate storyteller and humorist who became a full-blown comics *auteur* as soon as he had the chance to "do it all" (including, often, the lettering). Moreover, he showed that he had the ability to take

Left: Charlie Chicken, Andy Panda's buddy, compulsively counts his penny collection. From *New Funnies* #121 (March 1947). **Right:** The feisty rooster in the animated cartoon *Andy Panda's Victory Garden* may have inspired Stanley's creation of Charlie Chicken. Charlie made his debut in *New Funnies* #79, which went on sale on August 1, 1943, almost a year after the cartoon was released.

a character invented by someone else, and, while working within certain general parameters, find ways to develop and enhance that character.

John Stanley's association with Andy Panda in *New Funnies* lasted about four years. When Western wanted to see if Andy could support a comic book of his own, Stanley was enlisted to handle the second such tryout in Dell *Four Color* (#54, Fall 1944), which included his first attempt at a long story. "The Ghost Rider" stretched over thirty-four pages, playing on the widespread interest among children in all things set in the Old West. Even "The Magic Hat," the second story, is longish, running sixteen pages. It detailed Andy and Charlie's fall through a magician's hat into Hokus Pokus land, another type of story that became a Stanley

favorite, putting his protagonists in some sort of fantasy land filled with amusing, imaginative characters. The finished art in *Four Color* #54 was done by Dan Gormley, a cartoonist whose career seems to have begun in 1940 or 1941 on realistic comic books such as *Captain Midnight* and *Gang-Busters*. During and after the war, he did the finished artwork on John Stanley's *Andy Panda* and other stories, becoming a linchpin in Lebeck's operation.

Comic book script formats varied, but writers typically wrote at the typewriter, providing the captions and dialogue for each panel, and describing the action in verbal form. John Stanley didn't work that way. He sketched the action on each page on a blank sheet of paper, and wrote the words (in cursive) in balloons and captions where they were to appear. Stanley called these pages "storyboards," a carryover from his animation days. (Others have called them "layouts.") The sketches emphasized figure placement and gesture. They served as a guide for the finished art, which was done on large sheets of heavy paper about twice the size of a page in the printed comic book. The storyboards were made for his own use, but when Lebeck saw them (scripts were submitted in advance, especially for a new feature), he realized they would be helpful for other artists, too. If Stanley were freed from doing the finished artwork (penciling, inking, lettering), then he could move on to the next story. To Lebeck, Stanley was more valuable as a writer than he was as an artist, so as time went on, more and more of his stories were finished by others. (Unfortunately, while examples of Stanley's storyboards for some of his later stories exist, none from his early years in comics have survived.)[17]

Other features identified as Stanley work from 1943 through 1945 include *Lil' Eightball*, *Oswald the Rabbit*, *Hector the Henpecked Rooster*, *Johnny Mole*, *Blackie Lamb*, *Cilly Goose*, and *Flip and Dip*. Occasionally he would letter a story for a colleague, or apparently collaborate to "fix" or complete a story. Lebeck kept Stanley busy,

gradually increasing his workload. Given the vagaries of the business, there were times when it was mandatory that Stanley produce a story in a single day. He never let Lebeck down. In later life, he was asked where he got story ideas. Stanley responded, "[Story ideas] were just grabbed out of thin air, and done. In those days, I could write a six-page or an eight-page story in a day. No problem."[18]

AS 1944 ARRIVED, JOHN STANLEY continued to live with his family in the Bronx. They were worried about Jimmy, who was in the Air Force, now that the United States was finally launching attacks in Europe. The Allies landed in Italy, but the German forces were fierce. Second Lieutenant James F. Stanley was a navigator on a Consolidated B-24 Liberator airplane. Then the news came in a letter from the War Department, dated March 19, 1944.

Sometime between February 12 and 15, 1944, "while participating in sustained operational activities against the enemy," Jimmy Stanley went missing in action.[19] The family had to wait until July before he was declared dead. The War Department awarded the Air Medal posthumously to the young flier. The funeral service was at Visitation Church in the Bronx. Barbara Steggles said, "I remember going to church for his funeral. The coffin with no body inside was draped with a flag. I remember this, even though I was a little kid, because family members never seemed to cry, but they cried then. Everyone was crying. My grandmother never really got over that. My father [Tom] used to say, "Jimmy was a nice kid. He didn't deserve to die."[20]

At the time of this family tragedy, John Stanley had been creating comic book stories for a little over a year. After the slapstick of Tom and Jerry, and the domestic hijinks of Andy Panda—both started in comic books by others—Stanley was chosen by Lebeck to be the first to adapt a new character licensed from Walter Lantz Productions.

Just as Daffy Duck began as a chance appearance in a Porky Pig cartoon in 1937, Woody Woodpecker was intended as a one-time supporting character in an Andy Panda animated cartoon in 1940.[21] In *Knock Knock*, Woody was a crazy irritant to Andy and Papa Panda and was dragged off to the "funny farm" at the end of the story. He was created by Walter Lantz and storyboard artist Ben Hardaway, and animated by Ale Lovy. Mel Blanc provided his voice and trademark laugh. Even though he calmed down somewhat after getting his own cartoon series, Woody's brash, aggressive, screwball character remained. His cartoons began with Woody popping through the title, asking, "Guess Who?," followed by that staccato laugh. His wartime cartoon, *The Dizzy Acrobat*, was nominated

WAR DEPARTMENT
SERVICES OF SUPPLY
OFFICE OF THE ADJUTANT GENERAL
WASHINGTON

IN REPLY
REFER TO
AG 201 Stanley, James F.
PC-N NAT145

5 July 194

Mrs. James Stanley
2907 Heath Avenue
New York, New York

Dear Mrs. Stanley:

It is with profound regret that I confirm the recent telegram informing you of the death of your son, Second Lieutenant James F. Stanley, O-811,783, Air Corps, who was previously reported missing in action on 19 March 1944 over Italy.

An official message has now been received which states that he was killed in action on the date he was previously reported missing in action. If additional information is received it will be transmitted to you promptly.

I realize the burden of anxiety that has been yours since he was first reported missing in action and deeply regret the sorrow this later report brings you. May the knowledge that he made the supreme sacrifice for his home and country be a source of sustaining comfort.

My sympathy is with you in this time of great sorrow.

Sincerely yours,

J. A. ULIO
Major General,
The Adjutant General.

1 Inclosure
Bulletin of Information.

Clockwise from left: Stanley family photo ca. 1941. Baby Barbara Stanley is held by her aunt Marian, with Barbara's mother Margaret (Peggy) and uncle Jimmy Stanley completing the foursome. John Stanley, sometime during the dark days after his brother's funeral. Second Lieutenant James F. Stanley, and the government letter, dated July 5, 1944, that confirmed his death in air combat over Italy.

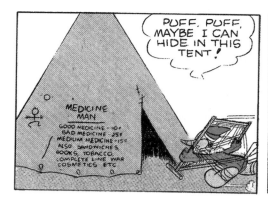

for the same Academy Award that Tom and Jerry's *The Yankee Doodle Mouse* won.

John Stanley warmed up with a simple one-pager in *New Funnies* #85 (March 1944). "What a nuisance I am!" Woody proclaims in the opening panel, and then frustrates a man working under an open manhole by fiddling with an underground pipe, creating a geyser in the middle of a city street. "Tsk, tsk. What's he sore about? I come along an' fix that well for him so's he gets plenty of water, an' he loses his temper!!" His first multipage story

in any comic book, in the following issue, has Woody attempting to join an American Indian tribe.

Woody appeared on the cover of *New Funnies* for the first time on #87 (May 1944), in the form of a headshot alongside others. His character was still in flux, and wasn't fully formed until Stanley had been on the strip for over a year. In some stories, he was an adult looking for work. In others, he was a schoolboy. As the Woody Woodpecker series evolved, one can feel Stanley's interest in the comics medium quicken. He became more focused on the

Top: Woody Woodpecker's second appearance in comic books, written and drawn by John Stanley, appeared in *New Funnies* #86 (April 1944). **Bottom:** By *New Funnies* #93 (November 1944), he was including disturbing elements in Woody's stories. **Opposite:** From *New Funnies* #127 (September 1947).

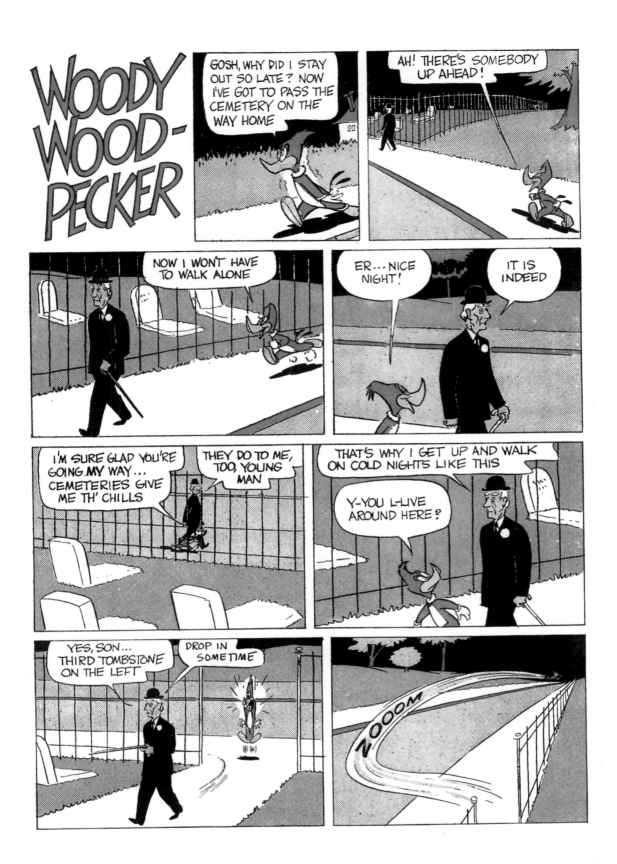

work, improving his cartooning (he did the finished art), making the stories more sophisticated and personal, and exploring the potential of comics in both form and substance. By *New Funnies* #93 (November 1944), Stanley's seventh full-length Woody tale, the series began to become something special.

This extraordinary story begins when Woody, in this case a student, decides to play hooky. He sneaks away from school, avoiding Truant Officer Ketchem. Happily, he makes it to a creek and relaxes with his fishing pole. "And so," a caption reads, "Woody falls asleep and dreams." In his dream, Woody is attempting to

escape over a wall from a school that resembles the island prison Alcatraz. As Woody swims away, he is pursued by Ketchem, a dark figure in a speedboat who fires a rifle at him. A desperate Woody flees by train, through a swamp and finally to Darkest Africa, where Ketchem is waiting for him, now wearing a skull-like death mask like something out of *Heart of Darkness*. Woody takes to the desert, and is dying of thirst when he spies an oasis. Even there, Ketchem is waiting with his rifle. "There's only one place left to go—the North Pole! Even if I freeze to death, at least I'm safe from Ketchem!—And school!" But no, at the top of the pole, Ketchem awaits, cackling, "Ha! Ha! Ha! Ha! Ha! Ha!," to which Woody yells "Yow!" He wakes from the nightmare, only to find the real Ketchem has found him. A subdued Woody submits, still in shock from the terrifying dream.

Woody's hooky nightmare is Stanley's first full-blown horror story. Although not unheard of in children's literature, that sort of thing was highly unusual in comic books, especially those from family-friendly Dell. Subsequent stories by Stanley included Andy Panda's encounter with a psychiatrist, and a disquieting story about the "suicide" of Hector the Henpecked Rooster. (Hector is a victim of spousal battery at the hands of his domineering wife, and fakes his suicide to get back at her.) From this point forward, dark elements become so common in his stories that it's clear that there was a mordant streak in his creative imagination. Still, while remarkable and unusual, the "Stanley darkness" would be expressed in terms that stayed within acceptable parameters for children's comic books.

How much of this reflected his own fears? In 1986, comic book historian Maggie Thompson wrote, "The fears [John Stanley] played upon in his days of comic book creation seem to be universal: fear of death, of loss of family, of the dark, of the familiar-turned-betrayer, of the dangerous unfamiliar. Did he use them because . . . he felt those nightmarish fears himself?" To this, Stanley responded, "It's possible. I still have nightmares and did as a child, and whether or not this had anything to do with it, I don't know."[22]

A cross pollination occurred between the Woody Woodpecker comics and the Walter Lantz cartoons. John Stanley's story in *New Funnies* #98 (April 1945), which recounts Woody's battle with an anthropomorphic weed that attacks his precious geranium, was used as the basis of the Andy Panda cartoon *The Wacky Weed* (released December 16, 1946). Obviously, the animators were reading John Stanley's work. Likewise, Stanley was paying attention to the cartoons, using the premise of the Woody Woodpecker cartoon *The Screwball* (released back in February 1942) for his baseball-themed story in *New Funnies* #126, his last full-length Woody tale. By this time, he was needed on another feature, so, after five more Woody one-pagers, he left *New Funnies* behind. He had been a major force behind it for nearly four years.

By the time he was finished with the anthology title, John Stanley had become one of the preeminent creators at Western Printing and Lithographing Company. Writers and artists at Western were encouraged to follow Stanley's lead. Woody Woodpecker is a case in point. Stanley made Woody Woodpecker work in comic books. His successor—the first Western artist to notably carry on the Stanley manner—was former Disney animation in-betweener (working under Jack King) named Dick Hall (b. Dick Marion), who imitated Stanley's work in such Woody stories as "The Evil Genius" (*Four Color* #169, October 1947), the first all-Woody comic book, and "Star of the Circus" (*FC* #188, May 1948), a thirty-two-page story. Hall's comics couldn't equal Stanley's work, but he managed (for a time) a reasonably faithful copy. Dick Hall was but the first of numerous Western writer-artists who were evidently urged to "do stories like John Stanley."

Woody's Stanley-written-and-drawn battle with an aggressive weed in *New Funnies* #98 (April 1945) was appropriated by the writers of the Andy Panda cartoon *The Wacky Weed*. **Opposite:** *New Funnies* #106 (December 1945) has John Stanley art.

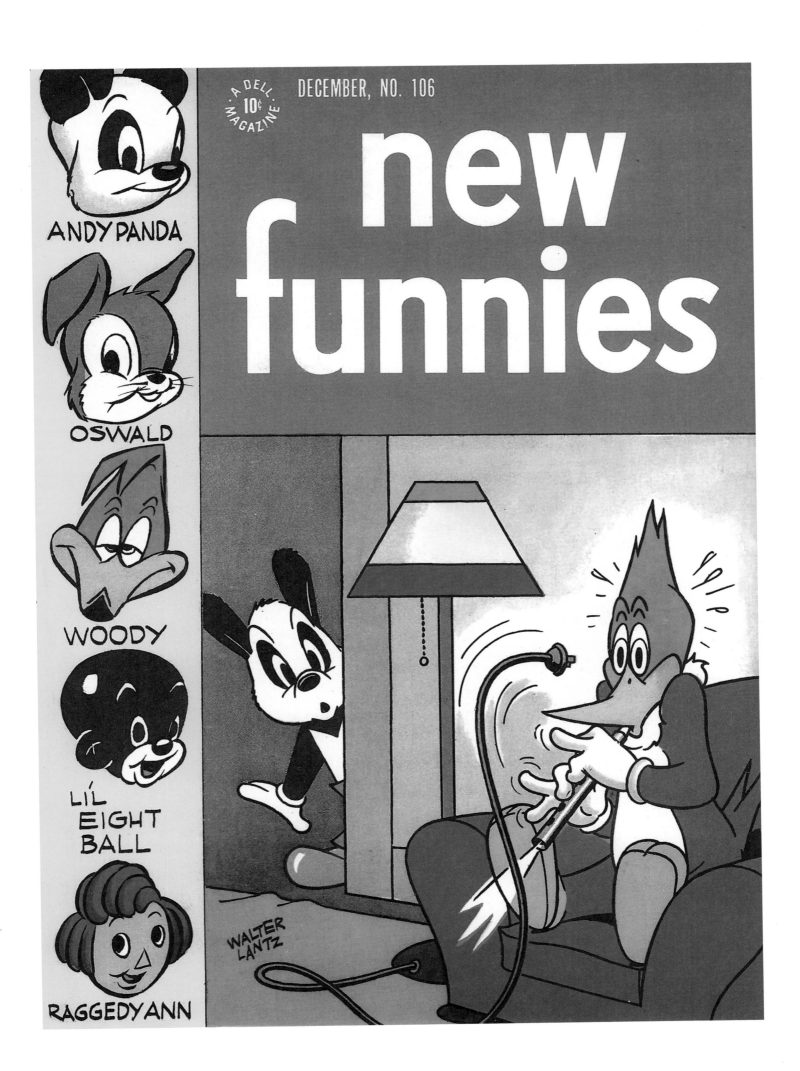

by Marge

LITTLE LULU

Little Lulu panels from the _Saturday Evening Post_. **Top left:** Little Lulu's debut appearance is in the February 23, 1935 edition. The cartoons had no captions but often incorporated words into the graphics as part of the gags. Marjorie Henderson Buell art. **Opposite:** The first _Little Lulu_ book reprinted panels from the _Post_. Rand McNally published it in 1936.

4

Giving Life to Little Lulu

HAVING REACHED THE top tier of Oskar Lebeck's staff of free-lancers, John Stanley had no way of knowing that, in the fall of 1944, he was about to be given a career-defining assignment. He was called upon to create a comic book version of Western's latest licensed property: Marjorie Henderson Buell's cartoon character, Little Lulu. As Stanley later put it, "Then Lulu came along, and the rest is history."[1]

Marjorie ("Marge") Lyman Henderson was born in Philadelphia on December 11, 1904, and grew up on a farm in Malvern, Pennsylvania. Her father was a Philadelphia lawyer who commuted to the city by train. As a child, she developed the ability to express her insouciant sense of humor in cartoon form, and precociously entered the ranks of professional cartoonists by selling her work to *Judge*, the popular humor magazine, at the age of seventeen. Before long, she was turning out cartoons, illustrations, and stories for *Life*, *Country Gentlemen*, *Collier's* and the *Saturday Evening Post*. In December 1934, when Carl Anderson's wordless *Post* cartoon panel *Henry* was sold to the King Features Syndicate (to be turned into a newspaper comic strip), the magazine's editor George Horace Lorimer asked Marge to create a replacement panel to appear in each issue.

"I brought in a number of roughs showing a mischievous little girl with corkscrew curls, and he liked them," she recalled.[2] "I wanted a girl because a girl could get away with more fresh stunts that in a small boy would seem boorish. The *Post* editorial staff named her 'Little Lulu,' which I've always thought was a very good name. I'd never done cartoons without words, and it sounded like fun. It was, and turned out to be no more difficult to do than cartoons with words. Occasionally I did a four-panel strip of Lulu to carry out an idea."[3] *Little Lulu* was introduced in the February 23, 1935 issue, with a cartoon of Lulu as a flower girl at a wedding tossing banana peels instead of flowers before the bride.[4] For the following nine years, Marge produced the weekly *Little Lulu* panel, which was unfailingly popular with readers. In 1936, she married C. Addison Buell, who (like her father) was a lawyer. They continued living in rural Malvern.

Lulu's character was in the tradition of other troublesome urchins in the early funnies, such as *The Yellow Kid* and *The Katzenjammer Kids*. According to the Meriam-Webster dictionary, "lulu" is slang for "one that is remarkable or wonderful."[5] Her antics included such antisocial behavior as cutting the tails off a

man's tuxedo with a pair of scissors, painting the fingernails on statues, taking a cat to a dog show, shouting into a doctor's stethoscope, and sticking out her tongue in a formal family photograph. Lulu's penchant to annoy was epic. It wasn't that she didn't realize her actions were objectionable. She just didn't care. In the *Post* of July 3, 1943, Buell said, "Lulu isn't mean except to stuffed shirts and Joe, her fat boyfriend, and she's only mean to Joe when he has been naughty or disloyal to her." Yes, there were consequences (sometimes) for her actions, such as the proverbial "good spanking," but even then, she put a sign on her bottom reading "Fragile." Buell's Lulu was a

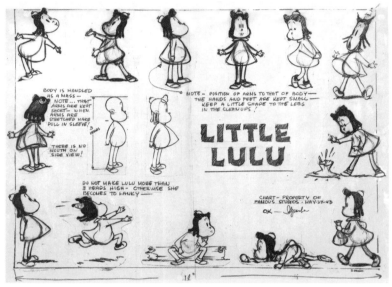

character, and seem to have (more or less) led to Lulu becoming the mascot of Kleenex tissues in a national advertising campaign. The lucrative Kleenex deal was predicated on Buell's participation as chief artist for all kinds of advertising: magazines, newspapers, billboards, display cards, bus signs, et al. This became her full-time job, just as her magazine panel was discontinued.

According to Buell, the *Post* was pleased with the idea of a Lulu animated cartoon series but became uncomfortable with the Kleenex deal (which would plaster Lulu's face across all media), so Buell left the magazine. "Our parting was a friendly one," she said, "and I've had no regrets."[6] Her final cartoon appeared in the December 30, 1944, edition, showing Lulu tossing away her New Year's resolution, which read, "I resolve to be a good girl in 1945."

Before ending the Lulu panel, Buell was approached by Western, and signed an agreement with them for the publication of "books, comics, magazines and other publications containing or featuring Little Lulu and various supplemental and subordinate characters which may, from time to time, become associated with Little Lulu in stories or in pictures or in any printed form."[7] The contract was dated March 25, 1944. The arrangement was expanded to include one-shot comic books in a second contract, dated October 23, 1944, which gave Western "the right to publish in printed form, in color or in black-and-white, comics magazines or comics [sic] books known as one-shots" starring Little Lulu."[8] The mention of "one-shots" may be a reference to the ongoing Dell *Four Color* series of comic books, where Little Lulu's adventures would appear. *Four Color* was referred to at Western as its "one-shot series." Buell would receive royalties of $500 for the first 300,000 printed, and one-quarter cent for each copy sold over that figure. She was paid an advance of $5,000 at the time the contract was signed, and would receive another $5,000 the following year. Marge would not write or draw these new comic books, although she had general approval of them. As she explained, "Having already signed a contract to do a large number of Little Lulu cartoons for Kleenex, it wasn't humanly possible for me to continue as writer and/or artist for Western's comic books as well."

pest, but a creative pest, whose actions reflected an above-normal intelligence. The readers loved *Little Lulu* from the start.

Marge retained ownership of the panel, and, as its popularity grew, she received offers from businesses that wanted to license her character's image. She accepted some of them. Rand McNally published the first collection of Lulu panels in book form in 1936. Five more similar books were issued by the David McKay company in the ensuing years. The Knickerbocker Toy Company manufactured the first Little Lulu dolls in 1939.

Richard Murray of Paramount Pictures met with Marjorie Buell in mid–1943 to discuss adapting the *Little Lulu* panel into a series of Technicolor, animated shorts. During a New York City meeting, Murray introduced Marge to William C. Erskine, who became her business representative. They struck a deal with Paramount for a series of Little Lulu cartoons, to be created by its animation division known as Famous Studios (successor to the Fleischer Studios, where Stanley worked a decade earlier). Her creative contribution was limited to providing model sheets to guide the animators. *Eggs Don't Bounce*, the first of the series, was released on December 14, 1943. The animated cartoons gained more exposure for Marge's

Kleenex ad from the March 10, 1945 issue of the *Saturday Evening Post*. **Opposite:** *Top:* Marjorie Buell in a 1943 Paramount publicity photo, which was used to announce its first Lulu cartoon. She is examining storyboards with Sam Buchwald, general manager of Famous Studios. *Middle:* Animator Joe Oriolo drew the Little Lulu model sheet, which is dated May 27, 1943. *Bottom:* Lulu in her first animated cartoon, *Eggs Don't Bounce* (December 1943).

John Stanley recalled, "Oskar handed me the assignment but I'm sure it was due to no special form of brilliance that he thought I'd lend to it. It could have been handed to Dan Noonan, [Walt] Kelly or anyone else. I just happened to be available at the time."[9] This typically modest comment made by Stanley after he retired from comics doesn't reflect the reality of the situation at the time. Dan Noonan was in the military, so he couldn't have been under consideration. Walt Kelly had his hands full with *Pogo*, *Our Gang* and other assignments, and his semi-illustrative approach was light-years away from Buell's more abstract, iconic style. Similarly, other artists on Lebeck's staff wouldn't be a good fit for Lulu. Comic art expert Hames Ware recently wrote, "The artist whose style might have come closest to Stanley's sparse, clean style would have been Oskar Lebeck himself. Lebeck had bowed out of art work for the most part by then, but, because of his instinctively wise artist choices, he probably realized immediately that Lulu called for John Stanley."[10] Later, Stanley acknowledged, "Somehow it suited me. They insisted that I do it."[11] Not only was Stanley's cartooning style right for Little Lulu, he was also one of Lebeck's best writers. Indeed, Lulu would be more about story than art. Lebeck knew that Stanley's hard-edged sense of humor and intellect were perfect for a feature coming out of a "class" magazine.

Roughly 200 days (a little under seven months) passed from the signing of the second contract and the date the first Lulu comic book was published, May 14, 1945 (just six days after V–E day).[12] This is more time than Stanley would normally need to produce work for a routine comic book scheduled to hit newsstands in May, but preparing the all-important first issue required extra care and planning. He had to create character designs and settings for the new medium, come up with a cast of supporting characters and conceptualize narratives that allowed Lulu to demonstrate her personality. That personality would have to go beyond what had been done before. It was his job to give "life" to Little Lulu.

Buell's creation of Lulu was fundamental, and creating a weekly panel presented challenges a-plenty, but it didn't require that she consider how her protagonist would speak and act in the course of a narrative. Fictional characters come most alive when they are revealed in a story, where their motivations are explored, where more complicated conflicts occur, and where greater verisimilitude can be achieved. Just as a movie has more life than a still photograph, so a sequential art story has more life than a single-panel cartoon. It was Stanley's job to flesh out Little Lulu as a fictional creature, giving her a kind of life she hadn't formerly enjoyed.

The first step was establishing a "look" for the artwork that sufficiently matched Buell's style, yet would be flexible enough to show Lulu and Tubby from all angles and positions. However, John Stanley wasn't the one who transformed Lulu from the tall, skinny, wraithlike character of the early *Post* panels. Marjorie Buell wrote, "Remember that Lulu appeared extensively in advertising after leaving the *Post*, starting in 1944. At that time, I changed the

Marge's Little Lulu

Full spread: John Stanley's first two pages as *Little Lulu* writer-artist are from Dell *Four Color #74* (June 1945).

appearance of Lulu considerably, changing her from a cartoon character to a real little girl. Plumper, shorter legs, wider dress, more attractive curls, big smile and the like. I also made some changes in Tubby at the same time. This new look was carried over into the comic books when they started in 1945, and it was generally felt that the three vehicles in which Lulu appeared—the *Post*, advertising and comic books, merged with each other in both appearance and personality of the characters."[13] An examination of Buell's early magazine ads for Kleenex show a Lulu that is almost identical to the way she looks in her first appearance in Dell *Four Color* #74 (June 1945). Nevertheless, Stanley was required to make the adjustments necessary to put Lulu through her sequential paces, and to express the intent of a writer who, inevitably, had a different creative sensibility.

Stanley's starting point was Buell's panels in the *Saturday Evening Post*. Now he studied them properly. He analyzed the basic types of gags that Buell used, and looked for specific ideas that could serve as springboards for stories. The most prevalent premises were inappropriate behavior in public, unorthodox uses of everyday items and unconventional money-making schemes. In addition, Lulu frequently interacted with animals, often at the zoo.[14] Numerous panels show Lulu using tricky methods to enter forbidden domains, such as a "boys only" treehouse. Although Lulu (according to Marge) was between seven and nine years

old, she was often entrusted with babysitting duties, and tended to come up with unorthodox ways of dealing with obstreperous children. Stanley was quick to see the potential in these situations.

Buell's panel offered much less guidance in terms of the supporting characters. Despite her claim that "Alvin, Gloria, Iggy, Willie, Dad, and Mother were seen in *Post* cartoons, gradually changing their appearances as years went by and adaptation to other uses took place," the fact is that (by her own admission) they weren't recurring characters, but "character types" with shifting appearances. The only supporting character whose look is relatively consistent, and who bears a name, was Joe, who was given a new name by Buell, although not quite as she remembered. Marge: "Tubby was renamed by me at the time—as I recollect—of the start of the Paramount animated cartoon series featuring Little Lulu and her pals."[15] Not so, unless the animators ignored her. Joe was renamed not "Tubby" for the Lulu animated cartoons, but (an unfortunate choice) "Fatso." Buell more likely came up with the "Tubby" name when she created model sheets for Western. John Stanley confirmed, "[Marge] gave us the name Tubby Tompkins. Maybe she changed it at the last minute, but that was his name, Tubby Tompkins . . . and Lulu Moppet. I think she supplied that [last] name too."[16] On another occasion, he was firmer: "Marge supplied their last names, Moppet and Tompkins. The rest of the characters, all of them, till the last issue done by me, were conceived, drawn and named by me."[17] That included Alvin, Gloria, Willy, Iggy, the West Side Boys, Lulu's parents George and Martha, et al.

With the model sheets and Lulu reprint books in hand, John Stanley got to work. He wrote, penciled, lettered and inked the entirety of the first issue, all thirty-six pages of it (there were no ads). Little Lulu's debut in Dell *Four Color* #74 (June 1945) is one of the most remarkable first issues in the history of the medium. It's a work of subtlety, masterful cartooning and expert story construction that is genuinely funny on every page. No other seminal comic book—not *Action Comics* #1 (the debut of Superman), not *Captain America* #1, not *Mad* #1—leapt into existence with such a fully realized first issue. Behind the cover were stories titled "Little Lulu" (ten pages), "At the Beach" (ten pages), "Minds Alvin" (eight pages) and seven one-page, wordless gag continuities.

On the surface, the first story simply titled "Little Lulu" is the least remarkable of the three. It starts with Lulu donning an angel costume made by her mother, which she is to wear to her friend Elsie Jones's birthday party. She and Tubby, who is dressed as Blackbeard the Pirate, go to that party, where they eat cake and play parlor games. It ends abruptly, seeming to run out of steam. Yet there's a great deal more going on in this simple narrative. For one thing, the first time we meet Lulu, she's in a cross mood (her most frequent state of mind in this first issue) because she hates the angel costume that she is forced to wear.[18] Why? Because she's worried about her social status, a common Stanley theme. Lulu tells Tubby, "If th' kids see me in that costume, I'll never live it down." When Tubby arrives in costume, he tells Mrs. Moppet,

"Don't be frightened! I'm only Tubby dressed up like Blackbeard th' Pirate." The first character trait he demonstrates is self-delusion (thinking his costume will fool an adult), suggesting psychological complexity from the start. To attempt to conceal her identity, Lulu commandeers Tubby's pirate beard for herself and he's helpless to take it back. This quickly establishes Lulu's primacy over Tubby. At the party, Lulu's "take no prisoners" personality is shown when she grows impatient when little Elsie can't blow out all the candles on her cake, and tosses a glass of water on the flames. She's such a disruptive presence that, when she's been blindfolded and spun around for pin the tail on the donkey, the other children open the door and guide her outside. ("You're getting warm! Warmer!") She ends up wandering through street traffic, which shows Stanley perfectly willing to put his character in mortal danger. But providence is also at work, guiding the blindfolded girl back to the Jones's home to finish the game. Stanley added subtle touches—such as hailing the beginning of the new series by having Tubby ask when Lulu will "get her wings." His knowing, unsentimental attitude toward children is refreshing and sets the right tone.

Having begun to lay the groundwork, his other two full-length stories are more ambitious. In "At the Beach," the reader discovers that despite their young ages, Lulu and Tubby have a great deal of freedom of movement. Their parents permit them to travel by bus to the beach unsupervised, which, given their penchant for getting into trouble, seems a questionable parenting decision. Somehow they manage to muddle through, by having a good eye to the main chance. Out of money, they fill their stomachs in the "Lost and Found" cabin, where children separated from their parents are treated to free food. They draw a number of adults into their maelstrom of meandering needs and wishes. Here Stanley shows his ability to create sustained sequences which have their humorous moments, but are more than gags strung together. This story signals that Stanley has elevated Tubby, an occasional supporting player in the *Post* and the animated cartoons, to costar status.

The last story in *Four Color* #74 is the superb "Minds Alvin." It's an ideal vehicle for Stanley to show the bland self-involvement of children, and to elicit gasps (as his stories often would) at their behavior. The premise: Lulu is saddled with babysitting her neighbor's little boy, Alvin Jones. This isn't the Alvin of later

Opposite: Little Lulu's first appearance in comic books. (Dell *Four Color* #74, June 1945). **Left:** "At the Beach" was the second Lulu story in *Four Color* #74. **Right:** One of seven single-page, wordless gag pages in that issue.

Pages 1 and 4 of "Minds Alvin," the last multi-page story in *Four Color #74*.

stories, who, while younger than Lulu, can talk. In this story, Alvin is pre-verbal, although he understands what they are saying well enough. Still, the essence of Alvin's personality is in place. As John Stanley later put it, "Alvin was the original rotten kid."[19] At this point, he's going through a "biting" phase. (Tubby: "G-gosh! Just like a snapping turtle!") After Alvin intimidates Old Man Gripe's bulldog, Lulu and Alvin put the "biting" Alvin between the bars of a lion's cage at the zoo. Alvin grabs a shank of meat from the lion and escapes with it unscathed. After they explain to his mother how Alvin got the meat, Stanley skips over her reaction, to the two of them scooting away, in what would become a typical Stanley elision. "I can't understand why she should get so excited," Lulu muses. Then she smiles. "It was nice of her though to promise she wouldn't ask me to take care of Alvin anymore." Fortunately for the readers, Mrs. Jones changed her mind in later issues.

In *Four Color* #74, Stanley uses techniques and ideas from his earlier Tom and Jerry, Andy Panda and Woody Woodpecker stories. One of the most obvious is the distinctive way he handles language. He commonly shortens words ("the" becomes "th'," "from" becomes "f'm," "come here" becomes "c'mere," "good night" becomes "g'night," "how are" becomes "how'r"). Words ending with "ing" are shortened (turning "getting" to "gettin'").

He invents words such as "sheddup" and "lookit." These shortened and conjoined "dual words" are his way of emulating the way children naturally speak. Favorite expressions ("Yow!," "A poke in the snoot!," "A fine thing," "I betcha," "One side," "That's all," "Phooey!") are in evidence. He frequently uses musical notes in word balloons alone (to convey humming) or with words (to convey a happy, singsong delivery, a perfect counterpoint to someone else's cross mood). Often sentences in word balloons end with no punctuation, and there are few captions (with notable exceptions, which came later). Also, there are multipanel sequences with no words at all. Stanley showed what he could do without words in the seven one-page continuities sprinkled throughout the issue. They are more "hit or miss" than his regular stories, and some of them are funnier than others, but all of them have a certain charm and diamond-like perfection.

The most important thing that Stanley brought to the comic books, which had not been a part of Marge's panels, was Tubby's personality. Marge's Joe was merely a foil for Lulu. With Tubby, Stanley created a character whose personality is so original, funny and complicated that he would almost immediately threaten to upstage Lulu in her own comic book. (More on Tubby's personality in Chapter 5.)

Even Lulu's personality changed noticeably. From panel one of the first story, Lulu is a much grumpier child than she was in the *Post* panels, frowning from the moment we meet her. Buell didn't use that facial expression often, but Stanley latched onto it, and used it on Lulu (and the other children) to great effect. It was a welcome change from the stereotypical "happy child" of other comic books and children's books. Stanley knew that a child who is often unhappy with the circumstances of her daily life would be more realistic, and intrinsically funny. Frowning suggests that expectations and hopes aren't being met. Thus, a problem must be solved or a conflict must be overcome, setting a story in motion. Most things presented by adults (even benign things) are met with that same frown. Showing "crabby" children made them more dimensional, granting them greater humanity. It also coincides with Stanley's own curmudgeonly tendencies.

Marge Buell: "It was clearly understood that I had the final word on the drawings and stories in the Lulu comics. Western sent drafts of each comic book for me to okay, and I returned the drafts, sometimes with suggestions for changes, but most of the time, without."[20] After completing the first issue, John Stanley visited her in Philadelphia to show her the finished art. This was the only time they met. He later recalled: "I went out to Philadelphia. I met her, and she was awfully nice and sort of bewildered by the whole thing. I really don't remember much of my stay there. She was polite . . . but gave me no instructions about anything. She had done her part, and she was perfectly willing to let it go at that, which I think is kind of nice."[21]

The cover of *Four Color* #74 is a simple image of Lulu walking, with a small dog trotting along beside her, against a Navy blue backdrop. The yellow logo is unimaginative, but at least it was large and hard to miss. Clues inside the issue suggest that Stanley also had input into the coloring design. The giveaway is the "rosy cheeks," which appear on the faces of Lulu, Tubby, Alvin and other characters, something picked up from Buell's *Post* panels. It's doubtful a colorist in Western's Poughkeepsie plant would introduce this time-consuming detail on his or her own. There are other eccentric oddities in the coloring that are unlike those in other Dell comics of the day, such as light blue or purple blotches in the white space around the characters in some panels, rather than a flat color evenly filling it in. Given the division of labor at Western, and how busy Stanley was at this time, he probably didn't color these issues himself, but passed along instructions to the colorists. (The "rosy cheeks" were phased out after the first few years.)

The Little Lulu stories by John Stanley are just as entertaining to adults as they are to children. The same can't be said of his work before Lulu. What changed? Was it a carryover from the *Saturday Evening Post* panel, which was read and enjoyed by people of all ages? Did he think the comic book would have a significant teenage and adult readership? At least a partial answer came years later, when Stanley explained, "I wrote for myself, my own enjoyment. Occasionally for Walt Kelly's enjoyment, but never the faceless mass of kids. I wanted guys like Kelly to say, 'Hey, you're great, man!'"[22] Stanley *was* writing for adults, because he knew his colleagues were looking over his pages as they came in, a common practice in the Western office. He wanted the respect of Kelly and his coworkers. His desire and capacity to entertain himself and other adults goes a long way in explaining why Stanley is remembered for his work on Little Lulu, whereas his work on Andy Panda or Woody Woodpecker has largely been forgotten. It also explains why he was able to invest as much creative energy as he did in Lulu, and why it sustained his interest as long as it did.

EVERYONE WAS DELIGHTED with the first Little Lulu comic book, but would it sell? Now the waiting began. If it didn't sell a high enough percentage of the copies that were distributed (publishers generally wanted a seventy-percent "sell through") then there would be no more. What worked in the *Post* or even in an animated cartoon wouldn't necessarily work in comic books. Buell, Lebeck and Stanley had to wait until fall for the sales reports from Dell's distributor, American News Corporation (ANC). Stanley handled assignments in thirteen subsequent comic books (issues of *New Funnies*, *Our Gang* and an Andy Panda issue of *Four Color*) before the fate of Lulu was known.

Sometime around October 1, the news came, and it was good. Exact sales figures aren't known, but there was no hesitation in putting regular follow-ups on the schedule. More *Four Color* Lulus would soon be appearing every other month, and they would be fifty-two page issues rather than the slim, thirty-six pages of the first one.

The big change with the second Lulu *Four Color* (#97, February 1946), which went on sale in January, was the cover design. Instead of the bright yellow, bouncy, block letters of the masthead on #74, this one introduced a new, graceful logo, in the style of cursive writing. Later, John Stanley wrote, "The masthead was done by a first-rate designer and letterer named Ed Marine. He did all the mastheads and color schemes for the Western Comics."[23] However, since it was clearly based on the lettering style that he'd used on the title of the opening story in *Four Color* #74, it can be considered initially created by Stanley, and adapted into finished form by Marine.[24] The other change on the cover was the addition of a decorative border framing the main illustration, with small images of Lulu in it. It gave the issue a distinctive look, setting it apart on newsstands from other comic books. The border/frame would be used on the rest of the *Four Color* Lulu issues, and on the first six issues of the upcoming, eponymously titled series.[25]

Could the second issue (Dell *Four Color* #97) possibly be as good as the first? Stanley had set the bar high, but something about Little Lulu inspired him like nothing had before. Virtually all of these early stories introduced new aspects of Lulu's and Tubby's personalities, new characters, settings and story concepts, and they are all gems. "Tubby's Travels" is a vehicle for us to learn much more about his personality, world view and quirks. It begins with Tubby's announcement to Lulu: "I'm gonna run away f'm home an' start life all over again." He has decided to roller skate

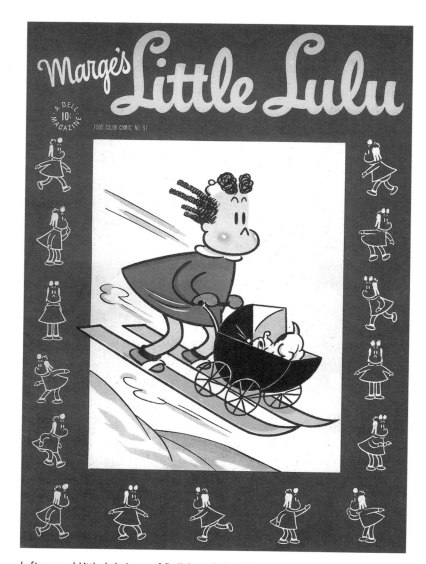

Left, second Little Lulu issue of Dell *Four Color* (#97, February 1946), and, *right*, page 1 of "Tubby's Travels." **Opposite above:** "Model Plane Contest" panel by Marge. **Opposite below:** Stanley adapted numerous situations in Marge's *Little Lulu panels* into full-length stories, such as "Enters a Contest" in *Four Color #97*. Pages 1 and 9 shown. Tubby scoffs but Lulu's unorthodox model plane wins the prize.

to Mexico "if my provisions hold out." However, he is ruled by his appetite, and eats the food he has packed before he gets more than a few blocks away. When Lulu convinces him that he can't go to Mexico because "it moved away," he decides to become a hobo. Lulu and Tubby encounter a hobo in the nearby woods. "I been all over the world," the hobo assures them. "Pittsburgh— Poughkeepsie." When Lulu announces that she must go home for supper, Tubby cannot resist the temptation of joining her. Neither can the hobo. The story ends where it began, at Lulu's house. Tubby's travel plans have given way to more pressing needs.

"Has Family Trouble," a story where Lulu must find homes for her cat's kittens, is a rare Lulu story without Tubby. Instead, it shows how Lulu gets along with her mother, and with other grownups in the neighborhood. In this story, we see that John Stanley's Lulu is a much better behaved girl than was Marge Buell's Lulu. Now, she is portrayed as "Lulu the problem solver," a role she will frequently play, as she must figure out how to get people to take four of the five kittens. "Goes on a Picnic" takes the reader on an adventure where we learn more about the way Lulu and Tubby interact, as they encounter various obstacles on their way to Moose Mountain, such as confronting a bull in a field,

crossing a stream, climbing a hill with a heavy picnic basket and exploring a cave where they meet a bear.

The most significant story in this issue is the one that starts it off. "Enters a Contest" was inspired by a Lulu cartoon in the *Post*. Lulu finds Tubby building a model airplane, which he plans to enter in a local contest. Tubby's misogynistic world view is revealed, after Lulu ventures, "Maybe I can help you make it." Tubby responds, "What? Are you kiddin'? Ha-ha-ha-ha-ha-ha! Girls can't make nothin' but fudge!" An infuriated Lulu decides to build her own model airplane, and, though tempted to buy a doll at the store, resolutely purchases an airplane kit. ("No one will ever know what a sacrifice I made. Sniff.") While Lulu's model isn't assembled quite as the instructions say, her airplane wins the contest, much to Tubby's chagrin.[26] Her prize money in hand, Lulu returns in triumph to the store to purchase the coveted doll.

"Enters a Contest" is the first of Stanley's Lulu stories with an underlying feminist theme. To what extent was Marjorie Buell a feminist? Her son, Lawrence, later wrote, "She knew she had created a feisty character and liked it. But she was not a conscious feminist. She didn't see life that way. She was like the mid–19th century women writers of best-selling novels who modeled (and imagined) a sort of feminism but were not feminist activists."[27] Still, there are feminist elements in Marge's panel. John Stanley made this an important theme, and would work many variations on it. It would soon expand beyond the push-pull relationship of Lulu and Tubby.

The third Little Lulu issue of *Four Color* (#110, June 1946) takes it a step further. The six-page story "The Working Girl" begins with Lulu noticing a "Boy Wanted" sign in a store window. She gets the job delivering a "Success" wreath to a new business across town. Although the wreath is destroyed when she gets caught in a revolving door, she gamely finishes the job, delivering its bedraggled remains. Beyond its "working girl" message, the story is also notable as the first extended Lulu story with no dialogue or captions. It's told entirely through the action in the panels.[28]

In "He Can't Hurt Us," Stanley also enters feminist territory. It begins when Lulu spies Tubby being harassed by a neighborhood bully. Without hesitation, she comes to Tubby's defense. When the bully leaves, using the excuse of not wanting to hit a girl, Lulu decides to teach Tubby how to defend himself. She has learned expressions like "put up your dukes" from her father, who has a pair of boxing gloves in the cellar. She knows who Jack Dempsey and John L. Sullivan are. More than that, she gives Tubby a punch (while wearing gloves) that knocks him onto a neighbor's rose bush, crushing it. As they run away, she allows that it's time to "practice

footwork." Finally, Lulu develops a scheme to get Tubby and the bully in such close quarters (inside a large box) that Tubby, who has the weight advantage, can get his arms around the boy and squeeze him into submission. Tubby doesn't deny Lulu credit for helping him defeat the bully. It simply makes no impact on

his male-centric world view. This becomes a pattern, which lets the boys vs. girls stories continue. Despite incontrovertible evidence to the contrary, Tubby's view of the superiority of boys over girls is unshakeable.

The third *Four Color* Lulu boasts five full-length stories in its fifty-two pages, including the uproarious, twelve-page "Stuff an' Nonsense," a slapstick tale which has Lulu bringing a horse into her house, and the fourteen-page "Lulu in Distress," when she tells Alvin a story, inaugurating a series that would be a part of nearly every issue to come.

This Alvin is a little older than the one in his first appearance. (He now seems to be about four, to Lulu's eight.) Lulu, the

marge's LITTLE LULU

'HE CAN'T HURT US'

Above: Lulu applies for a "Delivery Boy" job in "Working Girl" (*Four Color* #110, June 1946). **Below:** In that same issue, she gives Tubby a boxing lesson, in "He Can't Hurt Us."

babysitter, tells Alvin to behave. "I will if you tell me a story," he responds. Thus, Lulu concocts a long, meandering story, casting her as the protagonist who must deal with a wicked stepmother, and a nasty little brother who happens to be named Alvin. Her voice is conveyed in the captions, which understate what's happening in the images for a slyly comic effect. "After chopping the wood and stacking it in a neat pile, I would then set fire to it," Lulu says. But the neat pile looks to be about twenty feet high. "You see, Alvin liked to roast marshmallows." As Stanley explored Lulu's dreams and fantasies in this way, he found all sorts of ways the words and the images could work in counterpoint to each other. When telling these stories, he later commented, "[Lulu] enthralls herself. I mean, she's really talking to herself."[29]

THE FIRST THREE Little Lulu *Four Color* issues, all with Stanley's writing, finished art and lettering, are successful comic books on every level. The character designs work perfectly, and the storytelling is top-notch. Nothing in his work before Lulu had approached this degree of sophistication, focus and mastery of the form. The few flaws, like the abrupt ending of the first Lulu story, are insignificant.

His work reached a new level partly because of the aforementioned desire to gain the respect of Walt Kelly and the other cartoonists at Western Printing, but mostly because of the nature of the Little Lulu feature itself. He had created funny situations and stories previously, but doing stories about human beings rather than pandas, rabbits, mice and woodpeckers, released his full creativity as never before. Now he could make statements about the human experience in a way that he couldn't, with an attention to detail that helped the stories come alive.

With Lulu, John Stanley was able to tap into his own memories of childhood. Childhood issues such as bullying, getting the money to buy a birthday present, having accidents, competing with others, solving problems and learning teamwork are revealed by characters who are sympathetic but fallible, like all children. For, although Lulu and Tubby attempt to mirror the behavior of adults, which is their only guide, they do so while experiencing the attendant anger, happiness, frustration, envy, joy and disillusionment that are a much closer portrayal of the real childhood experience than the often sanitized, one- or two-dimensional images of children on radio, in the movies and in other comic strips. This evokes a shock of recognition in the reader, whether child or adult, creating an instant rapport. It's almost as if it opens a line of communication between the author and the readers, who feel that the storyteller understands them, and life.

In a way, Lulu, Tubby and their friends prefigure Charles Schulz's *Peanuts*, which was still five years away, by treating children as complex beings worthier of respect than they had generally been accorded thus far in comics. While the Lulu stories by no means eschew slapstick, it's like the difference between the slapstick of Charlie Chaplin compared to that of the Keystone Kops. Chaplin's slapstick had eloquence. The Kops, only chaos. Doing stories about human beings rather than talking animals brought Stanley down to earth, to the sidewalks that real children walk.

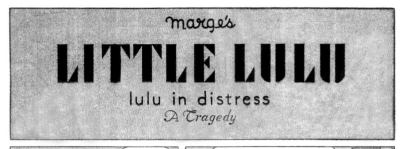

Above: In "Lulu in Distress, A Tragedy" (*Four Color* #110), Lulu tells a story for the first time to placate an unappreciative Alvin Jones. **Below:** John Stanley, mid-1940s.

LULU

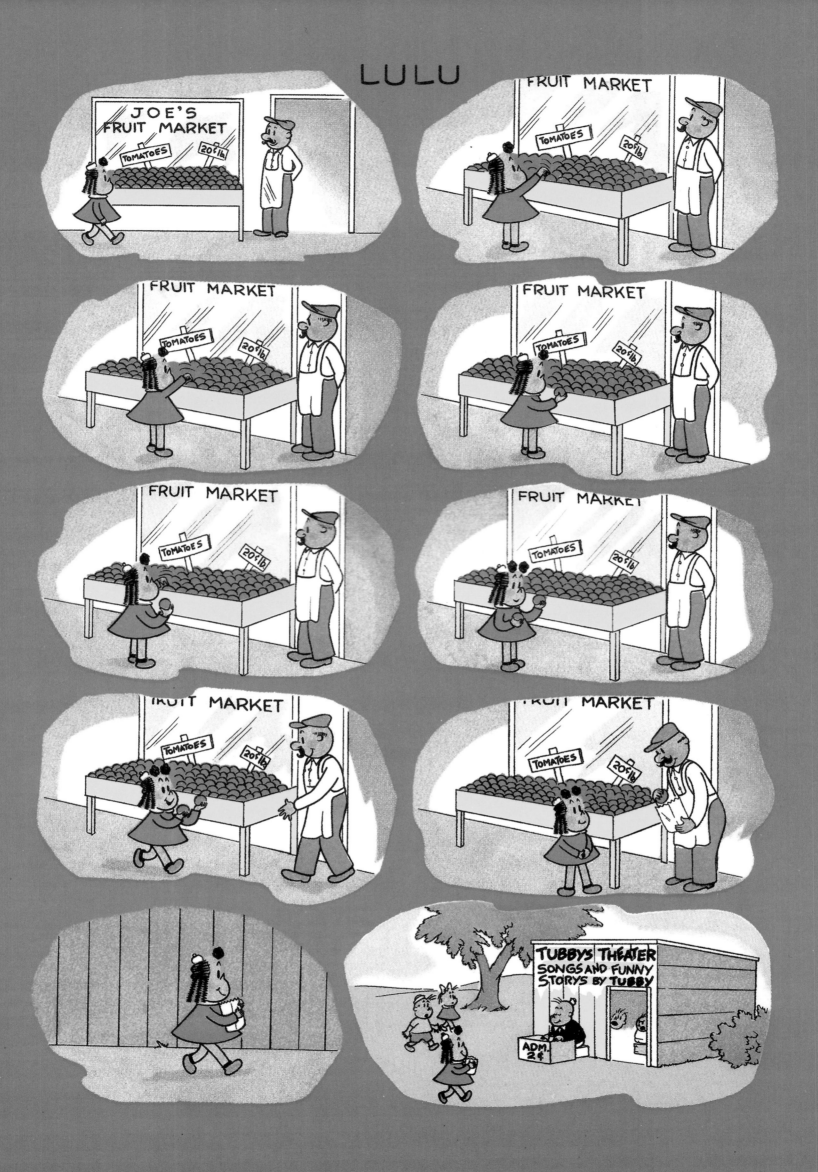

5

The Classic Lulu Years (1946–1949)

BY THE TIME JOHN STANLEY completed the first three Little Lulu issues in Dell *Four Color*, he had laid the foundation of the feature by deftly defining the personalities of Lulu, Tubby and Alvin and establishing their fictional environs. In the process, he had tapped into a fount of creativity that must have surprised him as much as it delighted his readers. The Little Lulu stories published from 1946 through 1949 are brimming with new ideas, new characters and new settings.

All five stories in *Four Color* #115 (August 1946) are outstanding. In "Fights Back with a Club," the "Men Only" treehouse is introduced, a prototype for the "No Girls Allowed" clubhouse of Tubby and his buddies that would become a staple of the feature in the coming years. In this story, Lulu responds to the all-male

club (officially called the Junior Paratroopers Club) by forming a "No Men Allowed" girls' club, to be called Lulu's Raiders. The members of the Boys' Club, an indistinct group at this point, pick Tubby to dress in girls' clothes to infiltrate Lulu's club and "learn all their secrets." Males forced to dress as females was a common comedic device in Stanley's stories.

In "Brings Some Friends Home to Dinner," Lulu feeds pigeons in the park, who follow her home and invade her house. In "Tells a Tall Tale," Lulu tells Alvin a story about the time she was marooned on a cannibal island. "A Problem in Box Tops" recounts the competition between Lulu and Tubby to submit box tops for a prize (a typical cereal promotion of the day). The story reveals that Tubby has a crush on Lulu and fantasizes being kissed on the

Opposite: Lulu thoughtfully shopping for tomatoes, from the back cover of Marge's *Little Lulu* #2 (March–April 1948). **Above:** Marjorie Buell originated Little Lulu's assaults on boys' clubs in her panels. John Stanley was quick to see the potential in this idea, beginning in *Four Color* #115 (August 1946).

Right: Stanley's penchant for ghost stories comes to the fore in "The Haunted House," in *Four Color* #115. **Opposite:** The script/layout for "Net Gain," a single-page *Little Lulu* gag continuity. Courtesy of Bob Overstreet and Ted Hake.

cheek by her. In the real world, most eight-year-olds aren't much interested in the opposite sex, but Stanley couldn't pass up the many story possibilities that would arise from such childhood crushes.

The final story is "The Haunted House," the first of the recurring ghost stories. Lulu and Tubby venture into an old, abandoned house and meet Timmy and Gertie, two "nice" ghosts who don't want to scare anyone. They also meet Kebel, "a nasty old ghost who lives in the attic." (Kebel is Lebeck spelled backwards, or close enough.) Lulu frightens Kebel with her "special loud screech" ("YE-EEEEE-YEOW!"), eliciting thanks from Timmy and Gertie, and an invitation to visit again. Significantly, the story isn't a dream or fantasy. It seems that "real" ghosts exist in Lulu's world.

Although Marjorie Buell seldom made any comment on the proofs of the stories that were sent to her for review, she noticed a change in the artwork in *Four Color* #115, and asked about it. Oskar Lebeck explained that two artists, Charles Hedinger and Irving Tripp, had begun helping produce the finished artwork on Little Lulu, working from storyboards by John Stanley. Irving Tripp later told comics publisher Bruce Hamilton, "When we got out of the

service, Charlie Hedinger and I, who were good friends, wanted something a little different to do and we went to Oskar Lebeck, Western Publishing's editor at the time—and we talked about it and he said he'd see what he could come up with. This was just about the time Stanley decided he wanted to do just the story writing . . . So Oskar gave Charlie and me the opportunity to do Little Lulu."[1] Stanley later confirmed that for the first three issues, "I did . . . the whole package myself. After that, the drawings were given to finishers, to other inkers, because I was too busy with other things. At that time, I had a half-dozen other magazines."[2] Lebeck assured Buell that outside of members of his own art department, no one but her had noticed the change. He told her that Stanley and his two new assistants were working efficiently and effectively, and that he was sure she would be pleased with the result.[3] Apparently she was, since the new production method went forward unabated.

Stanley didn't supervise Hedinger and Tripp. He remembered meeting Tripp "maybe two or three times at the Poughkeepsie plant. I never saw Tripp in the New York office. He was sent my storyboards, and enlarged and finished them. He did a good job, but he never added, subtracted or changed anything whatever.

I wouldn't allow any tampering with my work, and Lebeck, the boss, was totally supportive of this."[4]

Tripp: "[Stanley] turned [the storyboards] in to Anne DeStefano in New York and she checked them over and okayed them. Then she would send them to Poughkeepsie. I only had the opportunity to see Stanley three or four times when he visited Poughkeepsie for one reason or another. He came to Poughkeepsie with Oskar Lebeck on occasion, but mostly they were just having a good time."[5][6] Tripp admired Stanley, whom he called "Mr. Personality Plus."[7] When asked if Stanley's sketches were "rough," Tripp responded, "His were rough, but better than most. We'd get scripts from writers that were pretty crude, drawn with stick figures. They wouldn't even resemble the characters. In fact, the writer would have to label them. But you could almost reproduce Stanley's, they were so well done. But there again, if he was pushed for time—and he was always a little bit behind schedule—his scripts might come in a bit rough. But most of his, I would say ninety percent of them, were beautiful to work with. I mean, he had expressions! Everything was so clear and precise, you didn't have to go over it with a magnifying glass or ask questions about what did this mean or that. You knew."[8] Stanley summed it up: "For the thirteen or fourteen years I did them, all the stories, gags, etc., good and bad, were written entirely by me. The stories were done in storyboard form . . . and sent to the Poughkeepsie plant to be copied on large sheets of Bristol board, inked and lettered. All the front covers were drawn and finished by me."[9] However, it was Irving Tripp's artwork that delineated Stanley's stories for over a decade, and he deserves ample credit for his part in bringing those stories to completion.

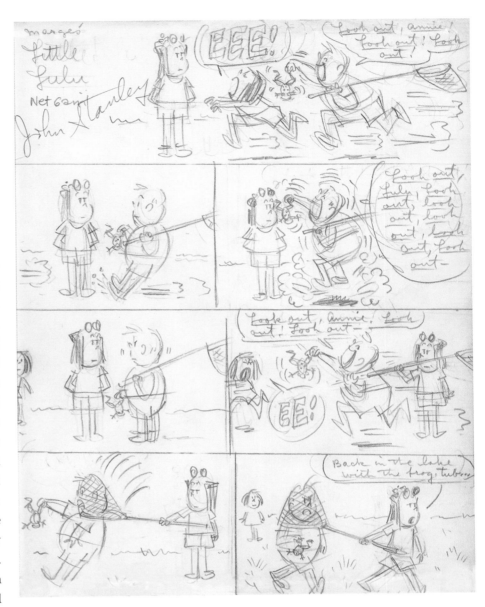

AS ONE READS the Little Lulu stories, and gains an appreciation for the creativity of John Stanley's writing—his ability to find humor in all sorts of everyday situations, his uncanny ear for the way children talk and his resourcefulness as a storyteller—one can't help but want to know about his creative methods. How did he develop the character of Lulu? Did his stories have autobiographical elements? How much did a story change from original conception to the completed form (his finished storyboards)? Did he, like some writers, create the beginning and ending of a story, then fill in the middle?

Only John Stanley could answer such questions, and he wasn't interviewed in any depth about his work in comic books until 1976, five years after he retired from the medium. (See Chapter 11.) Therefore, his recollections were colored by the passage of time, by certain unhappy events that eventually caused him to change occupations, and a persistent self-deprecating attitude about his own work. As Morris Gollub, a colleague from Stanley's days at

Western Publishing in the late 1940s and early 1950s, said in 1976, "[Stanley] has . . . an inferiority complex [about] his own work."[10] Also, his memory had dimmed, because he had given no thought to his early years in the business, and, most likely, because of chronic alcohol use. Nevertheless, Stanley made one thing abundantly clear: his creative methods involved a great deal of spontaneity and little, if any, preplanning.

Bruce Hamilton asked John Stanley to describe how he developed Lulu and Tubby. Stanley responded, "No stories had ever been written before, for Lulu or Tubby, so I started from scratch. I'm really not aware that there was any development. If you read the very first story I wrote, it's pretty much like the last one. The character is full-blown, such as she is, and that's it."[11] On this point, his memory was failing him. The Lulu of *Four Color* #74 changed considerably over the years, both in the way she was drawn and her personality. (More on Lulu's character in the discussion of Tubby's personality, later in this chapter.)

When asked by Tom Murray, a fan, "What is your thinking about the simplicity of style that you use . . . in your own work?," Stanley said, "Honestly, there wasn't any thinking. As soon as you begin to think about something, you don't do it right. I did it.

That's all. I did what I did, and I didn't have it in mind that they should be great or anything else, but just to make somebody read along. And to be interesting."[12] In terms of his settings, he added, "I tried to be economical, just because I was earning a buck and writing stories. Simple, keep them in the neighborhood, don't fool around."[13] The key thing to understand about Stanley's creative process is that he wrote instinctively. He knew that, for him, ideas and inspiration arose as he became absorbed in the story he was telling. Rather than maintaining a distance that allowed for calculation, he projected himself into the world of Lulu and Tubby. Each action and sequence logically led to the next. This is the source of those comics' believable character interactions, and uncannily real, cohesive "universe." Changes, new characters and settings emerged as each story unfolded. He never worked from a synopsis. "You know, you sit down, and [ask yourself], 'What's going to be interesting?' I start a story. I don't know how it's going to turn out. It just comes out in an organic sort of way. It works its way out. Someone else could do it better. But I do it that way."[14]

He discovered the end of the story at the same time as Lulu and Tubby. As he felt the end of the story coming (sometimes dictated by a required page count), he decided whether to end it with a gag, a twist or with understatement. If there was room, the story could have an extended denouement. Sometimes he only had room for an abrupt ending. His reliance on instinct was a conscious choice; not only because there wasn't time for preplanning, but because he'd learned by experience at Western that this was the way to summon his muse—or "you don't do it right." Not that it always worked. As he later revealed, "Sometimes I'd drop [a story] for a week or two, until I could carry it on. Speed was necessary. Many times, I sent in or brought in a story I didn't like. I'd bring in the whole magazine—thirty-two pages, whatever, in scripts—knowing that a couple of them weren't good, but one of them *had* to be good, the leadoff story."[15]

According to Stanley, the series with Lulu telling Alvin a story "just sprang into being. I have no recollection of how it came about. None whatever. I felt the magazine needed a change of pace . . . to get Lulu away from the neighborhood."[16] The desire for variety was the only reason that he cited. He rejected other ways of taking Lulu and Tubby out of the neighborhood, like having them travel to other parts of the country or foreign lands, because he didn't want to do the research.

When asked where he got his story ideas, Stanley said, "From within. It always comes from within."[17] He could write from the child's point of view because he was still in touch with his childhood self. Elements in the stories, apart from those derived from the *Saturday Evening Post* panels, are autobiographical. The environs are from John Stanley's "average childhood" in the Bronx of the 1920s. *Four Color* #74 alone shows such signs of urban life as houses with no front yards, just front stoops with a few steps down to the sidewalk, as well as street traffic (including trucks and taxis), alleyways, bus stops and a city zoo. Rural aspects of the Bronx can be seen in a city park, a creek that needs crossing or a pond that's frozen over for ice skating, all appearing in *Four Color* #97. We know that Stanley's youth included fishing and hunting trips, and other jaunts to the country, which could explain his protagonists' trip to Moose Mountain and encounter with a bear. As previously mentioned, the boys' clubhouse was inspired by similar clubhouses that Stanley recalled from his youth. So were Tubby's short pants, which were no longer regularly worn by boys after World War II.

Although Stanley lived in the Bronx all through the 1940s, visits with Lebeck in Croton-on-Hudson in the Hudson River valley—Stanley would eventually move there—and familiarity with the nearby town Peekskill, provided more source material. The Central Diner in Peekskill became the Sunset Diner in "Great Day," one of the most memorable Tubby stories of 1950. Many more places and settings in Peekskill found their way into Stanley's narratives in the coming years.

In 1968, John Stanley's coworker Dan Noonan described the effort Stanley put into his work: "Stanley always excelled as a writer. I think he could have been and still could be one of the top people in the field of comics. He was a hard worker. I went to Miami with him once, and I had the idea in mind that we were going to have a real tear-up time. But, come seven o'clock at night, he'd put his little steel-rimmed glasses on and sit down and go to work. And he'd work until one or two o'clock in the morning. And then he'd read for a couple of hours. I suppose he'd work the same way at home, too. He enjoyed his work."[18]

Whatever Stanley originally thought about working in comics, he'd learned to appreciate the medium by the time he came to Lulu. As Michael Barrier wrote in *Funnybooks: The Improbable Glories of the Best American Comic Books*, "There is in Stanley's best stories—as in Barks's best, not that either man ever spoke in such terms—an intensity of feeling arising from a wholehearted engagement with the comic book medium and a corresponding delight in its capacity for expression."[19] Stanley said that he didn't write for the readers, yet he later acknowledged that you had "to be aware of your readership, how they're going to react to your story. You have to bring them along."[20] Despite his obsession with social status, Stanley never seems to have felt that he was slumming in comic books. He appreciated books of both high and low literary value, loved newspaper comic strips and understood the need human beings of all ages have for stories, whatever the shape or form.

Stanley's stories in the remaining six Lulu issues of Dell *Four Color*—all "classic Lulu"—are fresh, funny, even outrageous. More characters, settings and situations are introduced in those issues, which had some of the finest Lulu stories of all time.

"Tuba Trouble" in *Four Color* #120 (October 1946) recounts not only Lulu's problems with the gigantic instrument, but shows Tubby with his violin for the first time. Lulu's last name, "Moppet," is revealed in this story. In the same issue, she placates Alvin with the story "Little Lulu and the Seven Dwarfs," the first fairy tale reference in the storytelling tales.

Borders on the Lulu covers gave her comic book a distinctive look on newsstands. *Top row: Four Color #120 and 131. Bottom row: Four Color #139 and 158.*

Left: Both Lulu and her readers have a hallucinatory experience in "Never Again" (*Four Color* #165); cover pictured below. **Right:** From "For President" (*Four Color* #158).

In "Is Taken for a Ride" in *Four Color* #131 (December 1946), an extra-long, twenty-one-page story, Lulu is abducted by two inept kidnappers. (Most Lulu stories are twelve pages or less. In this case, there's still room for two more stories and ten one-pagers.)

Four Color #139 (March 1947) has "The Big Snow Fight," the first full-length story involving snowballs and snow forts, natural for a writer who grew up in a city with consistently snowy winters. It climaxes with a snowball battle between Mr. Moppet and Mr. Jones, his neighbor, which gets out of control. Such winter-themed stories are among Stanley's best.

"For President" in *Four Color* #158 (August 1947) begins with Tubby announcing, "I think maybe I'll run for president of the United States!" When Lulu expresses the same desire, an incredulous Tubby responds, "Are you kiddin'? Tell you what—maybe I'll let you be the First Lady!" Her feminist ardor aroused, Lulu devises a scheme to show Tubby that he could never aspire to that high office. "Just a Gigolo" in that issue reveals that Tubby's appetite is a stronger motivator than the attractions of Dolly (a precursor of the attractive Gloria) or his friendship with Lulu.

Four Color #165 (October 1947) has three excellent stories. "The Case of the Purloined Popover" is Tubby's first foray into

criminology, a template for numerous tales of Tubby as an amateur detective. "Alvin's Solo Flight" has Lulu and Tubby on another jaunt to the beach, this time forced to take Alvin along. The issue also includes "Never Again," another wordless story in which Lulu tries smoking a bit of her doll's hair in her father's pipe. There's nothing anywhere else in the entire run of Lulu as strange as its ending sequence. The reader watches as a woozy Lulu's eyes move around on her face in impossible configurations. Indeed, since the reader is seeing something impossible, it's as if Stanley is giving the reader his or her own hallucinatory experience.

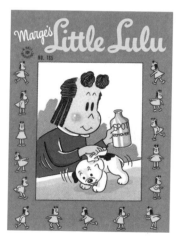

IN *FOUR COLOR* #146 (May 1947), John Stanley defines the character of Tubby in a way that sets the mold for the entire series. "The Kid Who Came to Dinner" is a comedy of manners. George and Martha Moppet have them. Lulu is manners-challenged. Tubby has none whatsoever.[21] It begins as dinner time approaches in the Moppet household. Mrs. Moppet takes Lulu aside and suggests that she tell Tubby to "go home—politely." Lulu turns to Tubby and says: "My mother says to go home politely." Unfazed, Tubby inquires what they are having for dinner, then invites himself for the meal, making one tactless comment after another: "I may not like the cookin'" . . . "Food is so expensive these days! Ha, ha!" . . . "Don't ferget I eat an awful lot!" Once seated, he demands everyone cater to his whims, and then, having stuffed himself (eating the baked apple dessert that Mrs. Moppet has fixed for herself), wails, "I been poisoned! I'm only a little boy and you poisoned me!" In actuality, he's merely overeaten. In this and other early stories, it becomes clear that Tommy "Tubby" Tompkins:

- Is aware of social niceties but is so self-involved that he has little or no consideration for them when he is going after what he wants. Yet, when others don't take his feelings into account, Tubby whines.
- Always seeks status, asserting (and assuming) his primacy, and claims to understand everything. That his concepts have little or no connection to reality never occurs to him.
- Aspires to be what a "man is supposed to be" from his kid point of view: a fireman, an Indian fighter, a hunter, detective, mountain climber, etc., pretending stoicism in the face of danger. Acknowledges no contradiction when he screams "MAWWWW" when he is even slightly hurt or afraid.
- Uses "kid logic" to interpret the world around him and solve problems.
- Absolutely believes in the superiority of men over women. He has to feel that he always has the upper hand with Lulu, even though it's clear that she has the upper hand most of the time.
- Far from feeling stigmatized by being fat, he feels it entitles him to more food than others. Food is the most important thing to him, even trumping status.

One gasps at Tubby's towering self-delusion, insensitivity, condescension and relentless double standards. In certain respects, he is much like the character of Lulu as she was conceived by Margaret Henderson Buell. Her Little Lulu didn't let social graces stop her from imposing her will on others. John Stanley has, through sleight of hand, made Lulu the voice of reason, an essentially "good little girl" who, while she still gets into trouble, does care about the people around her. Her errors, one feels, are an exaggerated but normal part of being a child, and we are confident the comic book Lulu will grow up to be a reasonably well-adjusted member of society. Tubby would seem to be heading for an adult life as a full-blown sociopath, although we forgive his flaws because he's "only a child" and is, essentially, likable.

Also in *Four Color* #146 is the important story "Crybaby," a "spanking manifesto" of sorts. When Lulu finds Alvin crying, and all her attempts to calm him are ineffective, she tells him a story about "what happens to people who go around crying all the time!" She recalls a time when she "used to be a crybaby," sobbing even when playing with friends, reading the funny pages in the newspaper, eating strawberry ice cream, etc., until the Moppet family is evicted from their home due to her incessant bawling. Finally, after they are reduced to homelessness, and are sleeping in doorways, "a change seemed to come over my father." Mr. Moppet takes Lulu in hand, and spanks her. Or, as Lulu puts it, "He placed me in a funny position over his knees and brought his hand up an' down on me very hard an' very often." And then, "I stopped crying." The story's message is lost on Alvin. "What a silly story!" he shouts. "I was cryin' *'cause* I got spanked!"

In Stanley's Little Lulu stories, a "good spanking" is a frequent parental response to a child's misbehavior and is never portrayed as harmful, merely a last resort for parents when other measures are ineffective or insufficient. Today, while legal in the United States, spanking children is considered unacceptable by a substantial percentage of parents and educators. However, the classic Little Lulu stories were written at a time when such corporal punishment was almost universally accepted by parents and children alike.[22]

Sales of *Little Lulu* were strong, and, although fan mail was reportedly arriving in increasing quantities, John Stanley saw little of it. "About one letter a month," he later said. "They withheld fan mail. They had them in the office. Everyone had their instructions: 'We'll give him one, a not-too-praising one. A little to keep him happy.' They didn't show you the bulk of it." Lebeck didn't show him specific sales figures, either. Stanley knew the comics were well-received in other ways: "They were nice to me, down there [at the office]. The editors used to buy me drinks and that sort of thing. You get the idea that you're doing all right."[23] He had to know things were going well when Little Lulu was given her own title independent of the *Four Color* series in late 1947, even though there were other factors than purely sales behind the decision.

At that time, Dell was in an expansionary mode. Promising postwar sales meant there was plenty of money to pay for Second Class mailing permits for individual comic book titles, and it made sense that its best sellers should have their own numbering systems. At the same time as *Marge's Little Lulu* #1 (January–February 1948), Dell published *Carl Anderson's Henry* #1, *Dick Tracy Comics* #1, *The Lone Ranger* #1, *Roy Rogers Comics* #1, *Smilin' Jack* #1 and *Tarzan* #1. Despite "graduating" in this manner, most of them, including *Little Lulu*, went from fifty-two to thirty-six pages in their own titles. This was less a cost-cutting tactic than a necessity, because paper supplies hadn't yet caught up to postwar demands.

The opening story in *Little Lulu* #1 showed that Stanley was prepared to stretch reality in Lulu's world. In "Mountain Climbing," Lulu and Tubby climb up the side of a city apartment building until they reach the top. The idea is that there are just the right brick extrusions for them to get hand and foot holds. As they climb higher, the absurdity of the situation grows, creating a tension that is perfectly counterpointed by comedic moments when they step through an apartment window for a drink of water, or

Left: *Marge's Little Lulu* #1 (January–February 1948). **Right:** *Marge's Little Lulu* #12. **Opposite:** Another Marge panel that inspired a John Stanley cover (*above*), and the first "Lulus Diry" entry (*below*).

Little Lulu #2 (March–April 1948) offered the memorable "Lulu's Conscience," with the good and bad in Lulu (depicted as angelic and devilish Lulus in her thought balloons) competing for control. It also introduced two new supporting characters: Tubby's and Lulu's teacher Miss Feeny, in "The Report Card," and Gloria, a pretty, blonde neighbor, in "Lulu's Heartthrob." Gloria is fated to suffer through Tubby's intermittent crushes from this point forward, and often uses them to manipulate him to get what she wants.[25] Tubby is much more outwardly smitten with Gloria—like Tom Sawyer for Becky Thatcher—than he is with Lulu.

Although the *Little Lulu* comic book only had thirty-six pages for its first fourteen issues, Stanley had room enough to return to ideas that had been introduced earlier, developing them into recurring elements in the series. One was the Boys'

for Tubby to make a phone call. Naturally, the people living in those apartments are startled and think they are seeing things.

Little Lulu #1 introduced a new, ongoing feature, titled, "Lulus Diry." When she saw it, Marjorie Buell asked for changes before going to press. Stanley: "When I did the early Dear Diry thing, [Marge] didn't like some of the wording I used, like cutting [the ends of] words off. I don't remember [exactly] what her criticism was, but I corrected it. It was a job, and you went along with it. But, for the rest of it, she never criticized anything I did."[24] His finished artwork accompanying these text pages had a loose, engaging quality meant to simulate the drawings of a child.

"No Girls Allowed" clubhouse, with Tubby's regular pals, Willie Wilkins, Iggy Inch and Eddie Simson (generally referred to as "the fellers"). Another was Tubby as a "junior" detective. Stanley was also able to indulge his penchant for ghost stories, although they were now explained as part of a dream, or in some other way. Dream stories, like the stories Lulu told Alvin, allowed Stanley to get Lulu out of her neighborhood. Sometimes a dream story became a nightmare story, giving him the opportunity to explore the dark side of his imagination. In "The Rocking Horse" in *Little Lulu* #5 (September–October 1948), Lulu no sooner enters another "haunted house" than she trips and is knocked out. Upon awakening, she discovers a rocking horse in a secret room. When she mounts the horse, it begins flying around the room and then out the window. At first terrified, Lulu discovers she can steer the horse through the air. Before long, she is flying next to an airplane, looking in the window. When a passenger screams "Stop the plane!! There's a little girl outside!," it's almost like the moment in the *Twilight Zone* when a passenger (played by William Shatner) sees a monster on a wing of the airplane. The thrill turns to terror when she descends to visit her mother, and the horse starts to fly away. Lulu grabs its tail, her mother grabs her leg, and the horse pulls them high into the air. Then the horse's tail breaks off and the two of them scream in terror as they're falling to their death. Next panel: Lulu wakes up in the haunted house, and realizes she has been dreaming. But then, how to explain the rocking horse tail in her hand?

The sales of *Little Lulu* were robust, so Western put the series on a monthly schedule with the seventh issue (January 1949), and upped the page count to fifty-two pages again, with *Little Lulu* #15. Wonderful stories kept coming, such as "The Beauty Contest" in #16 which introduced Lulu's best friend Annie Inch (Iggy's little sister, with buckteeth), and "The Deep Black River" in #17, one of the finest of the fairy tales.

JOHN STANLEY CONTINUED TO WORK at home, bringing his finished stories to Western Printing's office on Friday mornings. For Stanley, changes were seldom required. It was usually a simple matter of turning in the work and getting paid for it. If a new series required his services (apart from the Lulu work), he would step into Lebeck's office to discuss it.

All of Western's freelancers turned in their work on Fridays. Once everyone was squared away, Lebeck would take them to the Penthouse Club on the building's eighteenth floor for lunch and drinks. The group included some of the most talented people in comic books. One was Morris ("Mo") Gollub, who originally worked as an animator for Walt Disney on *Bambi* and other films. He was introduced to Oskar Lebeck after the war by Walt Kelly and went to work for Western as a cartoonist and

LULUS DIRY
PICTURES BY LULU TOO

May 1948

Dear Diry
It reelly isnt May but that is the only month i can spell rite because it is the shortest month in the year with only 3 letters in it. You will have to forgiv my spelling because i am just learning to be a tipriter and i cant spell so good on the tipriter like i can spell good riting with a pencil or a pen.

I always wanted a tipriter but Pop said he is very poor and cant afford to buy one. I felt so sorry for my Pop because he is poor that i cried and cried and he bought me this tipriter.

I cant wait to show it to Tubby. When he comes in i will make believe i dont know he is there because i am too busy tipriting. And he will say what are you doing because he is always nosy. And i will be polite and say what do you think i am doing nosy i am tipriting of course. Then he will say let me try your new tipriter and i will say no because you always break everything you touch like my Mother always says. Just a minute Dear Diry i hear Mother calling me. I will be rite back.

Here i am back. Mother wanted to know if i took the wisk broom and diddint put it back. Everybody blames everything on me. Yesterday i told Tubby that a wisk broom is no good to paint with but o no he has to borrow our wisk broom to paint the club house with and now i cant get the paint out of it. Everybody blames everything on me.

Well Dear Diry Tubby was here and he just left. He walked rite in like he always does just like he owns the place and said hi LULU. I made believe like i diddint see him because i was busy tipriting. He said he only wanted a glass of water and he went out to the kitchen and i heard him open the rifrigirator very quiet. But i heard it alrite and i hollerd what are you doing in our rifrigirator% And he said he was only looking and anyway he was going rite home to dinner in a minute. Then he came in to the room where i was tipriting and he said hey LULU i am going to visit my cousin in Vermont next year mabe whos name is Robert. And i said look at my new tipriter Tubby. And he said i havent seen my cousin Robert since we were little kids. And i said look Tub my tipriter rites printing just like in the newspapers. And he said my cousin Robert has a sailboat. And i said would you like to try my new tipriter Tub% And he said no mabe some other time because i have to go home to dinner rite away. Its a good thing he diddint ask me to let him try my new tipriter because i would have said no because you break everything you touch like my Mother always says.

It is now very late at nite Dear Diry. Almost 8 oclock. But Mother said i could tiprite for a little while before going to bed because i want to tell you what happened after Tubby left today.

Mother asked me to go to the store to get ½ pint of cream for Pops coffee and 50¢ worth of swiss cheese. I said o Mother why do i have to do everything around here espeshly when i cant have any coffee anyway. On the way to the store i met Geraldine from down the block who was going to the store to buy a loaf of bread which if it isnt fresh she will take it rite back. Geraldine says she has to do everything around the house too all the time. Her little brother Tommy who is almost 2 years old never does anything.

On the way back from the store Geraldine said lets walk by the pet shop which has white mice in the window that ride on a little ferris wheel. I said o lets go over there because i have never seen white mice that ride on a little ferris wheel. But when we got there we couldnt see so good because there were some big boys there who wouldnt let us stand in front of them. Then i said Geraldine lets go inside the store and look at the white mice over the little fence in the back of the window. So we went inside and asked the man if we could stand there and look at the white mice. He said alrite just dont touch them. Gosh they were cute and so white running around with little pink ears and pink feet. After we were there for a while i put the bag with the cream and swiss cheese down inside the window because it was gtting heavy and anyway there was plenty of room there with only 9 mice. We counted them. After a while some dogs in the store began to fight and we went over to where they were and the man said he would have to put them in seprate cages. Then we went back to the window and i took my bag out. Geraldine said gosh where are the mice they are not in the window. I said they are probly hiding some place but we couldnt see them. Then we left.

When i got home Mother said where have you been you took an awful long time. I said Geraldine and i stopped by the pet shop to see white mice on a little ferris wheel. Mother said o i am glad you have to go some place else to see mice because we dont have any in our house thank goodness. Mother took the bag with the cream and swiss cheese and went out to the kitchen Next thing there was an awful scream and when i ran out to the kitchen Mother was standing on the table. I said Mother what are you doing anyway% Mother said you wont have to go any place to see white mice anymore because we have plenty of them right here in the house now. She said the bag with the cream and swiss cheese was full up with white mice. They jumped out of the bag and ran all over the house. Mother was awful mad. Tomorrow i am going to ask Pop if he will buy me a little ferris wheel.

Thats all now Dear Diry because i have to go to bed.

Labels in illustrations:
MY POOR POP WITH A CIGAR
TUBBY WHO IS FAT
WISK BROOM
GLASS OF WATER
OUR CLOCK
GERALDINE
LITTLE TOMMY
BAG
DOG
MOTHER
WHITE MICE

Top left: John Stanley at Oskar Lebeck's house in Croton-on-Hudson with Anne DeStefano, Lebeck's secretary. Behind Stanley is Jane Werner (later Jane Werner Watson), who authored many children's books for Western. Jim Stanley commented: "My father never played an instrument, so the guitar photo is weird." Courtesy of Letty Lebeck Edes. **Bottom left:** John and Marian Stanley in Lourdes, France, 1948. Per Barbara Stanley Steggles: "[John] did take Marion to Lourdes. I remember when that was, because they went to London after that, and they were at Buckingham Palace on November 14, 1948, when Prince Charles was born. [They also] went to Ireland . . . and visited relatives there." This is John Stanley's only known trip outside the United States. **Right:** Publicity photo ca. 1950 of Oskar Lebeck (sitting), with Western freelance artists Mel Crawford, Dan Noonan, John Stanley and Dan Gormley.

painter. According to John Stanley, "Mo was one of those seemingly crotchety guys with a heart of gold. A nice man and a very meticulous draftsman. Some of his humor stuff had a Kellyish look to it but that was the Disney influence that Mo didn't particularly care for. He was actually a better draftsman than Walt Kelly but not as good a *comic* draftsman."[26] For his part, Morris Gollub liked John Stanley personally and was a great admirer of his work. "He was a sharp, bright guy who didn't babble too much. If you can remember the Arrow Collar type of individual, that's what he looked like—prematurely gray. He was a handsome son of a gun. He drank a little bit. He wasn't a lush or anything, but every weekend he'd hit a few, mostly because he couldn't sleep nights. All the restraints that his religious background [and] religious parents put on him seemed to have some negative effects that he could never really consciously offset, although he was not anything like religious."[27]

Walt Kelly was a regular at the Penthouse Club lunches. John Stanley recognized Kelly as a major talent: "Most of the artists were mainly concerned with their own stuff and there were some petty jealousies going on here and there, but when Kelly walked into the Western office with a stack of his art under his arm, everyone would stop what they were doing to read it. Everyone knew that he was something special. He loved to play jokes and, invariably, he would whip up some special drawing involving his intended

target. I must admit that Walt and I painted the town many times. He was a very enjoyable guy to be with."[28]

According to Gollub, Stanley had some problems with Kelly. "[Kelly] and Stanley got in a hassle," he told interviewer Michael Barrier in 1976. "[The] suspicion was that Kelly wanted to kind of take over and replace old Lebeck. I never could quite believe that. It probably came from Noonan, because Kelly wouldn't tell me that. Noonan had a way of ferreting those things out. [Kelly] couldn't have succeeded then, although later on anybody could have taken over from Lebeck [when] they were getting incensed at him up in Poughkeepsie, because he wouldn't follow directives. [Lebeck] insisted on being his own man. Stanley, whatever he thought, at least knew that Lebeck was square. He had a kind of contempt for Kelly." Stanley later told a friend that he witnessed Kelly pressuring a secretary to go out with him. When she wouldn't, Kelly had her fired, which Stanley thought was deplorable.[29] For his part, Gollub respected both Stanley and Kelly. "They were both very bright, and they both could be charming as hell."[30]

Despite these sorts of undercurrents, there was substantial *esprit de corps* at Western, per Dan Noonan: "We'd often stay and talk until late in the afternoon. The bull sessions sometimes lasted almost all day. There was a lot of ego deflating. Anybody who'd get to taking themselves too seriously was in for trouble, because laying in the woods were people like John Stanley and Walt Kelly.

And even they'd get it once in a while, too. It was really the heyday of the business. You were very well paid for the work, in those days. Western's page rate was good, and of course it was comparably higher in the '40s than it is now. Most of us would receive Christmas bonuses, too. And there were the Christmas parties up in the Penthouse Club. For the most part we'd see one another only on Fridays, which was payday and bull session day. There was Kelly . . . Stanley . . . Dan Gormley . . . Mo Gollub . . . Lloyd White, Jim Chambers, Tony Rivera . . . . there must've been eight or ten of us."[31]

Among the forms of approval that Stanley received from Western was what he later termed their "top rate." In the late 1940s, that meant $40 for a finished comic book cover, and $6.50 for writing and sketching each story page (combined).[32] He would have received about $30 a page if he had taken the interior pages to completion. (After the initial *Four Color* Lulus, that happened in only one other issue of the *Little Lulu* title.) He also received substantial bonuses at the end of each year, since *Little Lulu* was one of Western's best sellers. The bonuses were probably in the range of $1,000 to $1,500 a year.[33] Based on these figures, he made something in the neighborhood of $7,500 for work done in 1949 (including non-Lulu stories), a good (if not great) salary in its day. In current dollars, that would be about $75,000.[34]

By 1949, Stanley had reached a sort of summit in the comic book field. He was a well-paid professional who was the sole author and guiding artist of one of Western's best-selling comic books. With the Lulu animated cartoon series ending in 1948, Stanley was the only one writing new Little Lulu stories. Kleenex mounted a giant electronic billboard made by Artkraft Strauss in Times Square, New York City, featuring Lulu and Tubby. On October 20, 1949, Marjorie Henderson Buell was there to flip the switch to illuminate it for the first time. One wonders if Stanley was on hand to witness the grand event, and if so, how he felt about being the "man behind the curtain" of the ongoing adventures of one of America's most beloved comic book characters. For her part, although there's no record of Marjorie Buell referring to John Stanley by name, she was well satisfied with his work. Her opinion of the Lulu comic books: "I thought they were just great!"[35]

Sometimes Western artists put themselves or their fellow cartoonists in their stories. **Above:** John Stanley drew himself as a policeman in the Woody Woodpecker story in *New Funnies* #125 (July 1947). **Below:** Walt Kelly put "Perty Boy John" in this Albert and Pogo sequence from *Four Color* #105 (April 1946).

THIRTY CLASSIC LITTLE LULU STORIES FROM 1946 THROUGH 1949

FC = Dell Four Color [single series, tryouts]   LL = Little Lulu [her own magazine]

"FIGHTS BACK WITH A CLUB"—Introduces a "Men Only" club that meets in a treehouse. Prototype for the Feller's Club "No Girls Allowed" clubhouse. Lulu starts a "girls club." Tubby dresses as a girl to infiltrate it. Rare use of final "splash panel." *FC #115 (August 1946)*

"A PROBLEM IN BOX TOPS"—Reveals that Tubby has a crush on Lulu and fantasizes about her kissing him on the cheek. *FC #115*

"THE HAUNTED HOUSE"—Abandoned neighborhood house: Lulu and Tubby investigate. Meet boy and girl ghosts, Timmy and Gertie. Ghost Kebel is scary. How to get rid of him? Tubby suggests Lulu. "She's fierce!" Lulu uses her "special loud screech" and succeeds in scaring Kebel. Story not a dream. *FC #115*

"LITTLE LULU AND THE SEVEN DWARFS"—Story for Alvin. Evil Queen eats the poison cookie. Good example of contrast between Lulu's words and what appears in the panels. *FC #120 (October 1946)*

"IS TAKEN FOR A RIDE"—Lulu is too much for dimwitted kidnappers, extra-long story (twenty-one pages). *FC #131 (December 1946)*

"LITTLE LULU AND THE THREE BEARS"—Lulu completely forgets to include the bears in this story for Alvin. *FC #131*

"THE KID WHO CAME TO DINNER"—quintessential Tubby story that establishes his total, tactless self-involvement. *FC #146 (April 1947)*

"FOR PRESIDENT!"—Lulu: "I think maybe I'll be the president of the United States!" Tubby: "Are you kiddin'? Tell you what—maybe I'll let you be the First Lady!" *FC #158 (August 1947)*

"JUST A GIGOLO"—Blonde girl, Dolly, is a precursor to Gloria, though not rich. Bond between Lulu and Tubby is demonstrated when Lulu can't stand that another girl likes him. The clubhouse in a vacant lot/park is introduced, no "no girls allowed" yet. *FC #158*

"THE CASE OF THE PURLOINED POPOVER"—First Tubby-as-detective story. Popovers are missing, and Lulu, who is innocent, is punished. Tubby suspects Mr. Moppet, and sets out to prove his guilt. Turns out he's right. *FC #165 (October 1947)*

"ALVIN'S SOLO FLIGHT"—Alvin "flies" home from holding onto helium balloons. Use of unrealistic, fantastic element in story. Twenty-two page, extra-long story. *FC #165*

"NEVER AGAIN"—Another all-silent story, where Lulu tries smoking her doll's hair. She ends up hallucinating, and JPS does absurd things with her "high." *FC #165*

"MOUNTAIN CLIMBING"—Lulu and Tubby scale the side of a high-rise apartment building. Fifteen-page story. *LL #1 (January–February 1948)*

"THE REPORT CARD"—Tubby solo, backup stories begin. First mention of "the gang," although the kids are different. Early Miss Feeny appearance. Tubby gets all A's but wants to hide it from his friends so they won't think he's a sissy. *LL #2*

"THE TIMID GHOST"—Falling asleep while reading a book of ghost stories, Lulu dreams of meeting a timid ghost, who's afraid of her, and moans, "I try and I try, but people just won't stay scared!" *LL #4*

"THE ROCKING HORSE"—Boys won't let Lulu go to a supposedly haunted house with them. She scares them by pretending to be a ghost, then discovers a "secret room" where she finds a rocking horse that can fly. (Lulu was unconscious, after hitting her head, and it was all a dream. Or was it?) Stanley will use this device often for some of his most effective, imaginative and frightening stories. They often begin with a "secret panel" or "secret room." *LL #5 (September–October 1948)*

"THE ROBBERY"—Early "fellers clubhouse" story, now with "No Girls Allowed" written on its door, below the large word "clubhouse." *LL #5*

"THE GOURMET"—This six-page Tubby story echoes "The Kid Who Came to Dinner" from *FC #146*, and is almost as effective. In a restaurant, Tubby eats a struggling young couple out of all their money. *LL #5*

Left: "The Kid Who Came for Dinner" **Right:** "The Rocking Horse"

"BAD BOY"—Lulu and Tubby bring the ceiling down, but his mother thinks it was because of an earthquake. Stanley mistakenly refers to her as "Mrs. Trimble" (rather than Mrs. Tompkins) in the story. *LL* #6 (November–December 1948)

"THE UGLY DUCKLING"—Hans Christian Andersen fairy tale reimagined by Lulu for Alvin. Lulu is the ugly duckling, who is "discovered" by a Hollywood agent and made into a beautiful movie star. *LL* #6

Little Lulu is published monthly, starting with #7 (January 1949)

"DETECTIVE STORY"—Tubby "hires" Lulu as his sleuthing assistant. *LL* #7 (January 1949)

"SNOWBALL WAR"—The boys attack Lulu with snowballs. She vows to a friend, "I betcha we could show 'em … if we had a girl's army!" Indeed, they do. *LL* #7

"BEAUTIFUL LULU"—Lulu is upset when she hears the boys saying she's homely, but discovers being beautiful causes the boys to fight over her. In the end, she prefers to play with the boys rather than be put on a pedestal. *LL* #8 (February 1949)

"TUBBY MEETS A GHOST"—Tubby enters a graveyard to rescue a cat. He is scared by the caretaker, who he thinks is a ghost because of his long, white coat. *LL* #9

"THE PRINCE IN THE POOL"—Lulu tells Alvin a story, which features a "proto-Witch Hazel," wicked old lady. LL #11 (May 1949)

"HOUSEKEEPER WANTED"—Seminal Fellers Club story. Lulu is invited to join but must go through an elaborate initiation process. Fellers Club is more or less in place, with Willy, Eddie and Iggy there. Lulu finally passes all the tests, only to be told that she is vice president in charge of housekeeping. Hearing that, she socks them all and stomps off, telling them, "I Resign!" The boys, each with a black eye, vow: "Resolved—that no girl will ever become a member of our club again!" *LL* #11

"THE GREEN GIRL"—Lulu puts green ink in her weekly bath to simulate the ocean, and becomes green herself. This sets off a series of screwball antics: a doctor's appointment, Tubby charging people money to see her and, finally, a Bingling Brothers Circus job offer. She is "cured" by taking a second bath. *LL* #12 (June 1949)

"LITTLE LULU" [For some reason, Stanley left a number of stories around this time with no title other than the generic "Little Lulu."]—Lulu discovers a homeless ghost living in her dollhouse. Lulu finds him a new home, in a dark movie theater. Not a dream. *LL* #15 (September 1949)

"THE DEEP BLACK RIVER"—One of the best fairy tales. Lulu tells Alvin the story of a rich little girl held captive in a castle by a monster in a moat. *LL* #17 (November 1949)

"LITTLE LULU"—Lulu decides to give a poor little girl her old doll for Christmas, but is too attached to it. She gives away her new doll instead. A touching, Christmas-themed story. *LL* #18 (December 1949)

Clockwise from bottom: "The Prince in the Pool," *Little Lulu* #17, "The Deep Black River"

John Stanley gag continuity for the *New Yorker* magazine (March 15, 1947).

 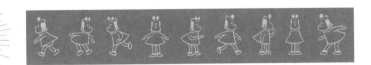

On the Side

A WELL-TO-DO MAN is asked by a poor man if he can spare some change, and acquiesces. The poor man enters a bar, but instead of spending the money on alcohol, puts it in the jukebox. Then he sits and listens to his musical selection, escaping, briefly, from his troubles.

This is the multipanel continuity by John Stanley in the March 15, 1947, issue of the *New Yorker*. Although he found his true calling in comic books, Stanley expended what seems to have been a substantial amount of energy working in the "gag cartoon" market after the war. His colleagues at Western Printing (in later interviews) alluded to other Stanley pieces appearing in the *New Yorker*, although they have never been found despite concerted searches of the magazine's postwar issues. The only surviving remnants of this work are a sheaf of sketched cartoon ideas, possibly rejects, found by Stanley's son among his father's papers. One is a "rough" of the published continuity described above.

Dan Noonan recalled, "His stuff, the ideas he sent to the *New Yorker* . . . I would say had as high a sales percentage as anything from anyone in their history. Very sophisticated gag ideas, all of

them. He sold quite a number of cartoon ideas to them. There were several that were drawn by Whitney Darrow."[1] Darrow is one of the best-known and most-celebrated gag cartoonists in the *New Yorker*, having had some 1,500 cartoons printed in its pages in the course of his multi-decade career.

Morris Gollub confirmed: "[John Stanley] was writing gags for other cartoonists occasionally. Jim Geraghty, the

art editor of the *New Yorker*, hired him and thought very highly of him. He was also doing these little title pieces between 'The Talk of the Town' in the *New Yorker* for a while."[2] By "little title pieces," Gollub was referring to small "space filler" images in the magazine. Jim Stanley found two finished images of this type among his father's belongings. Since Otto Soglow was the regular cartoonist for the Talk of the Town pages in the front section of each issue, space fillers by Stanley would more likely have appeared in other parts of the magazine. Despite the lack of hard evidence, Noonan and Gollub credibly establish that Stanley's contributions to the respected magazine extended beyond the single jukebox continuity, although they may never be identified.

JOHN STANLEY'S BREAKTHROUGH with *Little Lulu* ensured that his writing, layouts and finished artwork for the title were his top priority, but he continued to script *Tom and Jerry*, *Andy Panda* and *Woody Woodpecker*. He wrote for other subsidiary characters as well, including Walter Lantz's Oswald the Rabbit, from 1945 to 1948. Stanley began with the all-Oswald *Four Color* #67 (April 1945), which offered two long stories starring the ultra-cute Oswald and his buddy Toby (a bear), each more dimwitted than the other. In that issue's "The Secret Six," he managed to craft an interesting story by casting Oswald as the doppelganger of a heartless, penny-pinching business magnate, showing the corrupting influence of wealth, a familiar Stanley theme. Had Toby Bear been as sprightly and funny as Charlie Chicken, the series would have fared better. Nevertheless, Stanley did his best in two more Oswald issues of *Four Color*, and in the regular stories in the monthly *New Funnies*.

Between the success of Little Lulu and his "dues paying" on Oswald and other characters, John Stanley had earned the chance to create a strip of his own. Oskar Lebeck gave him a slot in *Animal Comics* to see what he could do. *Jigger*, his first original series,

"IS IT OKAY TO CHECK A CHIMNEY?"

Above: Early version of the continuity that, in more evolved form, appeared in the *New Yorker*. John Stanley art. **Below, next two pages:** Sketches and cartoons from John Stanley's papers, courtesy of Jim Stanley. The *New Yorker*-style gag cartoons and "space fillers" were most likely rejected. Otherwise, they wouldn't have been found among his papers.

"HOLD IT!"

"WHO THE HELL CARES WHERE THE SNOWS OF YESTERYEAR ARE?"

"A BEAUTIFUL SERMON THIS MORNING, REVERAND, AND YOUR PUT-DOWN OF THE HECKLERS WAS ESPECIALLY DEVASTATING."

Clockwise from top left: John Stanley created the *Hair-Raising Adventures of Peterkin Pottle*, which made its debut in *Raggedy Ann and Andy #32* (January 1949). Toby and Oswald "wait for the end" in *Four Color #67* (April 1945). Artist unknown. Jigger was John Stanley's first attempt at creating an original feature for comic books. Note the liquor reference in the name. *Animal Comics #28* (August–September 1947). **Bottom:** From *Raggedy Ann and Andy #33* (February 1949) and #36 (May 1949).

debuted in *Animal Comics* #24 (December 1946–January 1947) with an unremarkable story about the title character (a small dog) and Mooch (a large dog) searching for a buried bone. Stanley tinkered with the character designs for several issues, and retitled it *Jigg and Mooch* with #29. Unfortunately, his cartoon canines weren't much different than other routine funny animals. The feature never found its footing, and ended in the following issue with the book's demise.

A better-conceived, more mature, darker series created by Stanley appeared when Lebeck assigned him to the faltering *Raggedy Ann and Andy* comic book with #32 (January 1949). Stanley had watched as Walt Kelly regained ownership of his creation *Albert and Pogo,* and was preparing to launch it in a daily newspaper strip format in the *New York Star,* where Kelly served as art editor. *Pogo* ran in the *Star* from October 4, 1948, until the paper folded on January 28, 1949, which served as a springboard for its eventual national syndication. We know that Stanley later attempted to create his own syndicated comic strips (see Chapter 9), so it's probable that he began working toward that goal earlier. He may have thought he could follow Kelly's footsteps: creating and

perfecting a property at Western, then negotiating for the right to sell it to a newspaper syndicate.

Just as *Little Lulu* went monthly, Stanley's *The Hair-Raising Adventures of Peterkin Pottle* took over the cover and leadoff position in *Raggedy Ann and Andy* (an anthology title), relegating Johnny Gruelle's doll characters to secondary status. This was Stanley's big chance, his shot at the *Pogo* sweepstakes.

The premise is that Peterkin Pottle, a dull, antisocial boy, is teased and bullied by his fellow classmates, and escapes into daydreamed adventures, imagining himself as a hero who easily defeats his enemies. After an initial setup, each of the

Opposite: *Raggedy Ann and Andy* #33: John Stanley finished (penciled and inked) all the Peterkin Pottle art. **Above:** Peterkin Pottle in *Raggedy Ann and Andy* #33, pages 1 and 7.

ten-page stories shifts to "daydream mode" for the bulk of its pages. In the first story, he imagines himself as a fearless lion tamer, and in subsequent stories he's an Indian fighter, a pirate, a caveman, a strongman, a great white hunter and a lifeguard.

While *Peterkin Pottle* is much better than *Jigg and Mooch*, Stanley's bespectacled, gloomy protagonist is hardly the kind of boy with whom a reader would care to identify. The stories, which satirize the story tropes of boys' adventure stories, have a certain charm, but suffer from a lack of urgency because there's really nothing at stake. Occasional dreams could serve as welcome changes of pace; stories regularly based on daydreams quickly become tiresome. *Peterkin Pottle* has its virtues, not the least of them being finished artwork by John Stanley himself, but its protagonist was problematic. The pasty-faced, pathetic Peterkin virtually invites the readers' contempt, dooming the character to commercial failure. He was last seen in *Raggedy Ann and Andy* #38 (July 1949), just one issue before the book itself was canceled. Stanley wouldn't have the chance to create another feature of his own for over a decade.

How to explain his stumble on *Peterkin Pottle*, when he was able to turn the puerile *Raggedy Ann and Andy* in those same pages into something extraordinary with such apparent ease? This would be

a central conundrum in his career: his ability to successfully concoct stories for characters created by others, but difficulty achieving similar success on characters of his own. Yet there's no denying the effectiveness of the frightening stories Stanley gave Gruelle's protagonists, who seemed to operate on the age-level of most of their readers: that is, six to nine years old. Maggie Thompson read those stories as a child, and found them deeply unsettling. She wrote, "Consider the idea of a cave that seems only to be dark and deserted—but in which live the one-eyed wobblies which will get you, if they can. Or eating poisonous mushrooms and dying. Or entering a castle with endless rooms, from which you can never escape, not because it is locked but because the rooms form an endless bewildering maze. Now, *that* is scary stuff."[3] In #36, when Ann and Andy eat the poisonous mushrooms, they find they have sprouted angel wings, and are ascending through a series of ever-higher clouds on their way to heaven. But their progress appears to be thwarted by some playful cupids, who pluck their wings while they nap. The next time our protagonists try to fly, they fall back to earth. This proves to be providential, because they are able to return to their bodies, which revive after being given an antidote to the poison. The seven Raggedy Ann and Andy stories

Above: Raggedy Ann and Andy encounter the cave of the terrifying, one-eyed wobblies in issue #37 of their comic book (June 1949). Stanley art. **Below:** *Howdy Doody* #1 (January 1950) and *Henry Aldrich* #1 (August 1950). **Opposite:** Four of the fifteen pages of this story in *Henry Aldrich* #1, scripted by John Stanley and drawn (from Stanley's layouts) by Bill Williams, whose work Stanley admired. Pages 1, 3, 11 and 13 are shown.

written by Stanley comprise a small—but fascinating—part of his work "on the side" in the late 1940s.

MOST OF THE NON-LULU comics that Stanley would do in the coming years are "second tier" work: assignments that interested him personally in varying degrees, but don't rise to the quality he achieved in *Lulu*.

With *Lulu* he had a free hand, whereas most of his other assignments required him to adhere closely to source material, and thus, were more commercially compromised. Also, while he continued to provide his storyboards, Stanley did none of the finished art. He was there to get a projected series off to a good beginning. He later acknowledged his role as a series-starter: "I did the format, I did the writing and then we put it together," he recalled. "[Then] somebody else took over."[4] Much of this work was uncredited, until concerted study on the part of Frank M. Young led to their attribution to Stanley. They include comic books starring Howdy Doody, Henry Aldrich, Krazy Kat, Rootie Kazootie and The Little King.

Howdy Doody was the star of a popular children's television program originated by "Buffalo Bob" Smith and puppeteer Frank Paris in the late 1940s. Western launched the *Howdy Doody* comic book independent of its *Four Color* series, a practice that became more common when a property was thought to be sufficiently popular. Stanley was brought in to give it the best possible launch, although he may not have done all the stories. The series did well, running from #1 (January 1950) to #38 (July–September 1956), when Howdy "fever" had waned considerably.

Next came *Henry Aldrich*, a series more to Stanley's liking. The character was introduced in Clifford Goldsmith's Broadway play, *What a Life*, in 1938, and was successfully given his own radio program, movie series and television show. *The Aldrich Family* TV show, the prototype for teen-oriented situation comedy, made its debut in 1949. Henry, an awkward teen, is best remembered for this opening exchange. When his mother calls, "Hen-*reeeeeeeeeeeee!* Hen-ree Al-drich!," he answers in a breaking adolescent voice, "*Com*-ing, Mother!" It was licensed by Western Printing and given to Stanley to develop at the end of 1949.

What Stanley came up with was a not especially clever but enjoyable and amply amusing series of stories which captured the feeling of the *Aldrich Family* situation comedy. Presumably the comic book was named after Henry Aldrich, and focused almost exclusively on his antics with the other family members firmly in the background, in an attempt to sell it to those who were buying comic books starring Archie and other teenagers in the early 1950s. He did all but #3 of the first eight issues of this series in conjunction with an able cartoonist named Bill Williams, who was three years his junior.[5] (Stanley turned thirty-six in March 1950.) *Henry Aldrich* #1 (April 1950) offered a funny, well-constructed fifteen-page tale of a sleepless Henry getting up for a late night snack and somehow locking himself out of his house wearing only his pajamas. Not wanting to face the anger of his parents by waking them in the middle of the night, Henry runs the few blocks to the house of his best friend, Homer Brown, to borrow a ladder. There's much running back and forth between their houses as Henry and Homer borrow, then return, the ladder, including an encounter with a strolling policeman who gives chase. Also of interest in *Henry Aldrich*: the Homer Brown series in the back of the book, in which we meet another of Stanley's "rotten" kids. Homer's little brother Edgar, who makes life miserable for his brother, is what Lulu's neighbor Alvin Jones might become in a few years. Once *Henry Aldrich* was well on its way, Bill Williams drew scripts by other writers working (as best they could) in the Stanley manner.

Above: While working on *Little Lulu*, Stanley wrote other comic books on the side, such as *Krazy Kat* #1 (May–June 1951), *Four Color* #415 (August 1952), with Rootie Kazootie and *Four Color* #494 (September 1953) with The Little King. Other people finished the artwork. **Below:** John Stanley clowning around for the camera. Date and location unknown.

When the TV and radio shows went off the air, Western dropped the book (after twenty-two issues).

His third assignment (apart from Lulu) was *Krazy Kat*, when someone at Western thought it would be a good idea to do a comic book revival based on George Herriman's comic strip. Herriman's brilliant strip, which ran from 1913 to 1944, is known for its many variations on the mouse Ignatz throwing a brick at Krazy Kat, and an offbeat mixture of surrealism, idiosyncratic language and "anything goes" playfulness. The strip's main focus was on the relationship between Krazy Kat, a character of indeterminate gender (referred to as both "he" and "she"), and cranky mouse Ignatz. The third key character is Offisa Bull Pupp, who also loves Krazy. William Randolph Hearst, who syndicated (and loved) *Krazy Kat*,

canceled the strip after Herriman's death in 1944 rather than bring in a new cartoonist. Was it Stanley himself whose enthusiasm for Herriman's comic strip led to this odd revival, since we know he read the strip as a boy? Or was it Oskar Lebeck, who was unafraid to experiment?

Stanley completely redesigned Krazy Kat and his/her cohorts. From a purist point of view, the "new look" is a travesty. He attempted to evoke the language and absurdity of the original, but mostly relied on its slapstick elements. The results (seen first in *Krazy Kat* #1, May 1951) could almost be a brand new mouse-cat-dog feature. Nevertheless, Western made a substantial effort to put this new take on Krazy Kat over, in its own book and in *Four Color*. Again, not all of the stories are by Stanley, but the telltale signs are evident enough to include many of them in his credits, albeit as footnotes.

The same is true of *Rootie Kazootie*. Stanley worked on the first few Rootie appearances in *Four Color* to no great effect.[6] More interesting is his take on Otto Soglow's *The Little King*, the popular comic strip character syndicated by King Features, which ran from 1934 to 1975. The strip is notable for having virtually no dialogue. Unlike *Krazy Kat*, Stanley produced a book that was close in look and spirit to the ongoing adventures of the mustachioed, bearded Little King, whose childlike nature and curiosity are notably unkingly, except for one thing: it had a normal amount of dialogue. *The Little King* debuted in *Four Color* #494 (September 1954), and appeared in two

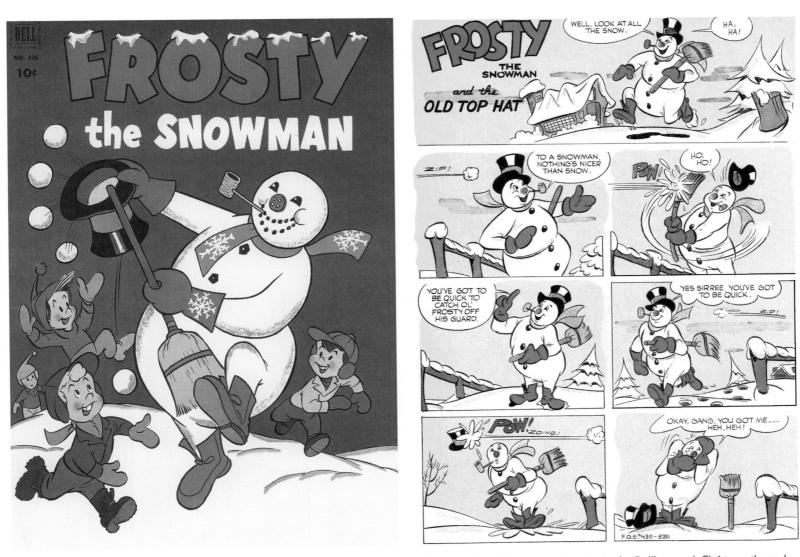

Stanley wrote "Frosty the Snowman and the Old Top Hat" in *Four Color* #435 (November 1952). He also wrote various stories for Dell's annual, Christmas-themed comic books.

more issues thought to be scripted by Stanley, #497 (October 1954) and #677 (February 1956).

WESTERN PRINTING PREDICTABLY produced Christmas-themed stories in many of its titles. It also put together an annual Christmas special in the Dell *Four Color* series called *Santa Claus Funnies*. John Stanley wrote some of the most charming stories in these holiday specials, having his sketched storyboards finished by Mel Crawford (who Stanley always called "the kid" because of his relative youth), Morris Gollub and Dan Gormley.

In *Four Color* #302 (November 1950), a fifty-two-page edition of *Santa Claus Funnies*, Stanley contributed "Teddy Bear in Toyland," with Teddy vying for inclusion as one of Santa's gifts to children. In that same issue, he may also have written "Santa's Christmas Presents," with Santa using an airplane to deliver his gifts on time. In *Four Color* #607 (December 1954), Stanley's "Christmas in November" has Santa dealing with Rufus, an elf whose near-sightedness causes problems, such as scheduling the delivery of Christmas gifts a month early (because he can't read the calendar). In the end, Rufus receives the gift of eyeglasses. In

response to the popularity of the song "Frosty the Snowman," which quickly became a Christmas standard, Western's holiday special in *Four Color* #435 (November 1952) was entirely devoted to the magical snowman's adventures. It was written by John Stanley and illustrated by Dan Gormley.

In succeeding years, Stanley wrote more stories for *Santa Claus Funnies*, always managing to deliver a fresh take on such holiday fare. He had reason to welcome these and his other assignments apart from his work on *Marge's Little Lulu*. They helped clear his creative palate and provided a change of pace. Moreover, they accrued extra dollars. But Lulu, Tubby, Alvin and the gang remained his top priority. By 1950, the world of Lulu's friends and neighborhood was fully formed, but Stanley was able to create unexpected new situations and characters. He just had to dig harder and deeper to find them.

Lulu and Tubby usher in the 1950s: *Little Lulu* #19 (January 1950). **Opposite:** An example of the *Little Lulu* daily newspaper strip (dated January 16, 1951), written and drawn by Woody Kimbrell.

7

Little Lulu in the 1950s

THE SALES OF *LITTLE LULU* and the other titles from Western Printing, which were often geared toward the youngest comics readers, were lifted by the postwar baby boom. Royalty statements sent to Marjorie Buell in the 1950s reveal that Western was printing more than a million copies of each issue of *Little Lulu*.[1]

Sales may also have been bolstered by the launch of the daily *Little Lulu* comic strip on June 5, 1950. It was produced by Western out of its West Coast office for the Chicago Tribune-New York News Syndicate.[2] The contest held to find a cartoonist to draw the strip was won by Woody Kimbrell, who ended up both writing and drawing it for fifteen years. Although Kimbrell's work couldn't come up to the quality achieved by John Stanley and Irving Tripp in the comic books, it seemed to satisfy the syndicate and the reading public, bringing Lulu and Tubby into millions of homes every day. This must have enhanced recognition of Little Lulu among newsstand browsers.

None of this should minimize how successfully Stanley's work attracted and retained readers. *Little Lulu* was a comic book with a special spark that delighted an extraordinarily high percentage of readers, and had them coming back for more. While it was about a self-empowered girl, boys liked it, too. Having Tubby as its prominent, cover-featured costar probably helped. Readers recognized, without understanding the mechanics of comic book creation, that "the people" who did *Little Lulu* were especially (and reliably) clever.

The rising tide of sales, in turn, helped Western keep the comic book at fifty-two pages until 1954 (except for a ten-issue run starting in mid–1951).[3] Most comic books had slimmed down to thirty-six pages by 1950. That made *Little Lulu* a better value than many of its competitors, just in terms of page count. Two fifty-two page issues of *Little Lulu* had as much entertainment as three issues of her thirty-six page rivals. (For example, the *Little Audrey* comic book from St. John had thirty-six pages in 1950.)

John Stanley kicked off his sixth year on *Little Lulu* with a 1950-themed cover, and a leadoff story featuring Tubby and his Junior Private Detective Kit.[4] Someone has gotten animal hair on Mrs. Moppet's hairbrush by apparently using it to groom the family dog, Mops. For this, Lulu has received a spanking by her mother.

Lulu: I didn't do it!
Tubby: Ha! That's what they *all* say!

Once Tubby accepts Lulu's innocence, his suspicions shift to Mr. Moppet. "I never *did* trust him! It's an open an' shut case!" Tubby conducts his investigation, discovering that Lulu's pop is indeed the guilty party. He has used the hairbrush to remove dog hair from his clothes when he couldn't find a whisk broom. George Moppet would be the "usual suspect" in most of the subsequent stories with Tubby-the-detective. *Little Lulu* #19 also introduces "fresh" Wilbur Van Snobbe, a rich boy who tricks Lulu

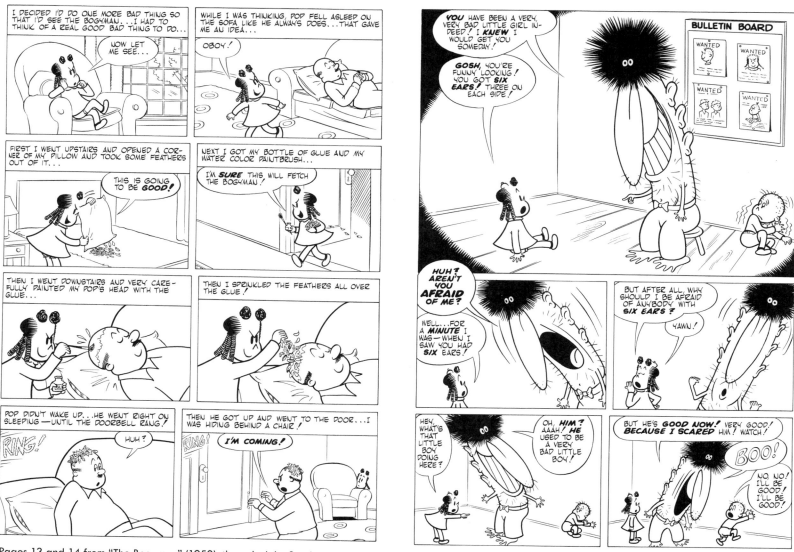

Pages 13 and 14 from "The Bogyman" (1950), the only John Stanley *Little Lulu* story Marge Buell rejected. It didn't see print until 1985, in Another Rainbow's *Little Lulu Library* series. **Opposite:** Pages 13 and 15 from "Five Little Babies" (*Little Lulu* #38, August 1951). "Yow! It's a wagonload of feet!!"

into paying for his soda, then mollifies her by giving Lulu his mother's pearl necklace. Lulu accepts it, grumbling, "It's better than nothing." Wilbur became a recurring character, a vehicle for Stanley to satirize the rich. The next issue brings another new character in Lulu's world: Clarence McNabbem, the bad-tempered, ineffectual, none-too-bright truant officer. (Shades of Woody Woodpecker's Mr. Ketchem.) School became a more important element in the Lulu and Tubby stories as time went on. Their teacher Miss Feeny often appeared in those stories, as did her parrot Percy.

Despite a certain *de rigueur* sensitivity to things that would upset parents, John Stanley obviously felt giving the readers a good scare was within the realm of acceptability. By 1950, ghosts and cemeteries had figured in a number of stories, with no negative reaction from Marjorie Buell or the readers. However, when he wrote a story intended for *Little Lulu* #26 (August 1950) titled "The Bogyman," with Lulu telling Alvin about a time when she behaved very badly, it was flatly rejected by Buell. "The Bogyman" was the only story nixed by her in all the years he worked on Little Lulu. (He never mentioned it, or his reaction to its rejection, in later years.)

In a letter to John Clark, editor of *The Little Lulu Library* reprint books, Marge Buell wrote that she "turned down 'The Bogyman' because it was an ugly, tasteless, scary story, entirely out of character and way below the high standards of the *Little Lulu* comics."[5] For his part, Irving Tripp didn't think it was beyond the pale. "It was a good horror story," he told Bruce Hamilton, "but it was about the Boogie Man [sic] and they didn't want it at all."[6] To fill the gap, the rejected story was replaced with a reprint of an Alvin tale from *Four Color* #110 (one with finished art by Stanley). Proofs of the finished pages of "The Bogyman" turned up years later, among the proofs for *Little Lulu* #26.[7]

If "The Bogyman" had just been a story with some unusually frightening elements, it might have gotten by, but Lulu's "bad behavior" in the story is out of step with anything else that Stanley had done with her. It counts as a lapse in judgment on his part. The story has Little Lulu performing all manner of deliberately cruel, destructive acts around the house (letting the bathtub overflow with water, breaking all the dinner plates, gluing feathers to her sleeping father's bald head). By this time, Lulu had shed most of her "bad little girl" behavior. Buell's *Saturday Evening Post* panels never portrayed Lulu as mean-spirited. Even though this is the

"fictional Lulu" of the "story time" tales, it's not believable that she would imagine herself this way. Even the Bogyman is afraid of Little Lulu!

Some of the frightening elements in the story are unusually disturbing. When the somewhat comical Bogyman is revealed in a large panel, there's a little boy cringing in the corner who looks like he's been through unimaginable horrors. It dramatizes the fear felt by a weak person when threatened by someone with greater power, an unsettling interpersonal dynamic that shows up in much of Stanley's work. Threats came in the form of authority figures, other adults, bullies and monsters from nightmares.

The misstep of "The Bogyman" is all the more surprising when one considers the sureness and confidence of Stanley's work in the early 1950s. His creativity was at its peak. In *Little Lulu* #38 (August 1951), he wrote "Five Little Babies," one of the best-known and funniest of the Lulu stories. It begins when Gloria passes by the boys, and Wilbur Van Snobbe points out that she says "hello" only to him. The boys taunt Wilbur by telling him that Lulu hates him, causing him to respond, "Hah! I betcha I could make her do anything I wanted . . . I could make her follow me around like a little puppy!" So outrageous is this claim, the boys agree to let Wilbur into their club if he can deliver on it. They have grossly underestimated Wilbur's ability to manipulate, and when

he does trick Lulu into getting on all fours, and wearing a collar and leash as he leads her along the sidewalk so the boys can see, they are forced to admit him to their club.

When Lulu discovers how she's been tricked, she devises a way to get revenge. While the boys are swimming in a local pond, Lulu steals their clothes, and offers them only diapers to wear while she takes them home in her wagon. She covers them with a blanket, assuring them that no one will see them dressed as babies. Instead of depositing them at their homes, however, Lulu pulls the wagon until she finds a group of boys playing in the street. When one of the boys curiously lifts a bit of the blanket to reveal some of the boys' feet, he yells: "Yow! It's a wagonload of feet!" Aghast at this grisly possibility, the boys summon a policeman and soon all the neighbors are crowding around the wagon. Then the policeman whisks the blanket away, revealing the boys in their infant garb to everyone. "I wonder why Lulu would do a thing like this to us?" one whines. "She's just mean, that's all!" Tubby responds. The End. Per Frank M. Young, "Five Little Babies" is the "ultimate battle of the genders comedy."[8] It was among the four Little Lulu stories reprinted in *A Smithsonian Book of Comic Book Comics* (1981) to best represent Stanley's work on the feature.

Nineteen fifty-one also saw the beginning of two new series of Little Lulu stories, one minor and one major. The minor one started with a five-pager in *Little Lulu* #35 that had no title (other than "Little Lulu"). In it, none of the boys will speak to a mystified Lulu. Annie informs her. "It's Monday for you and me, but for the Boys' Club, it's 'Mumday!' It's something new the Boys' Club made up! Every Monday—er—Mumday they don't speak to any girls! Anybody who talks to a girl on Mumday is fined five cents—and the money is used to buy baseballs!" It doesn't take long for Lulu to trick them into speaking to her, once again proving she can outsmart the boys. Stanley brought back the "Mumday" gimmick a number of times in the next few years.

A more significant series began in *Little Lulu* #39 (September 1951) with the first fairy tale featuring Witch Hazel, a cackling, shape-shifting crone who became fixated on Lulu. Hazel prototypes had appeared before, but now that Stanley decided that she would be an ongoing character, she needed a name.[9] He named her after Witch Hazel, the astringent topical medicine. Later, he commented, "I introduced the Witch Hazel stories for a change of pace. Just to get away from the neighborhood. And the best way [to escape] is through the imagination."[10] In "That Awful Witch Hazel," Lulu encounters a tearful Alvin who announces he's running away from home. Lulu tells him about the time she ran away from home, and was victimized by the devious Witch Hazel "who is always waiting in the woods to grab little kids." Hazel casts a spell on Lulu that imprisons her inside a large rock. Only a sculptor who finds the rock, and chips away everything non-Lulu, is able to free her. To this cautionary tale, Alvin responds, "Phooey!"

When Witch Hazel returns in *Little Lulu* #45 (March 1952) in "That Awful Witch Hazel Again," she pops out of a manhole next to Lulu's house to snatch her. Before long, Stanley was using the evil sorceress in every episode of the Lulu-as-storyteller series. (The name Witch Hazel was used in cartoons from both Walt Disney and Warner Bros. not long after she was named by John Stanley.)[11] Stanley loved witches and found ways to bring modified versions of Hazel into future projects whenever appropriate.

IN DECEMBER 1951, MARGE BUELL renegotiated her contract with Western Printing and Lithographing Company.[12] The improved terms of this new, six-year contract brought her $46,924.42 in royalties alone the following year, mostly from the comic books but also other Lulu items such as coloring books, puzzles, and so on. As Michael Barrier pointed out, "Even more than was true of Disney and the ducks, Marjorie Buell as the copyright holder reaped the benefits of popularity due overwhelmingly to the creative efforts of a cartoonist who had no ownership stake in what he created. But, as with Carl Barks, it is hard to argue that John Stanley was being exploited. Marge's Lulu, like Disney's Donald Duck, gave a gifted artist the head start he needed to do work that was far more impressive than anything he did, or may have been capable of doing, completely on his own."[13]

Had he realized how much Buell received, Stanley might have been upset, but there's no evidence that he did. He had to know, by inference or in general terms, that Buell was well compensated,

but getting Western's "top rate" seems to have satisfied him. Lebeck wouldn't have shared the specifics of Buell's contract. Why do something that could only breed discontent in one of his first-string talents? Besides, by the time of the 1951 contract negotiation, Lebeck was on his way out the door, and not of his own volition.

Oskar Lebeck had pushed ahead with a new kind of children's publication called Surprise Books, a sort of half-sized, semi-comic book designed to be sold on retail counters, rather than newsstands. It was a debacle. Upper management, which had found Lebeck autocratic and resistant to its control, used this failure as an excuse to push him out of the firm. According to Morris Gollub, the powers that be "simply fixed up the figures, behind his back, so he didn't have a chance. They dismissed him, bought out all his stock—he had a lot of stock in the thing."[14] The exact details and date of Lebeck's exit haven't been established, but his next project was writing the *Twin Earths* comic strip, which was drawn by Alden McWilliams. It was bought by United Features Syndicate, and made its debut in daily newspapers on June 16, 1952, and Sunday papers on March 1, 1953. Lebeck had used McWilliams as a freelancer at Western, and they had a comfortable working relationship. Lebeck scripted it until 1957, when McWilliams assumed scripting duties along with the art. Fifty-four years old at the time, the erstwhile editor lived another nine years, after moving with his wife to La Jolla, California, to be near their daughter. Little is known about his life on the West Coast, although it's thought that he had sufficient financial means in these later years, and could have simply retired.[15] Oskar Lebeck, the man who hired John Stanley to create comic books, died suddenly, on December 20, 1966, from unspecified causes. He was sixty-three years old. (The *Twin Earths* comic strip lasted until 1963.) Lebeck's editorial chair at Western was filled in mid–1951 by George E. Brenner, former editor of Quality Comics (*Plastic Man*, *Blackhawk*, et al). When Brenner died after a heart attack in September 1952, he was replaced by thirty-year-old Matthew H. Murphy, who held the post until 1970.

The "separation" of Oskar Lebeck from Western had a number of implications for John Stanley. First and foremost, Stanley had a great deal of loyalty to Lebeck and couldn't have been happy about this development: a good man forced out by people Stanley most likely didn't respect. Lebeck's departure also had an impact on Stanley's work on Lulu. Lebeck gave his work very little editorial review, and often none at all. "I don't think he ever *read* anything, except the first ones you did," Stanley said. "Lebeck figured you could handle it, and do it. If he trusted you, you had *carte blanche*. You could do anything."[16] Any creative person appreciates that kind of a vote of confidence. Now Stanley no longer had his champion as a buffer. Matt Murphy, a man of considerable native intelligence and an artist in his own right, understood that Lulu was "working" creatively and selling well. But this could also invite interference, in the cause of "protecting" an important asset. Suddenly, Stanley found his work subject to closer editorial scrutiny. He now had to field questions about aspects of his stories,

Original art from "Ol' Witch Hazel and the Dusty Castle" in *Little Lulu* #65 (November 1953). Courtesy of Glenn Bray.

and sometimes make changes. Once someone has enjoyed creative freedom, no editorial control, however benign, is welcome.

One of Oskar Lebeck's editorial decisions that didn't have John Stanley's wholehearted support was the selection of Irving Tripp to do the finished art on *Little Lulu*. Initially, Charles Hedinger had done the penciling; then things changed. Tripp later recalled: "In the early '50s, Charlie wanted to do story writing and I was given the job of doing both the penciling and inking of the Little Lulu characters and that went on for quite a while, until we were overburdened with a lot of work. After a while it just seemed to pile up, so eventually I did only the penciling and some of the inking. Lettering was done by Al Owens, backgrounds were done by Gordon Rose. When things really slowed down I eventually got to do the whole thing again." Although Stanley allowed that Tripp "did a good job," he said otherwise to Lebeck, and probably his successors: "I complained constantly trying to get a change of artist but to no avail. It was too static for me. I would rather have had faster movement."[17] Tripp later said, "I remember the first time he came up. Charlie was doing the penciling and I was doing the inking and he was very encouraging. We'd only been working on it a few months and I remember John saying, 'the inker can make or break a story,' so it was kind of encouraging. He complimented me on what I was doing and encouraged me to keep at it. I never got any criticism that [the characters] should be more active." For his part, Tripp had only one complaint about Stanley's storyboards: "Some of the writers would use a lot of close-ups in their scripts, just heads. [Stanley] used to put so many kids in them! That's why I had to work so much overtime! Boy, did he put the kids in some of those panels!"

To find out the approach John Stanley wanted for the finished interior Lulu art, one need look no further than *Little Lulu* #31, with five of the six stories finished by Stanley himself. (Tripp finished "Ten Pennies.") Stanley's bolder, more expressive brushwork was always on display on the covers, and in the illustrations accompanying "Lulus Diry," but here one can see him handling the same duties as Tripp—in a single issue—making it easier to compare their work.

"Adventures in Africa" (fourteen pages), in which Lulu tells Alvin about her trip across the Atlantic Ocean in a floating baby carriage, is one of his most freewheeling, wholly engaging Lulu stories. The first thing one notices is that Stanley's panels have a simpler look. He didn't have an assistant doing backgrounds. A greater difference is the lack of variance in the thickness of Stanley's brushwork. It may be that he was working quickly to complete the issue, and didn't want to expend the time or additional thought to devise a system of "thicks and thins." Nevertheless, Stanley's looser, freer inking style gives the story more zip and an air of spontaneity that "Ten Pennies" lacks. Tripp's thick-and-thin inking does give his pages a vibrancy and sense of visual rhythm that Stanley's lack, but it's a poor trade-off for the artistic virtues evident in the other tales in this landmark issue.

WHILE VISITING OSKAR LEBECK and his wife in Croton-on-Hudson, John Stanley fell in love with the area, situated midway between New York City and Poughkeepsie. Photographs show the two men enjoying a day at the river's edge, and in Lebeck's home with the stone edifice, at 126 Old Post Road. Such was his attraction to the area that Stanley bought a house in Croton-on-Hudson and moved his family there some time in the early 1950s. Having grown up in Adare, a small town in Ireland, perhaps Anna Stanley was all for returning to a slower-paced life. On the other hand, that meant his parents and sister would be leaving their Irish enclave in the Bronx.[18] James, Anna and Marian would live the rest of their lives in Croton-on Hudson. To the degree that John was still an avid fisherman and hunter, moving upstate brought him closer to regions where he could more easily pursue those activities. (He would move back and forth between Croton and the city twice in the coming years, but his parents did not.)

The address was 9 Darby Avenue. John Stanley's niece, Barbara, recalled, "My grandparents moved with John into a stone, European-type house. It was gloomy but probably expensive. John had a studio

Above: The Stanley home at 9 Darby Avenue in Croton-on-Hudson, New York. **Below:** John's late brother Jimmy's hobby was photography. Later, John became a shutterbug. His son, Jim Stanley, wrote: "He was very much into photography. There's a photo where he's taking a picture of a little girl on his doorstep at the first Croton-on-Hudson house. He has his Leica there. He definitely loved it as a hobby but pretty much gave it up by the time we moved back upstate to Horton Road."

Cover and pages 1, 4 and 9 from "Adventures in Africa" in *Little Lulu* #31, probably the only 1950s issue of that title with finished Stanley interior art.

Clockwise from top left: John Stanley at the beach with Oskar Lebeck, early 1950s. Courtesy of Letty Lebeck Edes. *Standing:* John Stanley. *Middle row:* Margaret (sister-in-law); Anna (mother); Barbara Stanley (niece); Margaret's oldest sister, Anne; Marian (sister) and Elsie Ryan. *Front row:* Tommy Stanley (nephew), Tom Stanley (brother). Photo of Anna at the Darby Avenue house. John and his sister Marguerite at 9 Darby Avenue. **Opposite:** First Tubby issue of *Four Color* (#381, March 1952). He is unforgettable as "Captain Yo-Yo."

there."[19] Living in Croton meant shopping in Peekskill, which was (and still is) the closest retail hub in the area. Barbara Steggles has one particularly vivid memory of visiting the Darby Avenue house: "He would have us pose for him. One time he was making Christmas cards or something, and he had us standing in a make-believe chimney in a drawing. It wasn't working out, and he was getting frustrated. But then he rewarded us. He had this giant glass jar of pennies, and he used to let us dig in there with our hands. Anything we could hold in our little hand, we could take away. This was a great source of amusement to him. He was kind of fun in his own way. He had a sense of humor."[20]

John (and his other family members) often visited his brother Tom's family, who lived at 10 Berkshire Road in Yonkers, a nice home in a quiet neighborhood. John was the godfather of his nephew Tom Jr. Barbara said, "He used to come and visit. There were a lot of family parties. At that time, you were really into the clan kind of thing, because these people had just arrived from another country. They were all like Ryans, and O'Neills, and they were all clinging together. Lots of weddings, that kind of stuff. We weren't like some Irish people who sang all the time. We just did a lot of eating, and talking, and of course, the adults were drinking."[21]

John and Tom got along, and did things together. Tom had read more widely than his limited education would suggest, and, rather than talking about baseball or football, the brothers had intellectual conversations about philosophy and literature. According to Jim Stanley, "My father was extremely well read and opinionated on a variety of subjects. If you disagreed with him on something, he could be very articulate and persuasive in explaining his views."[22] Everyone in the family respected the time that John needed to spend in his studio, sketching, writing and thinking. "He was always meeting deadlines," Barbara recalled. "When we were at his house, it was always 'he's got to get this work out.'"[23]

SUCH WAS THE MOUNTING POPULARITY of *Little Lulu* by late 1951 that John Stanley was informed before Thanksgiving that Dell had okayed tryout issues of a Tubby comic book in the *Four Color* series. Stanley was all for the idea. As he later told an interviewer, "I preferred doing the Tubby stories to Lulu. Why? I don't know. They seemed to come easier. Dealing with a little girl was a little more difficult."[24] The idea was that Lulu wouldn't appear at all in the Tubby stories.

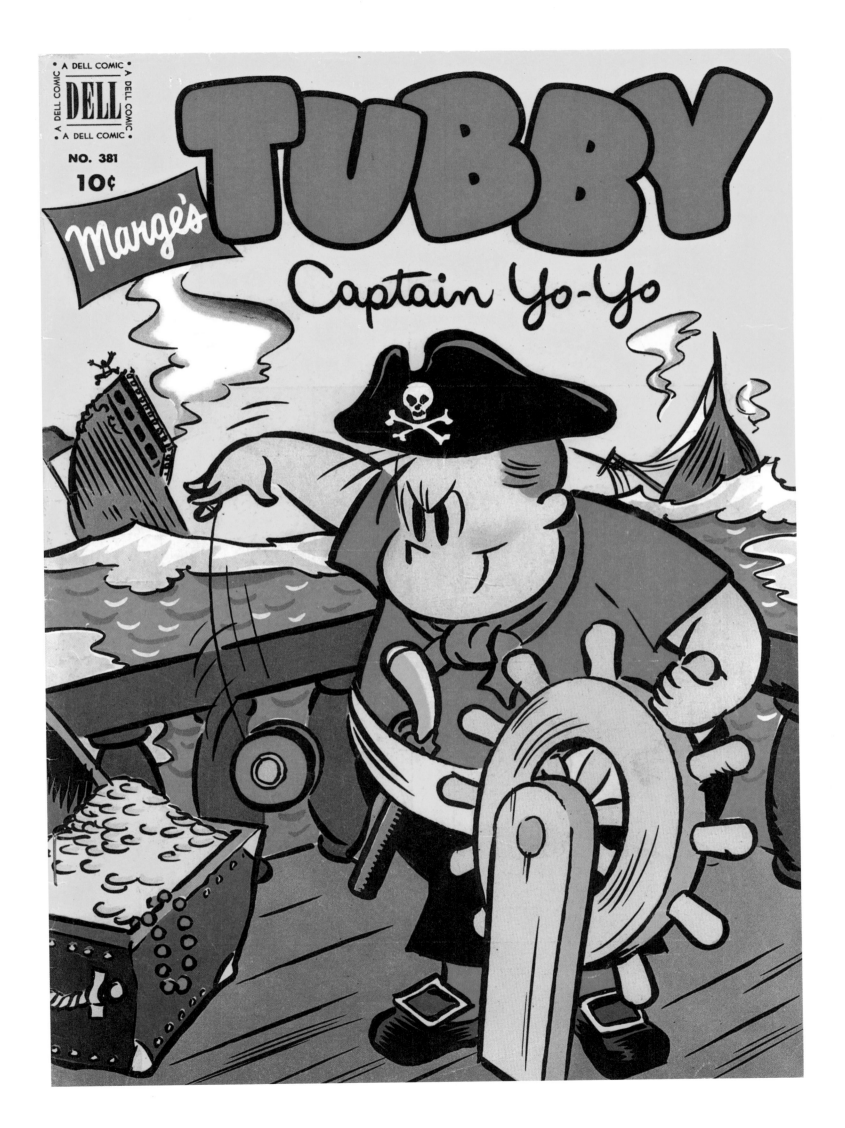

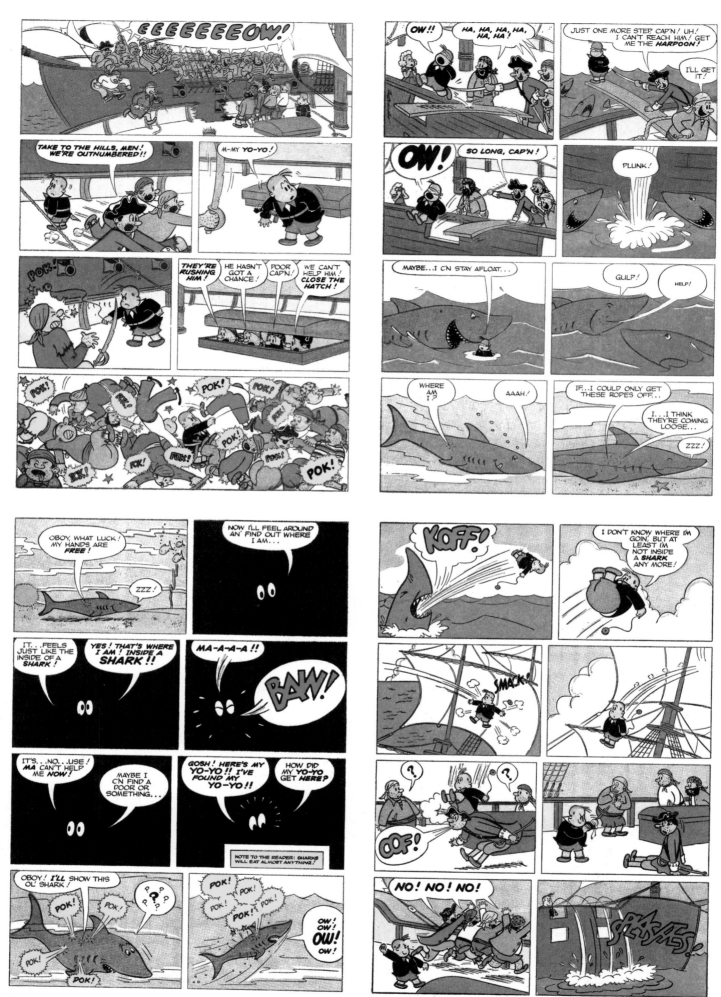

Pages 16, 24, 25 and 26 from "Captain Yo-Yo," written and drawn (including the finished art) by John Stanley.

Writing tales of Tubby Tompkins stimulated Stanley's imagination. Tubby was more "his" character than Lulu, anyway. Right away, a couple of key decisions made the Tubby stories different than those of Lulu. First was story length. Each of the four tryout issues had one long story, running thirty to thirty-four pages. (All Tubby comic books were thirty-six pagers. The first issue's thirty-four-page tale ends on the back cover.)

The series begins in *Four Color* #381 (March 1952) with the spirited "Captain Yo-Yo," a pirate fantasy along the lines of *Peterkin Pottle*. The interior artwork is by Irving Tripp. This story achieves a level of absurdity such that the reader gasps at its outrageousness even as he or she laughs out loud. The idea of fighting pirates with a yo-yo is the height of ridiculousness, something that could only happen in a boy's daydreams. When Tubby must walk the plank, and is swallowed by a shark, his escape via yo-yo (which forces the shark to cough him into the air) reaches a giddy crescendo in one of Stanley's finest stories. Then, beginning with *Four Color* #430, the second Tubby issue, come eight issues in a row written and entirely drawn—including finishes—by John Stanley himself. He had handled all the interior art in *Little Lulu* #31, but this was his only multi-issue run of "doing it all" since 1949 (on the aforementioned Peterkin Pottle series). *Four Color* #430 (October 1952) has the thirty-two page "The Shadow of a Maneater," which has a sequence with Tubby and Gloria trapped in a well. When Tubby figures out how to escape, Gloria marvels, "Gee, I always thought you were stupid!" *Four Color* #444 (January 1953) offers "The Bank Robber," a thirty-pager in which Tubby

Above left: In *Four Color* #444 (January 1953), Tubby reveals the name of his hometown. **Above right:** In *Four Color* #461 (April 1953), he is about to meet "the little men from Mars." **Below left:** *Four Color* #444. **Below right:** *Little Lulu Tubby Annual* #1.

tracks down three circus midgets who rob a bank in his neighborhood disguised as children. This story is especially significant because, on page twenty-five, he exclaims, "Those midgets! Don't let 'em get away! They held up a bank over in Meadowville where I live!" Suddenly, the town where Lulu and Tubby reside has a name. (However, the idea that they live in a small town is difficult to reconcile with the apparently urban milieu that Stanley had established.) These book-length Tubby tales sometimes meandered plot-wise, but the pacing was still brisk because they generally had a lower word count per panel than many of the shorter stories.

The bigger and more long-lasting change John Stanley brought to the stories in Tubby's solo comic book was a willingness to have fantastic elements exist in Tubby's waking world. He had done this a bit in the early Lulu stories (such as "The Haunted House" in *Four Color* #115), before relegating ghosts and flying rocking horses to the province of dreams. In Tubby's own book, there were still dream stories ("Captain Yo-Yo"), but with "Tubby's Secret Weapon" in *Four Color* #461 (April 1953), Stanley has Tubby meet tiny men from Mars in his "real life." They are drawn to him because of the destructive "super high-frequency sound

Full spread: Pages 4 and 8 of "Guest in the Ghost Hotel" from *Tubby* #7 (January–March 1954).

waves" of Tubby's violin playing, which wrecks the machinery on their spaceship. At one point, Gloria comments that it "must be a dream," but the Little Men from Mars become recurring characters in the series, which broke out of *Four Color* with *Tubby* #5 (July–September 1953). One can almost hear Stanley chuckling as he takes Tubby to Mars, and then puts him in the "Planet Control Room," where the eight-year-old steers the entire planet around the solar system like a giant rocket ship.

Once Tubby's own (quarterly, at first) title was underway, it wasn't long before Stanley began dividing each issue into three or four short stories. One of the most extraordinary is the terrifying "Guest in the Ghost Hotel" in *Tubby* #7 (January–March 1954). While trying to capture a frog to put in Gloria's lunch box, Tubby becomes stuck in quicksand. He manages to keep his head above ground until midnight. When he is about to be covered by the muck, he feels his foot touching something, which is rising up and lifting him out of the sand. A chimney, then a roof, then a whole house rises into the night. Trying to climb down, he enters the house through an open dormer window, only to discover it's a "ghost hotel," and once he has signed the register, he will turn into a ghost. Refusing to sign means he will be fed to Feer, a ferocious, man-eating furnace in the basement. Faced with that alternative, Tubby signs the register under protest ("BAW! I don't wanna be changed into a ghost!"). Fortunately, he misspells his last name in the register, so he remains human long enough to climb back outside to be rescued when the house rises again the following midnight. (This is the first time the name "Tompkins" is used as Tubby's last name.) Again, remarkably, this nightmarish story (there's little humor in it) isn't presented as a dream. In the Tubby-verse, it "really happened." It's the kind of story that could, and undoubtedly did, give young readers nightmares.

After Stanley did the finished artwork on eight Tubby issues (ending with #9, dated July–September 1954), a new finisher appears with #10: Lloyd White, whose work Stanley liked much more than that of Irving Tripp. In fact, Stanley told Don Phelps that White (whom he called "a dear friend") was his handpicked choice to take over the art on *Tubby*.[25] White has not been as popular as Tripp with John Stanley fans, but the *Tubby* comic book was, like *Little Lulu*, a top seller for Dell, so the artwork was

apparently effective enough not to detract from the average reader's enjoyment.

DELL CREDITED THE CREATORS of the *Little Lulu* comic book by name just once, on the inside front cover of *Little Lulu* #49 (July 1952). Why the sudden, one-time recognition? And why are the credits so frustratingly vague—listing Stanley among all the others who worked on the comic book, only singling him out as "cover artist"? Although Dell printed more detailed credits in three issues of *New Funnies* at this time, naming the writer of each story, they didn't do it for Stanley in *Little Lulu*, one of their top writers. It's a mystery.[26]

Tubby Tompkins remained as important in the *Little Lulu* comic book as ever, continuing to serve as the principle instigator in story after story. Some of the funniest are those with Tubby playing detective, when he called himself "The Spider" ("A spider spins a web to catch his prey!"), which hit a high-water mark in 1953. As a headstrong detective, Tubby has the perfect excuse for some of his most egocentric behavior, as well as his ridiculous disguises, which become increasingly absurd as time goes on. Other highlights are "The Super Long-String Yo-Yo" (*Little Lulu* #62) with incredible yo-yo antics explained as part of a dream, "Cousin Chubby" (*Little Lulu* #63 September 1953) that introduces the title character, Tubby's cousin, who is an exact double of him except younger and smaller, and "The Throw Rug" (*Little Lulu* #64, October 1953) when, again dreaming, Lulu discovers that the throw rug next to her bed is the entryway to an underwater world.

Little Lulu and associated characters created by Marge with art and story material prepared with the assistance of the following.

IN THIS ISSUE

• **The Case** of the **Pilfered Popcorn** •

• **The Working Girl** • **Little Lulu** •

• **20,000 Leaks Under** the **Sea** •

• **Lulus Diry** • **Tubby** •

STAFF WRITERS and ILLUSTRATORS

John Stanley • **Gordon Rose**

Irving Tripp • **Al Owens**

Front cover by **John Stanley**

MARGE'S LITTLE LULU, Vol. 1, No. 49, July, 1952. Published monthly by Dell Publishing Co., Inc., 261 Fifth Ave., New York 16, N. Y.; George T. Delacorte, Jr., President; Helen Meyer, Vice-President; Albert P. Delacorte, Vice-President. Re-entered as second-class matter December 15, 1948 at the Post Office at New York, N. Y., under the Act of March 3, 1879. Subscriptions in U.S.A., $1.00 per year, single copies, 10 cents; foreign subscriptions $2.00 per year; Canadian subscriptions $1.20 per year. Copyright, 1952, by Marjorie H. Buell. Printed in U.S.A. Designed and produced by Western Printing & Lithographing Co.

CHANGES OF ADDRESS should reach us five weeks in advance of the next issue date. Give both your old and new address enclosing if possible your old address label.

Above: *Little Lulu* #69 (March 1954). **Below:** This credit list, inside the front cover of *Little Lulu* #49 (July 1952), is the only time John Stanley is cited as a creator of the Lulu stories. **Opposite:** *Little Lulu* #47 (May 1952)

There were many important and enjoyable stories through 1953 and 1954, as Stanley worked toward completing the first five years of "Lulu in the 1950s." (See sidebar on the following page.) When a creator is working at such a high level, most issues have at least one or two notable stories, especially when the fifty-two-page issues of *Little Lulu* continued into 1954. More enjoyable Lulu and Tubby stories would come from the mind and pencil of John Stanley in the decade's second half, but, without question, his best years on the feature ended roughly with *Little Lulu* #70 (April 1954), the last of those generous, fat issues. Somehow, when the Lulu comic books dropped sixteen pages permanently, a little of the magic began slipping away.

LITTLE LULU IN THE 1950s

BEST OR NOTABLE STORIES FROM *LITTLE LULU* #19 (JANUARY 1950) TO #70 (APRIL 1954)—THE LAST FIFTY-TWO-PAGE ISSUE.

"LITTLE LULU"—Introduces Wilbur Van Snobbe, the rich boy who likes to play tricks on Lulu. *LL* #19 (January 1950)

"THE HOOKY PLAYER"—Introduces Mr. McNabbem, bad-tempered truant officer. *LL* #20 (February 1950)

"GREAT DAY"—Tubby achieves his dream of eating truck stop food alongside truckers. He overindulges. *LL* #23 (May 1950)

"THE DRAGON TAMER"—One of the finest of the fairy tales starts off the issue; another proto-Witch Hazel appearance. *LL* #25 (July 1950)

"THE BOGYMAN"—The "banned" Lulu story, with Lulu as a bad little girl who is kidnapped by the bogyman. Intended for *LL* #26 (August 1950): unpublished until its appearance in *Little Lulu Library* Vol. 5 (1986).

"LITTLE LULU" [Alvin's Record]—Alvin plays his "Mary Had a Little Lamb" record over and over, driving Lulu's father crazy. *LL* #28 (October 1950)

"IN NOTHINGLAND"—Lulu tells Alvin the story of a spoiled brat who hates everything, until she visits Nothingland. *LL* #29 (November 1950)

"SHE FLIES THROUGH THE AIR"—Lulu goes off a ski jump, flies across town. *LL* #30 (December 1950)

"ADVENTURES IN AFRICA"—Wonderful, fourteen-page stream-of-consciousness story. John Stanley is at his best. JPS did the finished art in most of this issue. Other stories are also excellent: "Little Lulu" [Tubby's Birthday Party"], "Crybaby," "Little Lulu" [Snowball Fighting], "Ten Pennies," "The Big Fish." *LL* #31 (January 1951)

"THE SPOOK TREE"—Tubby tells Lulu about the Spook Tree, in the cemetery. If you touch it, you can make any wish, but it's guarded by ghosts. *LL* #34 (April 1951)

"LITTLE LULU" [MUMDAY]—Introduces "Mumday," the day of the week when the boys won't speak to the girls. *LL* #35 (May 1951)

"FIVE LITTLE BABIES"—Lulu gets revenge on the Fellers by stealing their clothes and forcing them to wear diapers. Reprinted in *A Smithsonian Book of Comic-Book Comics* (1982). *LL* #38 (August 1951)

"THAT AWFUL WITCH HAZEL"—Introduction of Witch Hazel, who will appear in more issues of Little Lulu than any other character except for Lulu, Lulu's parents, Tubby and Alvin. *LL* #39 (September 1951)

"THAT AWFUL WITCH HAZEL AGAIN"—Second story with Witch Hazel. *LL* #45 (March 1952)

"THE GHOST TRAIN"—One of Stanley's most evocative, frightening fairy tales. Lulu is a poor little girl who picks up coal along the railroad track to survive. At night, she sees a ghost train, and meets its ectoplasmic engineer. He tells her where to find all the coal she wants. *LL* #47 (May 1952)

"LITTLE LULU" [AT THE BEACH WITH WILBUR]—Wilbur strands Lulu and Alvin on a rock at the beach, after the tide comes in. He steals their lunch, then gets in trouble himself. Also in this issue is the superb "Tubby" pantomime, shoeshine boy story. *LL* #50 (August 1952)

"THE GHOST IN THE BOTTLE"—Lulu meets a ghost in her dreams, who leads her to a scary old houseboat and a fight with the skeleton of Captain Kidd. The stuff of nightmares. *LL* #51 (September 1952)

"THE BALLOON DERBY"—Butcher Kohlkutz sponsors a cash-prize balloon hunt. *LL* #52 (October 1952)

The Sunset Diner in "Great Day" was based on the Center Diner in Peekskill, New York. Truant Officer Mr. McNabbem was introduced in "The Hockey Player." Panels from "Tubby's Doll" and "That Awful Witch Hazel." **Opposite, clockwise:** Tubby accuses Lulu's father of criminality because he has "beady little eyes!" in "The Spider and the Secret Six." Cousin Chubby debuts in *LL* #63. Lulu dives into her throw rug in *LL* #64. Cover of *Tubby* #5.

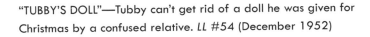

"TUBBY'S DOLL"—Tubby can't get rid of a doll he was given for Christmas by a confused relative. *LL* #54 (December 1952)

Tubby as detective "THE SPIDER" ("A spider spins a web to catch his prey!") is fixated on proving George Moppet is the culprit. Spider stories in 1953 are "The Case of the Egg in the Shoe" (*LL* #55, January), "The Case of the Well-Bred Worms" (#58, April), "The Outing" (#59, May), "The Spider and the Secret Six" (#61, July) and "The Case of the Head on the Stairs" (#62, August 1953).

"THE FORTUNE TELLER"—Lulu pretends to be able to see the future, with surprising results. *LL* #55 (January 1953)

"THE DOWNFALL OF MR. MCNABBEM"—The ineffectual truant officer loses his job. *LL* #56 (February 1953)

"RICH LITTLE POOR BOY"—Lulu sets out to show that she doesn't care about young movie actor Gregory Gallant, who is doing a personal appearance in Meadowville. *LL* #60 (June 1953)

"THE SUPER LONG-STRING YO-YO"—Tubby jumps out of a plane, trusting his super long-string yo-yo to save him on the upswing. Actually, a "dream" while being knocked out. Wonderfully absurd story. *LL* #62 (August 1953)

"COUSIN CHUBBY"—Tubby meets his cousin, who is a smaller version of him. *LL* #63 (September 1953)

"THE THROW RUG"—Lulu dreams that the throw rug next to her bed is the entryway to an underwater world. Story is an antecedent to the story "Mr. Green Must Be Fed" in *Tales from the Tomb* #1. *LL* #64 (October 1953)

"PAYS A SICK CALL"—Mr. McNabbem feigns illness to tempt children to pay hooky so that he can catch them. *LL* #65 (November 1953)

"OL' WITCH HAZEL AND THE GOLDEN EGGS"—Hazel's plan to get the goose leaves the poor little girl trapped in a treacherous grove of trees. *LL* #66 (December 1953)

"THE VISITOR"—With Tubby's famous anti-feminist speech. *LL* #101 (November 1956)

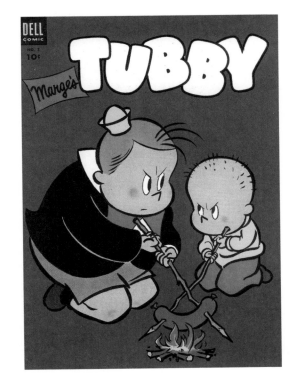

BEST OR NOTABLE STORIES FROM *FOUR COLOR* ISSUES STARRING TUBBY, AND *TUBBY* #1 THROUGH #7 (MARCH 1954).

"CAPTAIN YO-YO"—Tubby dreams of using his yo-yo as a weapon against pirates, in an issue-long, thirty-four-page story. One of Stanley's finest, funniest stories. *Four Color* #381 (March 1952)

"TUBBY'S SECRET WEAPON"—First "Little Men from Mars" story, which JPS allows to remain "real" as opposed to a dream story (although Gloria at one point comments that it "must be a dream"). First appearance of Tubby's violin teacher Professor Kleff/Cleff. Book-length story. The Little Men from Mars became recurring characters in the Tubby stories. *FC* #461 (April 1953)

Then, with *Tubby* #5 (July–September 1953), the first of his regular issues, before JPS lapsed back to his usual pattern of short stories of various lengths plus some one- and two-pagers, did a twenty-one-pager, "THE INDIAN FIGHTER."

"GUEST IN THE GHOST HOTEL"—Tubby is saved from sinking into quicksand by a "ghost hotel" that emerges under his feet from the swamp. He is almost turned into a ghost. One of Stanley's best, and most terrifying, stories. *First time Tubby's last name is given as Tompkins. Tubby* #7 (January–March 1954)

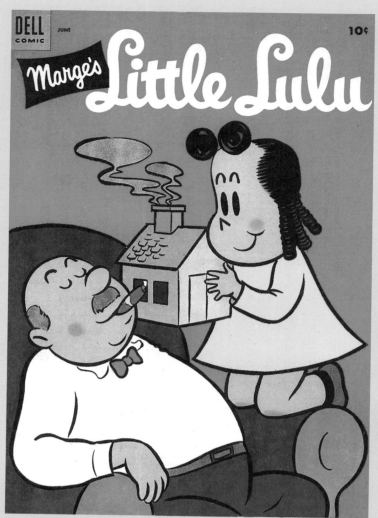

Little Lulu covers from 1954 or later. **Above:** *Little Lulu* #72 and 81. **Below:** *Little Lulu* #82 and 123.

From Lulu to Nancy

JUST AS THE LAST fifty-two-page issue of *Little Lulu* was published, the United States Senate was about to convene its "Subcommittee to Investigate Juvenile Delinquency" for two days of hearings at the federal courthouse in New York City. Criticism of violence in comic books, which was seen as contributing to the rising incidence of crime by American's youth, had reached a fever pitch. Now some felt it was time for the federal government to step in. The star witness was Fredric Wertham, M. D., whose indictment of comic books titled *Seduction of the Innocent* hit bookstores on April 19, 1954. Two days later, he was testifying before Senator Estes Kefauver and the subcommittee.

No one was more outraged by Wertham's inflammatory testimony than Dell Vice President Helen Meyer. Among her other executive duties, Meyer supervised Dell's comic book division. She knew there was nothing objectionable in Dell comic books, and, when she appeared before the committee on the second day of hearings, testified vigorously on the firm's behalf. She agreed that horror and crime comics were a blight on the industry, but maintained they were mostly published by small firms and generated low sales. Meyer objected to Dell Comics being painted with the same brush. Matt Murphy, who was there on behalf of Western Publishing, chimed in with what became the publisher's catch phrase: "Dell Comics are good comics."[1]

Although Dell refused to join the Comics Magazine Association of America, a trade association formed by comic book publishers after the hearings, and didn't submit its comic books for review by the Comics Code Authority, the company developed its own internal guidelines known as "Hints on Writing for Dell Comics." After suggestions on the kind of stories Dell wanted, the document included a section on "taboos," which began, "Avoid sophisticated and adult themes" as well as "anything dealing with minority races, politics, religion, labor, suicides, death, afflictions (such as blindness), torture, kidnapping, blackmail, snakes, sex, love, female villains, crooked lawmen or heavies of any race other than the white race." It also advised writers to "try to avoid atom bombs, Communists and international intrigue generally" and not to "make fun of the law or portray the law officials as stupid, dull-witted or cruel."[2]

When asked (years later) if the Dell "Hints" ever caused him problems, Stanley responded, "Not with the stories. Never with the stories. But there were some expressions that kids use all the time [such as] 'rotten.' Nothing doing. They didn't like that. And the word 'stupid' couldn't be used. Trying to deal with kids as they really are, that's kind of a problem. So I got around it by spelling it with two O's ["stoopid"] instead of a U. Everything had to be 'good' [because] they were trying to sell to parents."[3] Privately, however, Stanley complained that the internal censors at Dell intruded on his work in numerous other ways, and had been ever since Oskar Lebeck was sidelined.

Paraphrasing Stanley, who he met two decades later, Bob Overstreet stated, "He would send his stories in to the [Western] offices, and it got to the point where he would have to go into the office for a meeting—they must have had a psychologist on staff—and they would start changing his stories."[4] Sometimes stories were censored after completion. For *Little Lulu* #58 (April 1953), Stanley wrote a tale titled "That Ol' Witch Hazel and the Poisonous Mushrooms." It seems that he was harking back to an idea he had used in *Raggedy Ann and Andy* #36, when his

A PLEDGE **DELL** **TO PARENTS**
COMIC

The Dell Trademark is, and always has been, a positive guarantee that the comic magazine bearing it contains only clean and wholesome entertainment. The Dell code eliminates entirely, rather than regulates, objectionable material. That's why when your child buys a Dell Comic you can be sure it contains only good fun. "DELL COMICS ARE GOOD COMICS" *is our only credo and constant goal.*

protagonists eat poison mushrooms and almost die. But, what was permissible in 1949 was verboten a few years later. The finished artwork was altered by the time this Lulu story saw print, with the title changed to "That Ol' Witch Hazel and the Bad Mushrooms." The word "poisonous" was no longer acceptable. Other words and expressions in the story were also changed: "kill an elephant" became "fell an elephant," "wipe out an army" became "put an army to sleep," and "poisonous mushrooms are more poisonous than anything" to "bad mushrooms are more sickening than anything." Instances of internal censorship escalated after the "Hints" were instituted. Stanley reportedly told Overstreet, "Little Lulu couldn't be shown not wearing a top [to her swimming suit]. They had restrictions on how she had to be drawn, and what they could have and not have in the storyline. That really got to him, because he would go into these meetings where they would just slash his story. Then he had to go back and redraw it. So it got to be a big political thing to him."[5]

Meanwhile, years of anti-comic book propaganda from Wertham began to hurt overall comic book sales. The rising popularity of television also took a toll. Comic books, formerly a mainstream medium, were being marginalized. According to Michael Barrier, "By 1956 . . . comic books accounted for only nineteen percent of Western's revenues, down from thirty percent in 1952."[6] Barrier wrote, "The atmosphere was one in which even the most creative comics artists found it hard to avoid becoming a little more self-conscious and uncomfortable. Dell's titles were increasingly as uniform, stylistically, as those of its principal competitors, so that most of its animated character stories in particular shed the traces of individuality and even eccentricity that were common in the comic books of the 1940s."[7]

Walt Kelly never had to deal with Dell's writing "hints." With *Pogo Possum* #16 (April–June 1954), he ended his association with Western. The *Pogo* newspaper strip was firmly established, and he

wanted to give it his full concentration. With non-corporate points of view removed (Lebeck), and one of its most eccentric characters (Pogo) gone, the writers and artists who remained had no choice but to fall into line. Barrier: "Greater editorial control was resulting in a crudely efficient kind of storytelling."[8] Carl Barks, the writer-artist of Donald Duck in *Walt Disney's Comics and Stories*, and *Uncle Scrooge*, lost much of the creative freedom he had enjoyed at Western by mid-decade, as bureaucratic editors began picking away at his work. Like Barks, Stanley would attempt to match the Dell code's requirements, only to find, after turning in his work, that changes and new restrictions had been added.

The "Hints" made writing Little Lulu more difficult just as Stanley was teetering on the edge of creative burnout on the feature. Later in life, he expressed this theory regarding fiction writing: "Providing you have the imagination, you could write stories that take place in a small room for fifty years and make them interesting. People's relations with each other is all that matters."[9] However, he admitted how difficult it was to achieve this ideal: "Right from the beginning," he said, "I always felt 'I can't do another' at the completion of every book. There never seemed to be an idea left in me."[10] In light of the resourcefulness apparent in the first decade of Lulu stories, this would seem to be overstatement on his part. Nevertheless, his point was clear: in a business where deadlines were relentless, it wasn't long before he had worked through all the obvious story angles. After that, he had to use all his ingenuity to keep the stories fresh and maintain the quality of the series. According to Irving Tripp, as time went on, storyboards came in at the last minute or were sometimes late. "After a while," Stanley recalled, "I ceased to enjoy the writing of the strip because it was so hard to tap new ideas. There was only so much you could do with the neighborhood boy-girl format."[11]

Emblematic of incipient creative burnout was the way he handled the Alvin stories. *Little Lulu* #71 (May 1954), when the book

In *Little Lulu* #58 (April 1953), references to "poisonous" mushrooms were changed to innocuous-sounding "bad" mushrooms. The original wording was shown in the *Little Lulu Library* reprint edition (volume 14, 1986). **Opposite top:** As Stanley's work on Lulu drew to a close, he playfully referred to himself as Little Itch's father, and Witch Hazel's "half-witted half-brother, Stanley the sorcerer!" From *Little Lulu* #134 (August 1959). **Opposite bottom:** One of the last important characters Stanley created for Little Lulu was Gran'pa Feeb. He was introduced in *Tubby and His Clubhouse Pals* #1 (1956).

dropped to thirty-six pages permanently, was the last of his "fairy tales" without Witch Hazel. Lacking ideas for such tales (like "The Prince in the Pool"), Stanley put Hazel somewhere in almost every story that Lulu told Alvin after that, yet he brought nothing new to the character. Hazel's niece Little Itch made her debut in *Little Lulu and Her Special Friends* #3 (March 1955) and *Little Lulu* #82 (April 1955), but she also lacked dimension, and did little to enliven the

stories. The Witch Hazel stories were the most repetitive part of each issue.

Stanley was able to forestall total reliance on formula in the Lulu stories because of the size and variety of the supporting cast, which continued to grow. One of the most enjoyable additions was Iggy Magee's Gran'pa Feeble, known to the kids as Feeb. He was introduced in *Tubby and His Clubhouse Pals* #1 (1956), a Dell giant with all-new stories. Stanley later described Gran'pa Feeb as "an old-timer who impressed some people as being senile, but who was really blessed with a 'return to innocence' quality while retaining all his mental powers."[12] Given his playful, childlike qualities, Feeb fit in perfectly with the boys—in fact, he wanted to join their club in his introductory story. He falls in with their games easily, and claims to have met Kit Carson and other heroes of the past. One can never tell if he's putting them on, or really believes his tall tales. Inventing the new character helped Stanley fill up the 100-page comic book, for which he was most likely paid $12 a page.[13] He then put Feeb in the regular book, beginning with *Tubby* #22 (May–June 1957). By that time, the title had gone from quarterly to bimonthly, and Lloyd White was doing the covers as well as the interior artwork. Non-Lulu or Tubby work virtually halted, because Stanley had his hands full producing the eighteen books (plus annuals) per year starring the denizens of Meadowville. The popularity of Little Lulu and Tubby continued in the late 1950s, though probably (it hasn't been documented) sales gradually softened, like other Dell comics. In 1956, Dell published the paperback book *This is Little Lulu*, which reprinted a number of Stanley's comic book stories in black and white.[14]

ONE OF THE LULU stories at this time may have included a nod to an important event in John Stanley's life. In *Little Lulu* #102 (December 1956), Tubby has a toothache and is dragged to the dentist by Lulu. When he enters the office, he's greeted by a blonde receptionist, who says, "Go right in, Tubby. The doctor's waiting!" In real life, John Stanley met a blonde dental assistant about this time—and married her.

Barbara Tikoitin Widmer (b. 1929) was a young divorcee of Jewish descent, who was living with her mother Charlotte in an apartment at 880 W. 181st Street in Harlem. They had been among the last of the German Jews to escape Hitler's Germany, arriving in America shortly before the outbreak of World War II, when she was nine years old. "They were well-to-do German Jews," Jim Stanley later said of his mother's family in Germany. "She went from this privileged childhood in Germany, to having nothing, because they had to get rid of all their silver and everything to get a boat ride to America. She saw her father beat up by Nazis on Kristallnacht."[15]

The Tikoitin family struggled after arriving in New York City. Barbara married an Australian man named Widmer, but the marriage didn't last, ending before there were children. Then she met John Stanley. Although he was forty-two years old, the fifteen-year age gap proved to be no obstacle. His hair was mostly gray, but he was as handsome as ever. They began dating and soon were seriously involved, something that wasn't looked upon favorably by Anna Stanley, who didn't want her son to marry a Jew. Stanley's niece Barbara recalled, "At first, my grandmother would not let Barbara [Tikoitin] into the house. I don't think it was totally

because she was Jewish. I think it was more that she wasn't Irish Catholic."[16] Nevertheless, on December 19, 1957, John and Barbara obtained a marriage license. Four days later, they were married in city hall. Eugene Zion was John's best man, and Margaret Bloy Graham, his wife, was Barbara's maid of honor.

The newlyweds found an apartment at 172 Bleecker Street in Greenwich Village, above the Café Espanol, where they would spend the first year of their marriage. "They had gatherings when he lived on Bleecker Street, so he was probably more sociable at that point," Jim Stanley commented. "A cousin once told me he remembered 'the clinking of glasses' from that apartment."[17] Much of their socializing was doubtless with Zion and Graham, whose children's book *Harry the Dirty Dog* had been released to critical acclaim and sales success in 1956. Gene Zion, Stanley's best friend since his days at Textile High School, had graduated from the Pratt Institute, worked for Esquire Publications and CBS, then went freelance. In 1948, he married Margaret Bloy Graham, and they became collaborators, he the writer and she the artist, producing numerous, award-winning illustrated children's books.[18] Among them were several sequels to *Harry the Dirty Dog*.

The Stanley's life in the bohemian Village came to an end after the birth of their daughter Lynda in December 1958. He later said that he didn't think the neighborhood was the right environment for a child. "We felt we had to get out of the city," he said. "I was never happy there anyway."[19] They moved to a rural residential neighborhood in southwest Putnam County, New York, north of the city of Peekskill. (They had a Peekskill postal address.) The house was on Old Albany Post Road. There was a pond on the property with a rowboat and fish, and a little sandy beach. In winter, the pond would freeze and they skated on it.

Now, more than ever, Stanley had to keep up the volume of work. Not only did he have a new family to support, but he continued to provide money to his parents to maintain the house in Croton-on-Hudson. Eventually, Stanley moved his parents and Marian into a smaller house on Maple Street in Croton.

Despite his reliance on repetition and formula, there's still a lot to enjoy in Stanley's later issues of *Little Lulu*. One of the most memorable is "Hide 'n' Seek," a Tubby story in *Little Lulu* #79, in which a crazed neighbor

Barbara Tikoitin Widmer became John Stanley's wife in December 1957. Is that her in *Little Lulu* #102 (December 1956)? **Opposite:** Original art for the cover of *Little Lulu* #96 (June 1956), and his last *Little Lulu* cover (with a decidedly feminist theme) on #133 (July 1959).

dismantles his entire house, trying to find out where Tubby is hiding. Another is "Two Foots is Feet" in #94, where Lulu and Alvin decide the words "foot" and "feet" sound funny, and can't stop repeating them and laughing—and, in the process, become so annoying ("Foot! Foot! Foot! Foot!") that they instigate a feud between their fathers.

The end of John Stanley's run on *Little Lulu* and *Tubby* was coming. His last Lulu stories have a more manic, slapstick quality. There's more yelling, and more stories based on action rather than character. For example, the slapstick of "Camping Out" in #133 anticipates a trend that would become more pronounced and influence all his comics work of the 1960s, especially *Around the Block with Dunc and Loo* a couple of years later. It seems to have begun when Western was ratcheting up its control over his stories, and when he got married while still being at least partly financially responsible for his parents and older sister. Did it reflect suppressed anger at feeling hemmed in on all sides? But even in his last issue of *Little Lulu*, he was able to produce the thoughtful, remarkable "Alvin, Save That (Family) Tree," a seven-pager with Lulu teaching Alvin to appreciate his relatives, and be glad he's a part of a family. It's a rare case of a Stanley story with sentiment, hardly the work of an angry man. For this last instance of Lulu telling Alvin a story, "that awful Witch Hazel" is nowhere in sight.

Finally, Stanley told his editor that he was done with Little Lulu. Matt Murphy wasn't happy about it. On July 24, 1959, Murphy wrote him, asking if he had any more Lulu story ideas. "The last time we talked I know you were not interested but if you feel there are still some story ideas kicking around, we would be glad to have them."[20] Stanley demurred, and would never return to *Little Lulu*, which ran for twenty-four more years, except in the form of reprinted stories. Irving Tripp continued on the art. He also wrote scripts. Other Lulu writers after Stanley included Charles Hedinger, Carl Hubbel, Virginia Hubbel, Arnold Drake and Wally Green. They weren't able to generate the same kind of magic, although the post-Stanley issues had their charms. Much could be written about them, but that's outside the province of this book.

When *Tubby* #35 (July–August 1959) and *Little Lulu* #135 (September 1959) rolled off the presses, it was the end of one of the longest and most remarkable creative achievements in the history of comic books. Few titles were written by the same person for such a long period of time. Fewer still were as artistically satisfying and consistently entertaining as those of Lulu and her friends written and storyboarded by John Stanley.

DURING HIS LAST YEAR on *Little Lulu*, Stanley also wrote stories for another character: Ernie Bushmiller's Nancy. The *Nancy* comic strip began as *Fritzi Ritz*, a daily newspaper strip created by Larry Whittington, syndicated by United Feature Syndicate in 1922. When Whittington left to create another strip (*Mazie the Model*) in 1925, Ernie Bushmiller (b. Ernest Paul Bushmiller Jr.) ghosted *Fritzi Ritz* for a year, then took over officially. Four years later, he added a Sunday strip. Bushmiller introduced Nancy, Fritzi's niece, on January 2, 1933. She became so popular that she gained her own strip in 1938. (The separate *Fritzi Ritz* Sunday strip ran until 1968, although Bushmiller had long since handed it over to other artists.)

Nancy newspaper strips were reprinted in comic books published by United Features from 1949 to 1954, then by St. John Publishing. In 1957, St. John was winding down its comic book operation. Three comics featuring Nancy ended with July issues: *Nancy and Sluggo* (#145), *Fritzi Ritz* (#55) and *Tip Top Comics* (#210). Western Printing picked up the licenses to all three, with *Nancy and Sluggo* retitled *Nancy* (until #174, when it reverted to *Nancy and Sluggo*). John Stanley was assigned to *Nancy* in May. On June 2, 1958, Murphy sent him reference material on the supporting cast (Rosey, Lana, Rollo, Spike and Peewee). His first story appeared in *Nancy* #162 (January 1959). He later said, "I did [Nancy and Sluggo] from the beginning," but this is another instance when Stanley's memory was faulty. The first seventeen Dell issues of *Nancy*—#146 through #161—were written by others.[21] He wrote the Nancy and Sluggo stories in Dell's *Tip Top Comics* from issue #218 to #225. (Wally Green was named editor of *Tip Top* starting with #219.)

John Stanley's Nancy stories bore similarities to those of *Little Lulu*. Characteristically, he relied heavily on the supporting cast, and added to it in his first issue (*Nancy* #162) with a story introducing Nancy's spooky friend Oona Goosepimple. It begins with Nancy being saved from Spike, the bully, by a girl with strange-looking eyes who demonstrates the ability to control people's actions, and (apparently) read their minds. She's dressed in black, and resembles the girl Wednesday in Charles Addams's macabre cartoon series in the *New Yorker*. Oona lives with her Granny and Uncle Eek in a spooky old house. Granny, dressed in black like a witch, rides a unicycle around the house, and Uncle Eek stands about eight inches tall. Nancy is frightened, but when she tries to escape by running away, she finds the corridors of the house are a twisted labyrinth that take her back to her starting point. After she's finally able to leave, Nancy resolves to avoid Oona in the future. She doesn't succeed, because Oona is determined to be Nancy's friend.

It took time for Stanley to get his bearings on the feature. His early stories are laden with puns and weak verbal humor, and the characters are indistinct. As time went on, and he began utilizing the existing cast of supporting characters to better advantage, Stanley's interest quickened. His penchant for writing scary stories came to the fore in *Nancy* #169 (August 1959) with "Nancy Meets the Yoyos." When Oona Goosepimple's grandmother is away, she compels Nancy to accept her invitation to sleep over at her house. Once she's there, Nancy wants nothing more than to leave, but a mysterious force stops her. Later, she follows Oona behind the fireplace and becomes a victim of the Yoyos, inhuman beings who seem to want to make her their prisoner. Matthew Murphy requested changes in this story "to make [the Yoyos] sequence more 'believable' and eliminate the

more 'horrible' aspects.'"[22] He also rejected an entire story, titled "Bill Bumble's Birthday," because "we feel this tends to glorify a criminal hero (even though he ain't no criminal), and such antisocial activities as the jailbreak."[23]

Stanley later claimed, "I preferred Nancy and Sluggo [over Lulu and Tubby]. I can't tell you why, but it was more fun to do it. Maybe because Sluggo lived by himself in a junkyard, and I had this feeling about him, even though he got the worst of it all the time. Because Nancy was the main character, and I had to give her the best of it. But generally, I liked that strip better. I liked writing it. It was easy. And then I had a couple of good artists doing the drawings, like [Dan] Gormley, Lloyd White and a couple of other guys."[24] Stanley's avowed preference of Nancy and Sluggo over Lulu and Tubby seems perverse. Buell's characters, as he had developed them, were much more complex, interesting figures than what he was able to make of Bushmiller's. However good the Nancy stories became, the Lulu tales are generally superior in almost every way. In any case, he stayed until *Nancy and Sluggo* #185 (November–December, 1961), writing an entertaining—if uneven—series that, at its best, is well regarded by collectors and critics.

About a year and a half into his three years writing *Nancy*, Stanley produced the excellent, square-bound *Nancy and Sluggo Summer Camp* (*Dell Giant* #34, June 1960). Putting the covers and puzzle pages aside, what remains is a seventy-four-page story divided into fifteen chapters. It's the longest story he ever created, the closest he came to writing a graphic novel. The supporting characters are of prime importance, and they are many: Rosey

beautifully and logically. It may not have much adult appeal, but it's a flawless example of comic book-making for young readers. Even an eight-year-old can enjoy the cleverness of McOnion's relentless, plodding pursuit of Sluggo ("You're doomed, Sluggo . . . Doomed!"), and the absurdity of Rollo Haveall's luxurious private residence at Camp Fafamama.

This level of creativity makes is easier to believe Stanley when he said he preferred Nancy to Lulu. Or why, in a late-in-life interview, he said he thought this particular giant comic book had some of his best work. He had come a long way from the summer special just a year earlier (*Four Color* #1034), a joyless, contrived affair. In the 1959 camp comic,

(the homely girl), Lana (the best friend), McOnion (Sluggo's nemesis), Mrs. McOnion, Peewee (the littlest kid, and the youngest), Mr. Simply (camp director), Rollo (the rich kid), Keggly (Rollo's servant), Laura (a counselor) and so on. Oona Goosepimple also crosses paths with the campers. All the characters interact

all of the same elements were there (the characters, the setting), but used to much less advantage. Unfortunately, his summer special the following year (*Dell Giant* #45, 1961) represents a falling off from the standard of *Nancy and Sluggo Summer Camp* (1960), the apex of his work on Ernie Bushmiller's creation.

Above: Nancy cover roughs by Stanley. **Below:** Pages 1 and 2 from *Nancy and Sluggo Summer Camp* (*Dell Giant* #34, 1960), the apex of John Stanley's work on Ernie Bushmiller's creation. **Opposite:** In his first *Nancy* story, Stanley introduced the spooky Oona Goosepimple. From *Nancy* #162 (September 1957). All finished *Nancy* art by Dan Gormley. **Next two pages:** A chapter from the same *Dell Giant* shows Oona Goosepimple heading to summer camp. Gormley's finished art was based on Stanley's storyboards, which Wally Green sent to the fanzine the *Stanley Steamer*. They originally appeared in its December 1983 issue (#11). Courtesy of Jon Merrill.

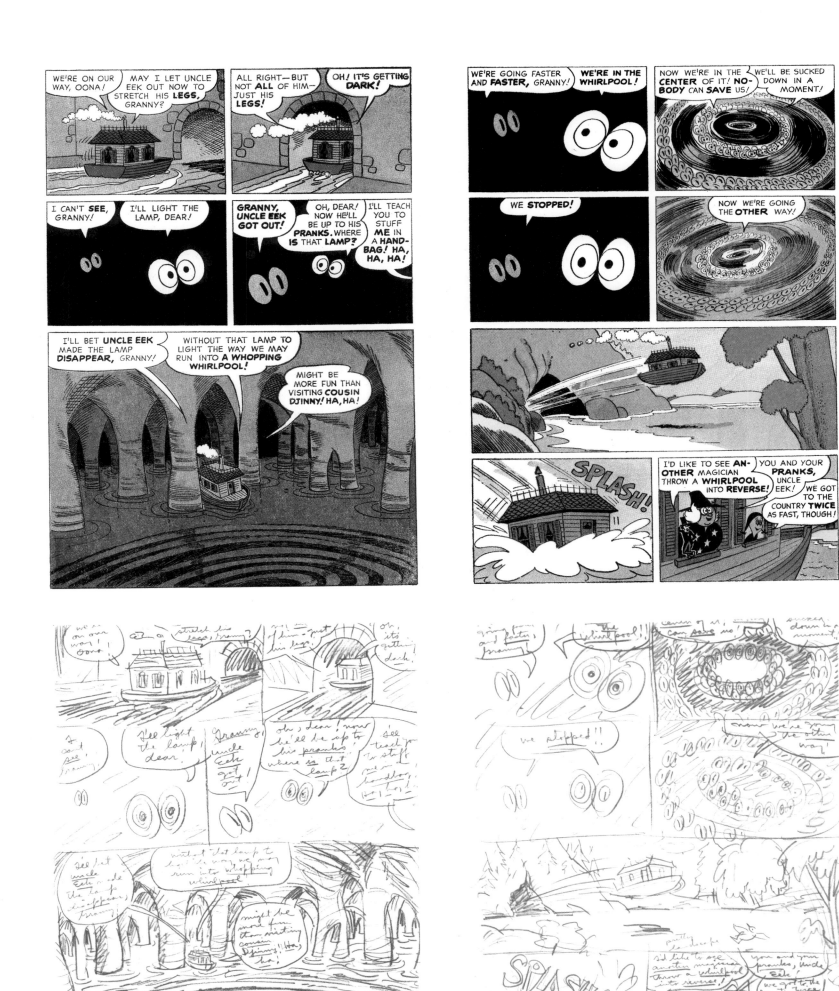

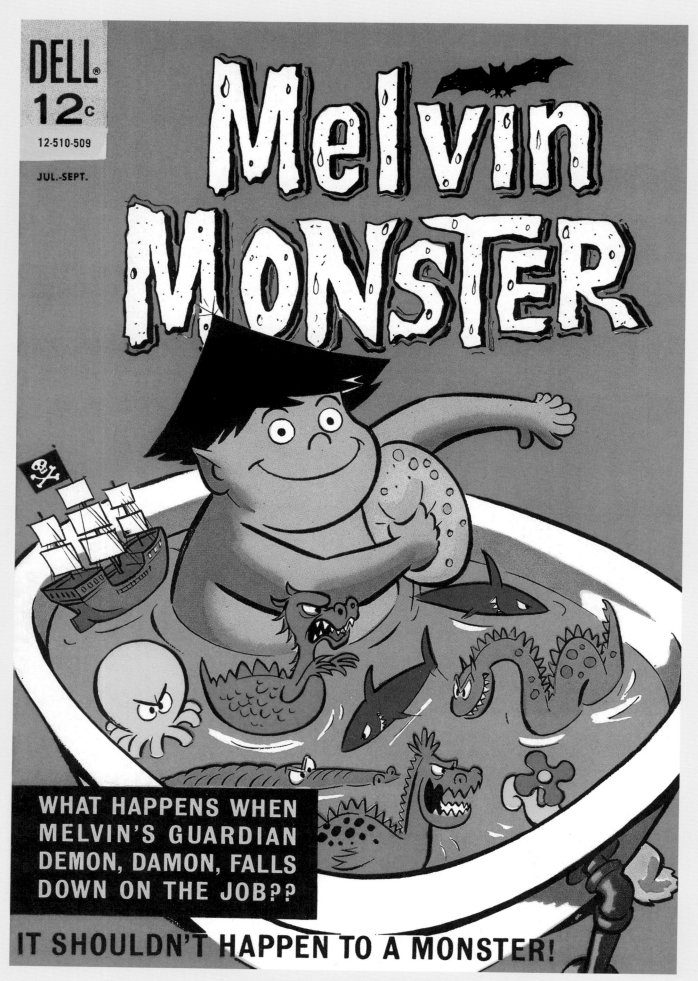

Melvin Monster #2 (July–September 1965). **Opposite:** Helen Meyer, courtesy of Robert L. Meyer.

9

John Stanley and the "New Dell"

IN 1961, JOHN STANLEY ended his eighteen-year working relationship with Western Printing. He seems to have gotten along well enough with editor Matt Murphy, but was tired of the increased scrutiny of his stories, the meetings and the requests for changes. The breaking point isn't entirely understood, although certain pieces of the puzzle have emerged. Stanley declined to explain what specifically led to the end of his relationship with Western, saying only, "I left Western. I had trouble with them— which [I] won't go into, because it's an involved, stupid thing."[1] According to Morris Gollub, "There were two or three people he used to deal with regularly, and the atmosphere deteriorated, and he'd kind of like to forget it, I think."[2] One of those people, it seems clear, was Lloyd E. Smith, who negotiated licenses for Western. On February 25, 1966, Smith wrote to Michael Barrier:

> John Stanley might still be working for us except for the fact that he made certain demands as to compensation which as a matter of business policy we were unable to meet. He even went to the extent of consulting an attorney in the matter, not so much to determine his rights, which were always clear and limited, but to insist that there was a legal obligation on our part to make a kind of standing arrangement with him. He found on consulting an attorney that this was not so but nevertheless he refused to continue with us and consequently he has not been engaged by us since that time.[3]

What sort of "standing arrangement" did Stanley want? Perhaps a statement made by Irving Tripp provides a clue. Tripp described one of Stanley's few visits to the Poughkeepsie plant: "One time, John was very disgruntled. I don't think he was happy and he also had these other characters that he wanted to get

involved in, too. He had some of his own."[4] On May 15, 1957, Stanley requested information of the copyright office of the Library of Congress, to which they responded on May 20. Unfortunately, the exact nature of his request has been lost. Was he hoping to claim ownership of characters he invented for Western?

As for the reported "demands as to compensation," Stanley may have wished to be paid when his stories were reprinted, as some of the Lulu stories had been in annuals and other places. He could well have asked for compensation when his stories were adapted to other media, as in animated cartoons. (He was likely aware that Famous Studios/Paramount had started working on new Little Lulu cartoons based on his stories. The first to appear was *Alvin's Solo Flight*, adapted from *Four Color* #165, which was released in April 1961. Another was *Frogs Legs*, adapted from *Little Lulu* #21, released a year later.) In any case, Stanley found no flexibility on compensation issues at Western.

Hence, John Stanley met with Helen Meyer, who had by that time ascended to the presidency of Dell Publishing. Dell and Western had renegotiated their arrangement, allowing for Western to act as its own publisher. Going forward, Western's licensed properties (from Walt Disney, Warner Bros., and others) would be published as Gold Key comics. If Dell wanted to stay in the comic book business, and they did, they needed to pursue other licensed properties. Meyer immediately launched initiatives in that regard, but knew that it was also important for Dell to develop properties of its own. If successful, the firm could reap additional revenue by licensing characters from such titles for toys, animated cartoons, television shows, etc.

Around the Block with Dunc and Loo #2 (January–March 1962), *Linda Lark Registered Nurse* #3 (April–June 1962), *Kookie* #1 (February–April 1962) and *Thirteen "Going on Eighteen"* #3 (May–July 1962). He only finished the art for the *Thirteen* cover. The *Around the Block* and *Kookie* covers are by Bill Williams. *Linda Lark* cover artist unknown. **Opposite:** *Dunc and Loo* #6 (April–June 1963). Bill Williams art.

Toward that end, Meyer met with Stanley at the dawn of the new Dell line.

From Meyer's point of view, Stanley's record as the creative force behind *Little Lulu* and *Tubby* made him a desirable catch for her new editorial staff, even as the editorial supervisor of all Dell comic books. Stanley: "They wanted me to do everything, and write everything. And start out a whole new line of books, because Western kept the copyright on all Disney stuff, Little Lulu, everything. So Dell was starting from scratch."[5] From John Stanley's point of view, Helen Meyer had the power to make a deal with him that would be more favorable than the work-for-hire arrangement that prevailed all those years at Western. (In brief, work-for-hire was the pernicious policy practiced by comic book companies at this time which made all work done by freelancers—including new characters they might create—the property of the publisher after a one-time payment.)

If Stanley assumed he would retain ownership of new characters he would bring to Dell (some which he had already worked up with Bill Williams, but had yet to be published anywhere), Meyer quickly disabused him of the notion.

This type of arrangement in the comics industry was decades away. (Walt Kelly was able to retain Pogo after leaving Western only because of his special relationship with Oskar Lebeck and others at the company.) What Meyer could do, when she asked Stanley to "start out a whole new line of books," was pay him to act in an editorial capacity, on top of what he would make as a writer, designer and artist. She could also offer annual bonuses based on sales, like Western. But basic work for hire prevailed, and, having hit the same wall at Western, Stanley accepted the status quo. He also accepted the role of a sort of editor in chief, although he didn't last long in that capacity, according Leonard Brandt ("L. B.") Cole's account to writer-photographer E. B. Boatner.

Cole, who had been a comic book artist and editor since 1943, was at loose ends in 1961 because he'd been let go by Gilberton (*Classics Illustrated*) for unspecified "irregularities" in the paying of freelancers. Cole, known for his braggadocio, stated, "[Dell] said 'we're going to take back our own editorial, and we want to get the best editorial and art director in the business.' I got the call. Now, I was not art director, I was [both] editor and art director. I took over the complete comics division, but when I got there, I ran into John Stanley, who was supposed to do the job."[6] Apparently, Stanley was ensconced in the Dell offices, busily working on ideas for new comic books, when he was informed that he would be sharing his office with Leonard Cole. Cole: "John Stanley quit after about six weeks because he had no more desire to be behind a desk. He was doing [comics stories], and he said, 'Helen, let Len do it.' And I think you know John had a slight problem at one time. At that time, he was fine, but he'd go off the deep end every once in a while and start screaming at me. And then he left and I took over the Dell Publishing Company comics line until the time I had a slight run-in with Helen Meyer about the royalties."[7] When Cole says "John had a slight problem" and would "go off the deep end every once in a while," he was referring to Stanley's alcoholism, which tended to lead to angry outbursts. Commuting to and from Dell's offices in Manhattan daily from his home in rural Putnam County couldn't have been pleasant for Stanley. He must have been relieved to return to his routine of working at home, and coming into the office once every week or two.

Whatever stresses Stanley was under, there's no question that the spring of 1961 saw the greatest creative explosion of his career. In those few months, he originated *four new titles*—each with lead and backup features.

On July 11, 1961 (or thereabouts), two new Stanley books hit newsstands, with the first comics characters created by John Stanley since Peterkin Pottle in 1949: *Around the Block with Dunc and Loo* #1 (October–December) and *Linda Lark Student Nurse* #1 (October–December). They were priced at fifteen cents, Dell's response to rising production costs. These, and all other titles Stanley produced directly for Dell, were published quarterly.

Around the Block originated from a couple of ideas Stanley had been working on for possible newspaper syndication, one in collaboration with Bill Williams. Stanley had liked Williams's art on *Henry Aldrich*, probably because of its looseness and dynamism. (He later described Williams as "a first-rate artist."[8]) An example of a daily strip starring the Loo character has survived, as has a

Full spread: Apparently, Stanley's teenage character Loo, who ended up in the Dell comic (with his pal Dunc), got his start as the star of a possible newspaper comic strip. Art by John Stanley. The other seven strips shown are for a Stanley-Williams strip submission about a shoeshine boy named Pepe. At this time, the Gus Edson-Irwin Hasen strip *Dondi*, about a war orphan of Italian descent, was at its peak of popularity.

finished sample daily starring Li'l Petey, who became the regular, secondary feature in *Around the Block*.

John Stanley: "[In] *Dunc and Loo*, I was dealing with teenagers . . . like Archie. I figured, 'I can do better than this. I'll show teenagers the way they really are.'"[9] Loo is a frenetic scatterbrain living in an urban neighborhood who drives everyone around him crazy, including his somewhat-more-sensible best friend, Dunc. The first story has Dunc entrusted with the running of Sid's soda shop while the owner deals with an emergency. Loo whips up chaos in the shop in nothing flat. The inside front cover of *Around the Block* #1 appears to be made up of two of the projected *Loo* daily strips. The backup feature, *Li'l Petey*, is a strip about a boy a bit younger than Lulu and Tubby who is growing up in the city. His debut concerns his attempts to sell newspapers on a street corner. Petey is a good-natured kid who is sorely put upon by the forces around him: his so-called buddies, other newsies, the cops and his customers.

Typical of Stanley's work at this point in his career, there's a lot of frantic activity, yelling and slapstick humor. Unlike Archie, who is caught between Betty and Veronica, Loo can't get any girl to give him the time of day. The inner city environment seems like a throwback to the 1930s, rather than the years of the "New Frontier"—after much of the country's urban population moved to the suburbs and were paying mortgages rather than rent. The real problem with *Around the Block* comes from its origins as a potential comic strip. It's gag-oriented rather than story-oriented, and Stanley's gag comedy ability is inferior to his ability as a storyteller.

Linda Lark Student Nurse #1 (November 1961–January 1962) was John Stanley's first attempt to create a serious comic book. The nurse subgenre of comic books was experiencing a boomlet in the early 1960s.[10] It carries the cover blurb, "The story of a young girl suddenly plunged into the drama and excitement of life in a great city hospital." Linda reports for her first day of nursing school, meets her homely, humorous roommate Charley (female), the handsome doctor Allen Mayne and her supervisor, Miss Dooley. The script meanders through semi-comical incidents, one life-and-death emergency, and a number of situations right out of a television soap opera. Stanley's script is clever. Maybe too clever—certainly for artist John Tartaglione, whose stiff visual style makes everyone look like an awkwardly posed manikin. But then, some of Stanley's more outré moments of dialogue must have mystified him, as they likely did the teenage girls who read the comic book.

John Stanley's third new book was titled *Thirteen*, and bore the subtitle "Going on Eighteen" although the title of record is just one word. Its publication date was August 17, 1961, about a month after Stanley's first two books had gone on sale. The lead character is Val, an impulsive, highly emotional thirteen-year-old. She's something of a tomboy, who wears her blonde hair in a ponytail, and whose principal moods are anguish and anger. She has her older sister, Evie, a high school student with a considerably more laid-back, mature personality, as a foil, as well as her chubby best friend, Judy, and her next door neighbor Billy Wilson. We meet Val's mother, but a father is nowhere in sight, nor is mention made of him. The series is basically about an awkward thirteen-year-old dealing with the difference between how she thinks her life should be versus its much-more-prosaic reality.

The artist initially assigned to *Thirteen* was Tony Tallarico, who may have drawn more pages for the new Dell line than anyone else. Beginning in 1953, Brooklyn-born Tallarico penciled and

Left: *Thirteen* #1 (November 1961–January 1962). Art by Tony Tallarico. (Courtesy of Michelle Nolan.) **Right:** Sequence from *Linda Lark Registered Nurse* #3 (April–June 1962). Art by John Tartaglione.

inked comics for lower-tier outfits such as Charlton, Trojan and Gilberton. He often worked with penciler William Fraccio, though Fraccio was generally uncredited. Tallarico's work was substandard, but he was fast, reliable and willing to work for low rates. Western Printing had held their rates steady as inflation caused other publishers to raise the amounts they paid writers and artists. By the early 1960s, the publisher's rates were below those paid by National and Marvel, and the new Dell offered similarly low rates. Therefore, the best artists worked elsewhere, or did rushed work for Dell. Tallarico found he had stumbled upon a good thing, which he described as his "best market in comic books."[11]

Tony Tallarico recently recalled working on John Stanley scripts for the first two issues of *Thirteen*: "I never met Stanley. I'd never heard of him until that time. I just got the assignment from Dell to do a book called *Thirteen*. Lenny Cole wanted me to illustrate it. I first worked with Cole when he was art director at Gilberton, on *Classics Illustrated*. Cole gave me the scripts for *Thirteen*. They were in typed form." Despite the fact that Stanley is on record as saying, "I always did my stories in storyboard form," Tallarico is adamant that the script was typed.[12] (It's possible Cole had someone create a typescript from Stanley's storyboards.) Tallarico remembers that he designed the characters. "I submitted sketches, which were approved by Lenny Cole and Helen Meyer, who was the head of Dell. I don't know if Stanley approved them. We did two issues. Then I found out that Stanley was upset. He didn't like the art. He was the only one who didn't like it. He went to Helen Meyer, who he was very friendly with, and she said, 'Sure, you want to do the art? Do the art.' So Lenny said to me, 'Don't worry about this. We've got tons of things to do here.' I got *Car 54 Where Are You?* and many other assignments.

"I saw a couple of Stanley's issues of *Thirteen*. I don't like criticizing him, but it was not well done. I didn't think he was an artist. It was crude. You know, we were supposedly competing with Archie and that type of book, and his was far from it. And that was it. It was a fun assignment. I had never done the Archie type of comic book. I was doing mostly realistic stuff, and *Thirteen* was a little different. I never knew what he didn't like about my work on it. I just knew that, all of a sudden, I didn't have the book anymore." *Thirteen* #3 (May–July 1962) became the first comic book Stanley both wrote and drew at the new Dell.

Stanley's approach to his finished artwork on *Thirteen* has nothing in common with the art in Archie comics by Harry Lucey or Dan DeCarlo, and more in common with his artistic approach to Little Lulu. His artwork on the new book is spare and energetic. The style of comedy is broad like *Around the Block*, but lacked the ingratiating comic detail of Bill Williams. Its sparseness and repetitive visual iconography put the focus almost entirely on the stories, and the emotions of the characters. As Val gropes with what it means to be a "good friend," or how to relate to boys, she takes on a reality that makes "better artwork" unnecessary. Val isn't "pretty" or "cute." She's a force of nature.

Teamed with Bill Williams, *Kookie* is Stanley's fourth new comic book for Dell. Its first issue was dated February–April 1962. Kookie is an aspiring, young actress working at Mama Pappa's Expresso [sic] shop in Greenwich Village. She and her roommate Clara interact with all manner of beatniks, artists, musicians and poets in the shop, allowing him to draw on his memories of the Village. Her blonde innocence is a perfect foil for their eccentricities. The backup feature is "Bongo and Bop," the misadventures of two ne'er-do-well, bearded beatniks. The stories aren't as incessantly frenetic as *Around the Block*. Kookie is a charming young woman, and the stories are genuinely funny. While the scene in the Village had already changed somewhat in the years since John and Barbara had moved to the country, the stories and characters feel like they reflect a reality known by the writer, not viewed from afar by a stuffy adult. He obviously had a certain amount of affection for the bohemian lifestyle. Sadly, inexplicably, *Kookie* only lasted one more issue. This was too soon for sales reports to have dictated its demise. Did naming the lead character "Kookie" lead to confusion with the role Edd Burns was playing on the popular TV show *77 Sunset Strip*? (There seems to have been some confusion regarding that television program's comic book licensing. The new Dell published an issue, and then the title switched to Gold Key.)

As it turned out, only one of the four Stanley titles was successful enough to warrant continuation: *Thirteen*. *Around the Block with Dunc and Loo*, his self-professed humorous version of the way teenagers "really are," didn't click with readers. The comic, which bore the shortened title *Dunc and Loo* starting with #4, reported an average sale of just 222,865 copies as of September 20, 1962, in a sales report published in #6 (April–June 1963). We don't know the percentage of sales, only that the comic book wasn't sufficiently profitable, because it was canceled with #8.

The same fate befell *Linda Lark, Student Nurse*, after going through two title changes. (It became *Linda Lark Registered Nurse* with #2, then *Nurse Linda Lark* with #6.) It too was canceled after #8 (August–October 1963). With its shifting tone and stories that made little sense, *Linda Lark* is a failure on all levels, except in one respect: its unusual backup feature *Tramp Doctor*, which ran from #3 to #8 in four page installments.

Tramp Doctor was something brave and fascinating: the story of Dr. Ivar McCutchin, who has taken refuge (or found himself stranded) on the small island Gorbu in the Fiji Islands. He has "occasional problems with alcohol," the reader is told, because he blames himself for the loss of his wife and child who both died in childbirth, although it wasn't his fault. He stays at the Gorbu hotel, owned by a lovely island woman named Tisara Lister and her young brother Mikeli, who says, "He drinks whiskey once in a while, and the people here call him tramp doctor . . . but he helps us all and we love and respect him." Although McCutchin is prone to self-loathing ("Once a drunk, always a drunk," he tells himself in a morose moment) and even thoughts of suicide, he becomes a hero when the islanders are in danger. In the superb fourth installment, "Tidal Wave," when the

John Stanley's remarkable *Tramp Doctor* was a backup feature in the *Linda Lark* comic books. Was there any other ongoing character with his own series who went on recurring alcoholic benders, yet was shown in a positive light in comic books of this era? From *Linda Lark Registered Nurse* #3. (It's mostly likely penciled by John Tartaglione, according to Frank M. Young.)

people of the village don't believe his frantic warning that a tidal wave may be coming, he slugs the town constable and sets off the storm siren to get the residents to move to higher ground. By saving their lives, he permanently endears himself to the people of Gorbu.

Tramp Doctor is a series that couldn't have existed in a Code-approved comic book. The tales of McCutchin (another Irish "Mc" name, like McNabbem and McOnion) ask the question—not inapplicable to John Stanley's own life—"Can an alcoholic who falls off the wagon from time to time be a worthwhile, respected member of society?" *Tramp Doctor* explores how such a person can live with himself, and how he finds meaning in a life that others might consider meaningless.

OF ALL THE STORIES written by John Stanley for the new Dell, possibly the most revered by comics aficionados are those in *Ghost Stories* #1, the first of an ongoing series, and *Tales from the Tomb*, a one-shot, that appeared at almost the same time. In them, he demonstrated a talent for full-blown horror stories that's unsurprising, considering the many frightening and/or disturbing tales he'd written for *Little Lulu* and *Tubby*.

The kernel of the idea may have come from L. B. Cole, one of his last editorial acts before exiting Dell in April 1962. While editing comics for Gilberton Publications, Cole had overseen the publication of *The World Around Us*, an anthology comic book that studied various aspects of nature and science. Somehow he was able to shoehorn an issue titled "The Illustrated Story of Ghosts" into the natural science series (#24, August 1960). Its cover featured a haunted house with an ethereal ghost hovering nearby, pointing an accusatory finger at the reader. That cover was the work of Cole's friend Norman Nodel, according to Gilberton expert William B. Jones Jr.[13] Its interior was made up of tepid "true stories" of ghosts, poltergeists and hauntings.

The first issue of Dell's *Ghost Stories* featured a cover that copied the one by Norman Nodel on *The World Around Us* #24, although the figure of the ghost is reversed. (The artist of the copy is unknown.) The twelve-cent title went on sale in the summer of 1962. It has perhaps Stanley's best, and best-remembered, horror story for these new comic books: "The Monster of Dread End," a terrifying tale of a monster living in the sewer, whose reptilian arm reaches from an open manhole into the windows of tenement apartments to kill neighborhood children. Everything about the story is outstanding: the way the story is set, the horror of the monster squeezing children to death (off stage), and then the main part of the story, when a boy finally sees the slithering arm with its clawed hand, and it pursues him through the alleys and streets. Gerald McCann, an artist who had done numerous issues of *Classics Illustrated*, employs a crude, bold style that suits the story well. "Dread End" is the stuff of childhood nightmares, and must have caused many among the young readers who innocently plunked down their twelve cents that summer.[14]

Tales from the Tomb (October 1962) is a giant, eighty-four-page comic book of (mostly) supernatural stories, some truly

Stanley created *Ghost Stories* for Dell and wrote at least two of the stories in its first issue (September–November 1962), including the terrifying "The Monster of Dread End." The cover was a poor copy of Norman Nodel's cover for Gilberton's *The World Around Us* #24 ("The Illustrated Story of Ghosts," August 1960) by an unknown artist, probably engineered by editor L. B. Cole. Gerald McCann drew "Dread End."

frightening, that goes well beyond what could be done under the strictures of the Comics Code. While Stanley was scripting it, Cole hired artist John Schoenherr to paint a suitably macabre cover.[15] The twenty-five cent comic book features ten stories (and a few one-pagers) drawn by artists such as Frank Springer ("Mr. Green Must be Fed"), George Evans ("The Mudman"), Tony Tallarico ("Crazy Quilt" and "The Cat That Was Part of the Night") and other unidentified artists. Tallarico recalled, "I enjoyed doing these. *Tales from the Tomb* and *Ghost Stories* #1 might have been the last two books that were edited by Len Cole. The scripts were in standard, typewritten format, as were all the scripts for the stories I did for Dell." The first story, "Mr. Green Must Be Fed," uses the same rug with concentric circles as did the Little Lulu story "The Throw Rug" (#64, October 1953). This time, a fearsome green monster ("Mr. Green") emerges from the rug to eat lodgers in a rooming house. In "Still Life," a haunting painting of a cursed tree stump causes the painter to hang himself. In "Oh, How We Danced," a man discovers that the beautiful woman with whom he has danced was killed in a car crash two years earlier. In "The Mudman," a mud-monster comes out of a swamp to kill a boy's faithful dog. There's no blood shown in any of the stories, but the level of horror inherent in them is startling for a 1962 comic book.

These two comic books elicited a huge, negative reaction from parents. Of *Tales from the Tomb*, Stanley said, "It sold like nothing I've ever done. But, it horrified all sorts of people. We got letters—a ton of letters—from parent groups, and associations and whatnot, who told Dell they were going down the drain to print stuff like this. I was called into the office, Mrs. Meyers' office, and [asked], 'How could you do a thing like this to us?'"[16] Stanley was delighted! Jim Stanley recalled, "My dad was really tickled by the protests against *Tales from the Tomb*. He relished doing that kind of material. I remember him telling me Dell had to take him off the horror stuff because they received so many complaints from parents. I think he was kind of proud of that. He was never a huge fan of the artwork in those comics. Personally, I thought it was quite effective."[17]

Whatever fallout came Dell's way didn't prevent *Ghost Stories* from continuing. Unfortunately, its second issue (April–June 1963) doesn't live up to the potential of #1, nor did the ones that followed. They're credited to Carl Memling, writer of Dell's *Ben Casey* title, also known for writing many of the Little

Full spread: Two climactic pages from the John Stanley-Gerald McCann collaboration, "The Monster of Dread End."

Golden Books in the 1950s and 1960s. Perhaps, as Jim Stanley says, his father was taken off the book because of the complaints. Or, perhaps it was a result of L. B. Cole's sudden departure. When asked why Cole left, Tony Tallarico said, "All I know is that one day he was gone, and his assistant, D. J. Arneson, took his place. And Arneson didn't even know why Cole left. It was a big surprise." Arneson later said, "In April 1962, Len Cole was—let's say—let go, without getting into the details there. My understanding is that he was 'let go' but what the actual circumstances were, I do not know."[18]

This led to Arneson being given Cole's job as editor in chief of the entire Dell comic book line, after being there just one month (and being new to the comics field). He later explained, "Helen Meyer called me into her office and asked me if I was capable of

doing [the job as editor in chief]. I said, 'Yes I am,' and she said, 'Okay, you are now my comic book editor.' So I didn't come into comics with a long history of working in them. I came into the publishing industry and it turned out my entry was through Dell Comics. I was there until I moved to Europe [in the early 1970s]." Therefore, it was Arneson who hired Carl Memling to write the *Ghost Stories* series. Of John Stanley, Arneson said, "I did not know

John all that well. He was an established writer long before I met him. He had a close relationship with Helen Meyer."

Meyer's decision to entrust the top editorial position to a neophyte proved to be disastrous for Dell's comic book line. The twenty-seven-year-old Arneson had no writing experience, and no knowledge of comic book scripting and art. Despite the low page rates Dell was willing to pay, an experienced comic book

Full spread: Beneath John Schoenherr's painted cover for the 84-page *Tales from the Tomb* are fourteen horror stories (from one to fourteen pages in length) written and storyboarded by John Stanley, with finished art by such artists as George Evans, Frank Springer and Tony Tallarico.

professional with a modicum of taste could have put together a more attractive, salable line than the dismal fare that doomed Dell to comic book extinction. They had a few decent sellers (such as *The Beverly Hillbillies* when the show was on the air) and a few worthwhile original titles (*Combat*, with art by Sam Glanzman, and John Stanley's *Thirteen*), but most of their line was dreck. It sputtered to an ignominious end in the early 1970s, whereas Western's Gold Key line, also operating on a low budget, lasted ten years longer. (*Little Lulu* was one of their last titles, under their Whitman label.) Meyer was by all accounts a smart business person, but even smart people make mistakes.

THE STANLEY FAMILY EXPERIENCED typical developments and passages in the early 1960s: Barbara and John had their second child, a son names James (Jim) on April 16, 1962. He was born in Peekskill Hospital. James Stanley, John's father, passed away less than a year later.

By the time John's niece Barbara was married on August 10, 1963, his wife ("the other Barbara") had been accepted by Anna Stanley. The Irish matriarch and Jewish daughter-in-law would never become close, but they saw a lot of each other at family gatherings. Niece Barbara married a British student named Steggles, who was working on his master's degree at Columbia University business school. "I felt like I escaped in 1963," she recalled. "It was an Irish clannish life, and not how I wanted to live." She went on to get a degree in economics at Columbia. The two of them would live for many years in Europe.

Above left: 1965 photo of the Stanley home on Old Albany Post Road in Putnam County, New York. John is with his young son, Jim, and a cousin (unidentified). **Above right:** John with his parents ca. early 1960s. **Below:** Drawing by Margaret Bloy Graham of "The Happy Stanley Family" ca. 1962. Courtesy of the Estate of Margaret Bloy Graham.

Work continued on *Thirteen*. The book evolved. In the beginning, Val's best friend Judy was overweight. *Thirteen* became fully realized about the time Judy slimmed down, starting with #6 (February–April 1963). The stories, simply titled "Val" or "Judy" or "Val and Judy" vary in length, and allow for short encounters, longer adventures and half-page gag strips. Val's need for attention and drama cause her to devalue her neighbor friend Billy as "boyfriend material," along with just about any other boy around, causing an ongoing cycle of stories on the theme of getting the "right" boyfriend that runs through almost every issue. For the most part, Val's pursuit is frustrated, usually by her own behavior. Stanley does accord her one perfect moment, when time seems to stand still in the midst of Val's typical tumult: a romantic first kiss with her Prince Charming, the handsome Paul Vayne.

The backup feature stars Judy Junior, a chubby little girl whose mission in life is to completely dominate her neighbor Jimmy Fuzzi, which makes his life a living hell. She's like Tubby in her self-delusion and self-involvement, but much worse: in short, a monster. But who exactly is she? Is "Judy Junior" supposed to be Judy when she was eight or nine? Stanley never explains. The reader keeps rooting for Jimmy Fuzzi to best Judy Junior. She's so self-righteous and insensitive that she deserves to be taught a lesson. Jimmy's victories are few and far between. The Judy Junior strips are darkly humorous, but a little uncomfortable to read because the reader feels Jimmy Fuzzi's pain.

A momentous event occurred with *Thirteen* #12 (August–October 1964): the cover is signed by John Stanley—the first time he had ever put his name on a comic book cover. Beginning with that issue, he signed nearly all of the subsequent covers. Yet, strangely, it didn't mean much to the cartoonist, or so he said: "They insisted I put my name on covers, hoping [it] would sell a couple [more copies]… but I didn't want my name on these things. Somehow, I felt that it wasn't important. It didn't matter, one way or the other."[19] For him, working in comic books was about making a living. Recognition might be nice, but not that important.

Gregory Gallant, the cartoonist known as Seth, is a fan of *Thirteen*. He wrote: "I like Archie comics quite a bit . . . but I have to say, these characters are weak ciphers when compared with Stanley's lively creations. Val, Judy, Wilbur, etc.—these are not complex characters by any stretch of the imagination, yet they have

Above: Val's "one perfect moment" with Paul Vayne (*Thirteen* #6). **Below:** Jimmy Fuzzi and his nemesis Judy Junior in "Idle Hands" (*Thirteen* #6).

an inner life lacking in the Archie gang. You would have no trouble imagining any of Stanley's teens and their private worlds. It might be because Stanley was interested in eccentricity. His characters are natural oddballs, peppered with personal quirks. Because of this, Val and Judy are as real to me as other beloved cartoon characters like the *Peanuts* gang. Stanley so ably breathed life into them that they seem to exist outside of the crumbling yellow pages of these old comic books. A wonderful alchemy occurs where they seem to continue living even after you close the book."[20]

AFTER ALL THE COMIC BOOKS he created except *Thirteen* were canceled, Stanley needed more work. He filled in by writing five issues of *Clyde Crashcup* in 1963. Stanley's stories of the crackpot scientist from the 1960s animated television series *The Alvin Show* were drawn by Irving Tripp. Stanley also wrote much of the exhaustively titled *Alvin and His Pals in Merry Christmas with Clyde Crashcup and Leonardo* (February 1964).

Then he saw a new show on ABC-TV called *The Addams Family*, which made its debut on September 18, 1964. It cleverly adapted Charles Addams's macabre family from the pages of the *New Yorker* into an original, droll situation comedy, starring John Astin as Gomez and Carolyn Jones as his wife, Morticia. A week later, *The Munsters*, starring Fred Gwynne and Yvonne De Carlo as Herman and Lily Munster, a more cartoonish show about a

Above: Original art for *Thirteen* #14 (February–April 1965), courtesy of Gary Brown. *Thirteen* original art on is 14" by 20," or double the size of the 7" by 10 1/8" comic books. **Below:** In addition to the comic books Stanley created, he did other work for Dell on such characters as Clyde Crashcup, Deputy Dawg and Nellie the Nurse.

From *Melvin Monster* #1

family of monsters, made its debut on CBS-TV. It wasn't hard for Stanley—creator of *Tales from the Tomb*—to see the commercial potential in a similar comic book. He got to work.

Stanley named his character Melvin Monster, no relation to the Atlas character in 1956 (who was a Dennis the Menace imitator). The first issue of Dell's *Melvin Monster* (April–June 1965) was rushed to the stands, going on sale on February 9, a little over four months after *The Addams Family* was first broadcast. It's another title that Dell could publish because it wasn't a signatory of the Comics Code, which prohibited "scenes dealing with . . . walking dead, torture, vampires and vampirism, ghouls, cannibalism and werewolfism."[21]

In the first story, "Like a Little Monster Shouldn't," we're introduced to the Monster family: Mummy, Baddy and Melvin. Stanley quickly establishes the backwards aspects of their world. Melvin wants to go to school. His parents urge him to play hooky. In "Teacher's Patsy," Miss McGargoyle (who looks ever so much like Witch Hazel) screams "Get lost!" when Melvin reports to The Little Black Schoolhouse. "In Human Being Land," Melvin finds himself in our world, captured by an eccentric millionaire for his private zoo, then returns to Monsterville to deal with a diminutive

flying demon named Damon. It's an impressive, astonishingly creative beginning to the last major comics series that John Stanley would essay.

Melvin Monster might have worked better if it hadn't fallen victim to its creator's unbridled penchant for wild yelling and frantic action, but one can enjoy it for Stanley's emphatic, dynamic artwork. It's the opposite of the spare look of *Thirteen*. This time, he gets out his thicker brushes and goes to town using heavy strokes to create contrasts and visual excitement. Each story has a splash panel, and well-worked-out, highly visual situations, displaying his particular ability to work variations on a theme. One needn't read the dialogue. Simply turning the pages, following the story visually, is a great deal of fun, and a lesson in how to design pages and move a story along from someone who had mastered the form, and attacked the pages with vigor.

First four pages of "Human Being Land," a key story in *Melvin Monster* #1. Melvin is flung into the "real world" and into the clutches of a crazed "monsterologist."

Top left: Melvin playing with his "pet" alligator, Cleopatra: from MM #1. **Top right:** Single gag continuity from MM #9. **Bottom row:** "Overtime" story, also from MM #9.

Opposite: Although *It's Nice to be Little* was generally well received, a reviewer for *The Kirkus Review* felt differently: "Hindsight is supposedly better than foresight, but the little ones who don't find life one big cream puff aren't likely to take much stock in this idealized, backward view of their world. If they do, the concluding news that 'never, never again will you have the fun you had when you were little' is chilling." By the mid-1960s, John Stanley found writing and drawing comic book stories increasingly difficult. In August 1965, the *Peekskill Evening Star* interviewed him about his writing career, including his recent children's book, *It's Nice to be Little*. The photo of Stanley at his drawing board appeared with the newspaper interview.

10

Leaving "A Young Man's Game"

JOHN STANLEY'S FRIENDSHIP with Eugene Zion and Margaret Bloy Graham opened a door to the world of writing children's books. In 1964, he collaborated with Jean Tamburine, an established artist of such books (*Milkman Bill*, *Almost Big Enough*) on *It's Nice to be Little*, published by Rand McNally and Company the following year. Stanley said, "[It's] for very little children. It is simple, as all things should be for very little people."[1] The book is small, just 7.25 inches horizontally and 5.25 inches vertically, and thirty-two pages long.

Stanley wrote in *It's Nice to be Little*: "Being little is the time when every day is for play—when you are closest to your best friend, to flowers, apples that fall to the ground, and lost nickels. Never, never again will you have the fun you had when you were little."[2] That's its theme, in a nutshell. It's a sweet, unpretentious book, which rather wistfully celebrates the innocent pleasures of youth. (His daughter Lynda was just entering grade school, and Jim turned three when it was published.) A reviewer in the *Morning Record* (Tamburine's

local paper in Meriden, Connecticut) wrote: "In a world in which the young are trying hard to grow up too fast and the old, or at least the middle-aged, are trying to recapture their youth, it is nice to find a book which bespeaks the fun of childhood, especially a book for children."[3]

On the dust-jacket flap, the biographical note on the writer describes him as "a freelance commercial artist and cartoonist [who] decided to try his hand at writing his first children's book—a happy decision that should be the beginning of a new and successful career."[4] It wasn't, even though *It's Nice to be Little* went back to press in 1966 and 1967. He never did another. As with his gag cartoons for the *New Yorker*, Stanley would seem to make an inroad into a new type of work, only to pursue it no further.

Reporter Dorothy Krumeich mentioned the children's book when she interviewed him for an article which appeared in the *Peekskill Evening Star* on August 11, 1965. It was the only time when Stanley was interviewed for publication. To her question about the anti-comics furor of the 1950s, he responded: "Watching television is now the thing kids do that parents and teachers and educators disapprove of. Comics at their worst never approached the mayhem rampant on the TV screen today. There is much good in television but it's up to mother and father to guide the selections."[5] He is described as a putterer around the house—"and he loves it." Stanley: "When my daughter first went to school and the kids were asked, 'What does your father do?' her answer was: 'He fixes things.'"[6]

It's NICE To Be LITTLE

by John Stanley
pictures by JEAN TAMBURINE

STANLEY WORKED HARD to put *Thirteen* over. In its third year, sales perked up. For most of 1963, they had averaged fifty percent of 381,191 copies. As better issues arrived through 1964 and 1965, the percentage of sales steadily rose, till it reached sixty-three percent of 325,204 copies for issues on the stands during most of 1965.[7] These are not great results, but they were enough to keep the comic book going and suggested that sales might continue to improve. Instead, in the fall of 1965 and winter of 1965–1966, despite the series hitting its creative peak, sales were dropping. The same was true of *Melvin Monster*. By summer, Stanley knew they were slated for cancellation. Having produced nothing for Dell with real sales vitality, he was dispirited and depressed. That most comic books fail was a lesson he hadn't learned during the halcyon years at Western.

He and his family moved back into the city, to an Upper East Side apartment at 152 East 94th Street. The reason for the move isn't clear, only that it took place sometime during the summer of 1966, ostensibly in time for their daughter to begin her school year there. (There would be no Catholic schools for the Stanley children. They attended PS 198, two blocks from the apartment.) With

Above: *Thirteen "Going on Eighteen"* is the most successful comic book John Stanley created, sales-wise (apart from *Ghost Stories* #1 and *Tales from the Tomb*). Then, between issues #15 (May–July 1965) and #17 (January 1966), shown here, sales began declining, and the title was doomed. **Below:** *Thirteen* #14 (February–April 1965)

YVETTE KAPLAN ON *THIRTEEN: "GOING ON EIGHTEEN"*

Cartoon historian Jerry Beck wrote:
Animation director Yvette Kaplan (*Beavis and Butt-Head*) not only grew up reading John Stanley's stories, but his influence has inspired her storytelling talents and her career as an animation director. I asked her to explain her passion for Stanley's comics and what animators can learn from his work.

Yvette Kaplan:
I first became aware that I had a knack for comedy timing in 1993 when I started directing on Mike Judge's *Beavis and Butt-Head* series for MTV. Luckily for me, I had been reading John Stanley's brilliant, and insanely funny, *Thirteen: "Going On Eighteen"* for years. I have no doubt whatsoever that I learned—or more accurately—absorbed the essence of comedy timing from inhaling pages just like this one:

Judy has convinced Wilbur that she just fed him his ratty old hat for dinner. Note the big reactions . . . expressive poses . . . unexpected pauses . . . rapid mood swings . . . And—lots of yelling.

As far as I'm concerned, Wilbur stopping in the midst of his agony to stare pensively at a motorcycle is comedy timing at its best. A single panel, that's all. He doesn't notice it as he passes, doesn't turn around and go back. We don't see him stop, he's just there. (Cue the soundtrack of your choice. Sometimes I hear a soft whistling, sometimes crickets, sometimes Muzak.) And then he's screaming his head off again a panel later. Ah, the beauty of manic behavior!

limited space in their new quarters, Stanley set up his drawing board in the children's bedroom. When queried about his earliest memories of his father, Jim says, "My earliest memory is standing on my father's feet, and he would walk around with me, holding onto his legs. I also remember my parents arguing, in a good way, in the house on Old Albany Post Road. I used to whack him in the butt when they were doing things like that. I have early memories of him drawing. When we moved to the city, his drawing board was in the same room as my bunk bed. I would pop my head up and see him working."[8] One comic book with his father's work that Jim remembered is the *WHAM-O Giant*.

WHAM-O Giant Comics #1 (April 1967) was an enormous comic book that measured 14 by 21 inches—one of the largest comic books ever published, in terms of dimensions—put together by WHAM-O Manufacturing Company, probably to exploit the comics craze initiated by the Batman TV show in 1966 to sell its toys.

It's an uneven affair highlighted by a couple of brief stories by legendary comic book writer-artist Wallace Wood— and, a single page by John Stanley: *Bridget and Her Little Brother Newton the Nuisance*. The story costars yet another of Stanley's annoying, overbearing kids, and is drawn more or less in the style of *Thirteen*. He never said how he got this one-off job, but in so doing, he became part of a unique comic book. (It wasn't intended as a one-shot, but that's what it was. The odd size made it difficult to display.)

The last issues of his two Dell titles trickled out. Both *The Addams Family* and *The Munsters* TV shows aired their final episodes in the spring of 1966. *Melvin Monster* lasted for another year. Although the lively, emphatic cartooning by Stanley never flagged, the stories became increasingly manic and unfocused, almost deconstructing before readers' eyes. Melvin, Mummy, Baddy and Miss McGargoyle shouted their last in issue #9 (August 1967). *Melvin Monster* #10 is a reprint of the first issue.

In the spring of 1967, Stanley penciled and inked thirty-two pages of artwork for the concluding issue of *Thirteen*. It was the final go-around for Val, Judy, Evie, Billy and Wilbur. On the last page, Judy Junior is about to punish Jimmy Fuzzi for outdoing her on ice skates. John Stanley left poor Jimmy suspended for all time in purgatory, perpetually in retreat from his nemesis. The Dell era ended for John Stanley with *Thirteen* #25 (December 1967), although it continued through #29 with reprints of the first four issues. By the end of 1967, the new Dell line was on the road to extinction. D. J. Arneson's editor in chief position was reduced to a part-time job. The publisher's output diminished and became erratic, with nothing on the newsstands for a month or two, then

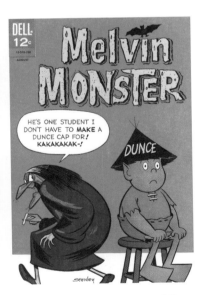

Above: Original art (courtesy of Gary Brown) and printed cover for *Thirteen* #23 (June 1967). **Below:** Stanley's Miss McGargoyle, Melvin's reluctant school teacher, resembles Witch Hazel from *Little Lulu*. From *Melvin Monster* #9, the last new issue, dated August 1967.

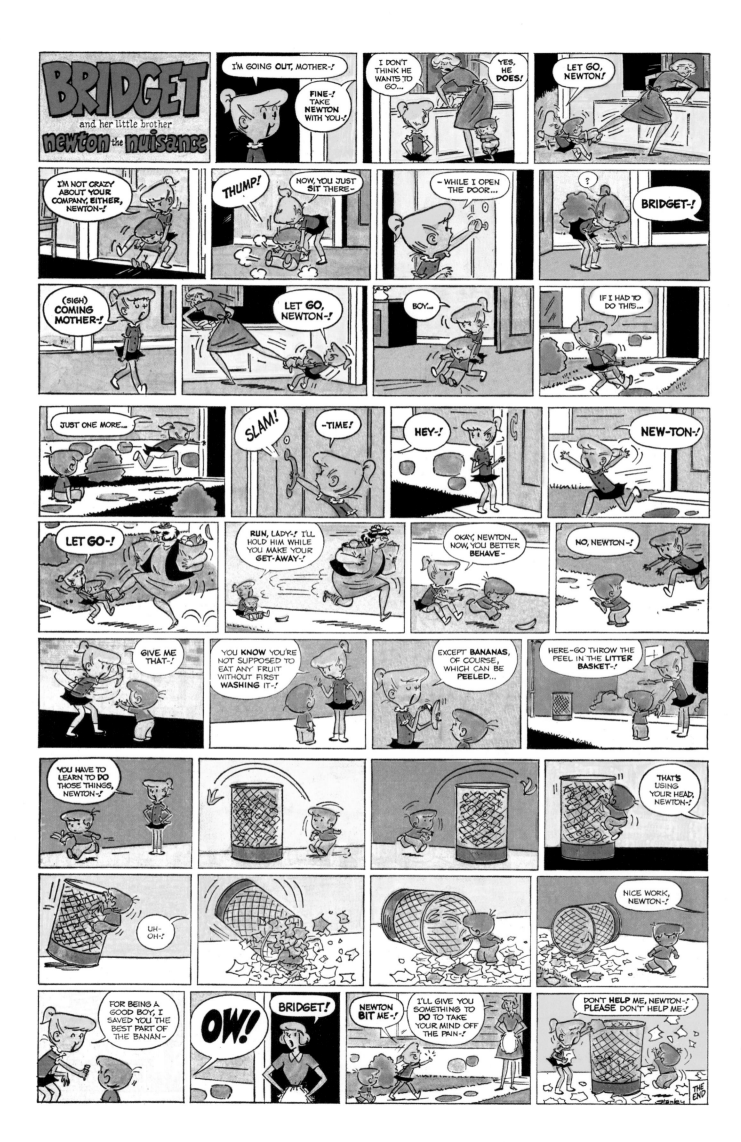

Opposite: Stanley's *Bridget* page. Above: John Stanley left poor Jimmy Fuzzi suspended for all time in purgatory, perpetually in retreat from the monstrous Judy Junior, in the final issue of *Thirteen* (#25, December 1967). Below: Stanley's last two comic books: *Choo-Choo Charlie* #1 (April 1969) and *O. G. Whiz* #1 (February 1971).

a large group appearing at virtually the same time, like the death throes of a fatally wounded animal.

John Stanley needed work. Unfortunately, as with the years before he started with Western, late 1967 and 1968 is a "mystery period" in Stanley's life. His son says that his mother didn't have a job at this time. What were they doing to pay the bills? (Split royalties for the third printing of *It's Nice to be Little* couldn't have amounted to much.) Were there proposals for new comic books that didn't fly? Eventually, Stanley reached out to Western Publishing. Matt Murphy was still an editor there, as was Wally Green. The logical thing would be for Stanley to return to *Little Lulu*. After all, Gold Key was often using reprints of Stanley stories in their Little Lulu books. The twenty-five cent *Marge's Little Lulu Summer Camp* #1 (August 1967) was a reprint of most of John Stanley's *Lulu and Tubby at Summer Camp* #2 special (October 1958). *Little Lulu* #186 December 1967) consisted of reprints from *Little Lulu* #52 (October 1952), #70 (April 1954) and #99 (September 1956). Of course, it was galling to Stanley that he received nothing for this reprinted work. (Soon Marjorie Buell would be out of the picture. With royalties for *Little Lulu* drying up, she retired and sold the rights to her creation to Western Printing in December 1971. The comic book dropped "Marge's" from its title with #207, September 1972.) Instead, in late 1968, Stanley landed the most meager of assignments: the commercial one-shot *Choo-Choo Charlie* which saw print with an April 1969 cover date. Charlie was the railroad engineer in television commercials for Good & Plenty candy. It was up to Stanley to come up with some sort of a story. As it turned out, he both wrote and did the finished art for it, and the results were lighthearted and charming. He wrote at least part of another issue, which was never published.

John Stanley's last new comic book work appeared in November 1970. *O. G. Whiz* #1 (February 1971) was the sixth title he created (eighth if you count *Tales from the Tomb* and *Ghost Stories*) since 1960, the story of a child genius put in charge of a toy company by an eccentric millionaire.[9] After writing the story and lettering the first issue, he walked away. Gold Key was left to find others to produce the succeeding eight issues (there were a total of nine, plus a reprint of the first issue in #10) before it died. His son later commented, "Since he stopped [doing comics] when I was in second or third grade, my memories of him actually creating comics are pretty dim. I remember him working on the Gold Key stuff — *Choo-Choo Charlie* and *O. G. Whiz* — when I was eight or nine, and that's about it. It's too bad, because I wouldn't fully appreciate his gift and stature in the comics world until much later in life. [I did know], growing up, that he was exceptionally talented and had this

From *Choo Choo Charlie* #1 (April 1969).

other previous life and body of work that he was renowned for, and I was proud of this."[10] John Stanley said that he left comics because he was tired of the pressure of producing new stories to meet deadlines. When he did the cover art for *O. G. Whiz* #1 in 1970—the last piece of finished artwork of his twenty-eight-year comic book career—he was fifty-six years old.

DURING HIS DIFFICULT last years in comic books, John Stanley's behavior toward family and friends seems to have gone off the rails. He became so estranged from his brother Tom that his son Jim didn't even know he had an uncle until he was much older.

(Tom had problems of his own, also being fond of alcohol, but was steadily employed by New York Transit, like his father.) Stanley also became estranged from his friends Eugene Zion and Margaret Bloy Graham, who were divorced by this time. Graham remained friendly with Barbara Stanley, but Gene Zion dropped out of John's life not long after the children's book *It's Nice to be Little* was published.

In the 1960s, imipramine (marketed as Tofranil)—the first medication that dealt directly with clinical depression—came on the market. Many found great relief in this and variants that followed. John Stanley wanted nothing to do with it. Even years later, when he understood depression better, Stanley resisted any sort of treatment: "I don't believe in psychiatrists or 'pills,'" he told fan Bradley Tenan. "Nobody can tell you what to do or how to conduct your life. Like any physical sickness, you just have to let the depression run its course until it goes away."[11] In short, there could be no solution at all.

Of his father, Jim Stanley said, "When he was happy and not overcome by his demons, he was a loving, caring and funny person. By 'demons,' I mean mainly that he suffered from depression and alcoholism, and surely they exacerbated each other. He also smoked pretty heavily his whole life, and tried unsuccessfully to quit numerous times.[12]

"He was a charming guy. He loved women. He had a charming way with all women. He liked older women, and he liked younger women. I remember my second grade teacher in the city, a blonde whose name I've forgotten . . . and I remember him either charming her, or talking to her about me."[13]

Finally, after their children's school year ended in 1970, John and Barbara Stanley agreed to a sort of separation. "[Dad and I] moved back upstate when he left the business," Jim recalled. "From the city, we moved to Horton Road [with a mailing address in Cold Spring, New York]. And I remember moving there just with him. And staying there, and practically living off the land. The house was a real fixer-upper. Now, in hindsight, my parents must have been really fighting a lot, so there was kind of a cooling-off period. I stayed up there quite a while with him, just getting the house ready."[14] It was located in a residential-rural neighborhood. Jim has happy memories of going fishing with his father, driving to the local deli Sunday morning for rolls and watching television together.

The move upstate was made possible because Stanley found a job in Cold Spring. He began working as a silk-screener for Fairgate Rule, a company located in a single-story facility in a residential neighborhood. (Its white, clapboard edifice with awnings over two doorways looked more like a duplex rather than a commercial business.) The firm made all sorts of precise rulers for architects, engineers and others. Jim Stanley recalled, "His post-comics career was unfortunately spent in a small factory building in Cold Spring, New York, churning out silk-screened aluminum rulers. Even there, the company's owner . . . recognized his abilities and tried to convince him to run the company for him—but my father would have none of it."[15] Fairgate Rule was a small business with fewer than ten employees, in addition to the British-born owner Charles Brody and his sister. John was the screen printer, a key position, and was one of the few employees who only did one job. Jim Stanley wrote to Michael Barrier, "I think at [my father's] core he was an artisan, a perfectionist who wasn't afraid of getting his hands dirty—so it isn't a stretch to understand where he ended up. He used to complain about the cranky old S.O.B. who owned Fairgate Rule. He did some advertising artwork for him as well. Later in life, I ran into locals who worked alongside him as young guys in their twenties, and they made it a point to say what a great guy he was. Hard to reconcile with the nasty stuff at home, but I can understand it now."[16]

Tim Lahey was one of those locals. He worked with John Stanley at Fairgate Rule for two years. He recently wrote, "I knew John Stanley in the early 1970s when he was working as a silk-screen printer. I had recently graduated from college with no idea what I wanted to do and in a poor job market. I was hired as a backup printer to John, who taught me the basics of screen printing in a short time. I printed for him when he was on vacation or out sick and, at times, when two of us were needed to print. John didn't much like working there but he was always meticulous in his work and he had a real ability to manage the often finicky screens so they didn't stretch or shrink during the day.

"The screen printing was all done by hand with a rubber squeegee. The rulers were printed on plates of various sizes depending on the ruler. Rulers varied from six inches to eight feet. We made a variety of specially curved rules that were used in the garment industry as well as straight rules used in graphic design and for general use. Silk-screening required standing all day, and the floors were concrete, but we had rubber mats in front of the screens to stand on. It was mind-numbing work, and John felt the same way I did. As he said to me one day, 'I never thought I would be doing something like this in my declining years.'

"He was one of the most fascinating people I have ever known. He did talk about his comics work and, early on, he told me that he had written the Little Lulu comics. I recall him telling me about the tremendous stress of producing a comic story every two weeks, especially when he was doing the drawing and the writing. He said it was 'a young man's game' and he just couldn't continue to produce on a schedule. His prodigious wit constantly entertained me and often it was spiced with some bitterness toward the publishing industry. I remember him discussing that all he ever got for his creative work was a regular paycheck.

"I was aware that [Stanley] suffered from alcoholism although I never saw any signs of it in his work. I do know that he left the shop every day at noon time and went to a local bar. He always returned on time and I didn't notice any effect on his work. Of course, I was barely twenty-one years old and probably would have missed some subtle signs. Most mornings when I got to work he would be sitting in his new Volkswagen Beetle reading the *New York Times* before the shop opened. I remember discussing a book by Tom Wolfe that I had just read, *Radical Chic & Mau-Mauing the Flak Catchers*. He really appreciated Wolfe's writing style, particularly Wolfe's ability to puncture the façade of some pretty self-important individuals.

"John had a wonderful sense of humor and a broad knowledge of our culture. His sense of humor really appealed to me because he seemed so unlike others of my parent's generation. He could comment sarcastically on the absurdities of our work situation as well as view his own life with a sense of irony. It was a privilege to know him."[17]

11

John Stanley and Comics Fandom

JOHN STANLEY WAS DONE with comics, but like the ghosts in his stories, his four-color past came back to haunt him. In the 1960s, a fandom formed by people who read comic books in the 1940s and 1950s was growing by leaps and bounds. One of the fans' missions was to find out who had created the objects of their fascination, since so many of the writers and artists worked in anonymity. Fans of certain Dell Comics wondered, "Who was 'the Good Duck artist?'" and "Who (really) did Little Lulu?"

Carl Barks wrote and drew the adventures of Donald Duck and Uncle Scrooge for seventeen years before he was "discovered" by John Spicer and others in 1960. This changed his life. By then, his best years on the Walt Disney characters were behind him, and he was grateful for the praise and appreciation of his newfound followers. A decade later, when Barks was in the last phase of his career in comic books, fandom gave him a social network and a way to make money by selling paintings of the ducks.

While the professionals working for DC and Marvel comics became aware of fandom (because much of fans' attention was focused on the super hero comics that were taking over the marketplace), Stanley was off to the side, writing and drawing *Thirteen* and *Melvin Monster*, and had no awareness of fandom. He never dreamed that one day, the grown-up fans of Little Lulu would come calling. That is, until he began receiving a few odd letters. Perhaps the first was from someone named Michael Barrier, who lived in Little Rock, Arkansas.

Barrier's primary interests were animated cartoons and the duck comic books by Carl Barks. He was also a fan of *Little Lulu*. "After I began collecting old Dells again, around 1963, I wanted to compile a list of the Dell one-shots, and that somehow led me to the Catalog of Copyright Entries in the University of Chicago's library. Stanley is credited in the copyright registrations as the author of the Lulu *Four Colors*. Soon after I learned that, I saw my first issue of Don and Maggie Thompson's fanzine *Comic Art*. That

was when I learned Carl Barks's name. I wrote to the Thompsons soon thereafter, probably in early 1965. I think it was then that I told them about Stanley."[1] Seeking Stanley's address, Barrier queried Marjorie Buell's agent William Erskine, and Lloyd Smith of Western Printing, to no avail.

The Thompsons were prominent comics fans who were also working on an index to the Dell *Four Color* series. In *Comic Art #6* (July 1966), they began taking advance orders for this index, which was still taking shape. (Since the *Four Color* series ran for more than 1,300 issues, it was a big job.) Despite the input of Barrier and others, there were still many questions and gaps in their list. Prompted (apparently) by Barrier, they wrote, "Can anyone give us the address of John Stanley, the cartoonist and, we believe, writer of *Little Lulu* and *Jiggs and Mooch*?" They also asked, "Who or what is Oscar [sic] Lebeck? Is he still alive? Does anyone have his address?"[23]

Somehow, Barrier obtained Stanley's address (he doesn't recall how), and sent him a letter in 1967. The cartoonist was then living at 152 East 94th Street in the Upper East Side in New York City. He didn't receive a reply. Others, such as the Thompsons, wrote him, too. While these erudite comics enthusiasts' letters reflected their maturity and appreciation of Little Lulu and Stanley's other work, they made no more headway than Barrier.

Stanley didn't want to be found. He was in the final, wrenching stages of his comic book career, and smarting from the cancellation of *Thirteen* and *Melvin Monster*. For him, comics had been simply a way to make a living, and he harbored resentments over the way things ended with Western. As a result, his relationship with fandom was problematic from the start. When Maggie Thompson was finally able to speak with him in 1974 for an article in Michael Barrier's *Funnyworld* magazine titled, "The Almost-Anonymous Mr. Stanley," she wrote, "Those of us who collect his work have to be pretty good detectives—and even then we'll have to work

Dear Mr Bray,
Sorry for the delay. It took a while to recover from the trauma of being asked for an autograph — It's the first time that I can recollect.

Somehow I never managed to hold on to a single copy of Little Lulu — or any other comic I've done. It's nice to know somebody else has done so.

Thanks, and the very best to you.
Sincerely,
John Stanley

GLENN BRAY
14460 Tyler Street
Sylmar, California
91342

without his help. He says that one reason he doesn't answer his mail is that so many letters ask questions like, 'What stories did you script in *Little Lulu* #75?'—and he has neither the comics, the data nor the interest to answer."[4]

The earliest known instance of John Stanley replying to an entreaty from a fan occurred in early 1971. Comic art collector Glenn Bray sent him a piece of artwork and asked him to sign it. Stanley complied, and wrote:

> Dear Mr. Bray,
>
> Sorry for the delay. It took a while to recover from the trauma of being asked for an autograph. It's the first time that I can recollect.
>
> Somehow I never managed to hold on to a single copy of *Little Lulu*—or any other comic I've done. It's nice to know somebody else has done so.
>
> Thanks, and the very best to you.
>
> Sincerely, John Stanley[5]

His return address at the time was "Horton Rd., Cold Spring, NY."

By this time, Carl Barks was doing lucrative art commissions for fans. He had more orders for duck paintings than he could fill, and before long, new paintings were only available via auction. Glenn Bray, who had been involved in the Barks painting enterprise, thought John Stanley could do the same. Bray offered money to Stanley for a painted recreation of a favorite *Little Lulu* cover, and suggested he do more paid commissions for others. "I proposed to him that he do some cover recreations. But after he

started working on mine, someone . . . got in and swayed him to do auction-only. So, I sadly never got the cover I requested."[6] Once word got out that Bray had received a response, more fans began writing to Stanley. Sometimes he would answer, sometimes not, according to his whim. One he did answer was Denis Kitchen.

This was in the early days of Krupp Comics Works, Inc., a publisher of underground comix in Milwaukee, Wisconsin. On November 8, 1972, Krupps owner Denis Kitchen wrote Stanley, inviting him to produce new material for one of his comix. A month later, Stanley responded:

> Dear Denis,
>
> I've been out of comics about three or four years now. At present, I'm drudging at silk screening—it's sort of a living and a little easier on the nerves. I must confess I've never seen a comic of the underground variety! Would you send me a couple? If I can come up with something I'm not too ashamed of I'll send you roughs. Thanks for the letter.[7]

Kitchen sent him a group of underground comix, including *Smile* #2, *Snarf* #1 and #2, *Mom's Homemade Comix* #3, *Bijou Funnies* #5 and #6, and *Fever Dreams*. He wrote, "*Bijou* #5 contains a parody of 'Little Lulu' which, although fairly crude, you might find amusing."[8] He also included a current Krupp catalog, and offered to send along anything that interested Stanley.

The Little Lulu parody in *Bijou Funnies* #5 (December 1970) was "Little Poo-Poo" by Justin Green. In the six-page story, Chubby, Spiggy and the rest of the members of the Boys' Club are

When Denis Kitchen was trying to get John Stanley to create some new comics for Krupp Comics Works, Inc., in 1972, he sent him *Bijou Funnies #5*, with Justin Green's "Little Poo-Poo, War Against Weenies." Cover art by Skip Williamson. **Bottom left:** "Stanley confirmed that he painted the cover of this Little Lulu coloring book sometime in the 1950s. Courtesy of Bob Overstreet."

smoking marijuana in their clubhouse when they are challenged by Little Poo-Poo to a 'Battle of the Sexes' at nearby Miller pond. The girls attack en masse, shouting "Up from under!" and "No vaginal orgasms!," quickly overpowering the boys. As in Stanley's original Lulu strips, the boys assert their superiority, and the (all-male) police lock the girls up. However, the boys bail out the girls, Poo-Poo and Chubby French kiss, and the groups unite. The story ends with Little Poo-Poo exhorting, "We must bypass all conditioned responses towards our masculinity and femininity so that at long last our very humanity will supercede [sic] all divisive sexual motives!"[9]

According to his son, Stanley was fascinated with the samples that Kitchen sent him. Stanley later stated, "I saw one . . . underground magazine. It had a semi-pornographic treatment of Little Lulu. I wasn't the least bit disturbed about it. It wasn't my character and I didn't particularly give a damn."[10] Even so, Stanley didn't write back, or respond to follow-up notes from Kitchen.

A year and a half later, Kitchen wrote Stanley with a new idea. He proposed that Stanley do a small self-portrait for his Famous Cartoonists button series. "I know you've ignored previous pleas for material, but please consider doing this one small thing." On July 1, 1974, Kitchen received a package from Stanley.

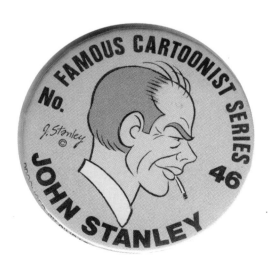

Dear Denis,

Here's the drawing—The first I've done in years. My kids thought it crummy, so it's got to be a fair likeness. I'm still hopeful I'll be up to doing comic book work for you soon. Best of luck with your button project.

Sincerely, John Stanley

P. S. Hair gray, eyebrows darker, skin standard comic book pink.

A delighted Denis Kitchen responded in his letter of July 30, 1974, thanking Stanley: "Your kids may think it was crummy, but I think it was damn good." But then Kitchen dropped the ball. The Famous Cartoonist Series was duly produced, with the numbered buttons featuring cartoonists from comic books (No. 4: C. C. Beck), comic strips (No. 10: Al Capp), underground comix (No. 13: R. Crumb), and *Playboy* (No: 28: Harvey Kurtzman), in alphabetical order. John Stanley was button no. 46. However, Kitchen failed to send samples of the button or payment to Stanley.

Almost two years later, Stanley's niece wrote to Kitchen asking for some of the Stanley portrait buttons. On April 7, 1976, Kitchen wrote to Stanley, stating that the niece "mentioned that you never received a sample of [your button]. The series has been out for quite a while. I'm sorry if you didn't get one right away. Here is one if you didn't." He offered to send more, and again entreated Stanley to work on some new comics.

This inadvertent slight seems to have soured John Stanley on Denis Kitchen. So, most likely, did the button itself, which showed his hair as brown, not gray as the artist had specified. When Kitchen heard back, the letter came from Stanley's wife Barbara. On July 8, 1976, she wrote,

Denis,

It was nice to hear from you and to receive the button. I must say that we were rather surprised to find out from our niece that the buttons were indeed being sold. My husband never received any thanks or acknowledgement [sic] for his drawing from you much less any royalties as you had promised. But then this is the type of transaction he has come to expect from those connected with comics and the reason he is so disillusioned. It would have been nice to at least receive several of the buttons for our fourteen-year-old son.

Very truly yours, Barbara Stanley

On July 12, Kitchen responded, apologizing for the delivery of the buttons falling through the cracks. He wrote that no more than twenty-five or thirty of the John Stanley buttons had been sold. He explained that at royalties of twelve percent of each $1.00 retail button, the amount would be embarrassingly small. He then said that he would send some extra buttons. He also offered to

prepay on any comics work that Stanley would produce for him in the future. "I am anxious to restore your faith in me as a comix publisher, if not as a 'button magnate.'"

Barbara was conciliatory in her letter of August 13, 1976: "I realize very well that this is not a money-making proposition and was just a little upset that you never acknowledged receipt of the drawing. Thank you again, the buttons were much appreciated." Actually, Kitchen *had* acknowledged it, in the letter of July 30, 1974, that somehow went astray. This was the last contact he had with the Stanleys.

WHAT FANS HAD NO way of knowing is that John Stanley's health began deteriorating in the 1970s. As his son later told interviewer Michael T. Gilbert, "I'm sure his drive and desire to turn out work were severely hampered by his drinking, depression and failing health. He suffered from severe headaches that were debilitating."[11] His father blamed his smoking for the headaches.

When Stanley was able to keep his alcohol and mental problems at bay, he could be a good father. Jim attended Millbrook School, a prep school in Millbrook, New York, for grades nine through twelve. "My friends all loved my dad because he had a great sense of humor and could be 'one of the guys.' He had a great way of relating to teenage boys, in a sort of 'I know what you guys are up to . . . wink-wink' sort of way. He loved the reading material I brought home in the '70s, such as *Mad* and *National Lampoon*.

"He did relate well with children and he had a terrific sense of what appeals to children and understood their thinking. Was he child-like? Yes and no . . . he could be very stern and no-nonsense, and 'authoritative' with my sister and me, yet other times he could also have a silly sense of humor, singing and carrying on when he was in a good mood. He also could have a fearsome temper and put the fear of God in us just by raising his voice. So his mood really made the difference, and it could go far in either direction."[12]

How could the Stanleys afford to send Jim to Millbrook School? It was Barbara Stanley who was determined this would happen, because the local high school had a terrible reputation. Since Stanley's salary at Fairgate Rule was substantially less than he had made in comics, Barbara had gone back to school, and by this time had become a kindergarten teacher at Woodside Elementary School in Peekskill. Jim Stanley said, "She was always a hard worker. She was driven. So she went to SUNY [State University of New York] in New Paltz in her forties, got her teaching degree and then she got her master's."[13]

Another reason for Stanley's "hot and cold" attitude toward fan contacts and doing further work was that by 1974, his marriage was coming apart. The major point of contention seems to have been finances, as well as his drinking. Of his parents' marriage, Jim said, "Dad had about fifteen or so good years with my mom, but then the marriage started to disintegrate around the time that he left the comics business. They went from having huge fights to long stretches of silence, until he finally moved out to my aunt's house in Croton."[14] Marian was living there with Anna Stanley, who was in her nineties. The matriarch passed away in 1978, leaving her two eldest children to live in the house as companions for the rest of their lives.

Despite these difficulties, Stanley did respond to contacts from some fans. He answered Maggie Thompson's questions for the aforementioned article in *Funnyworld*, and became friendly with Craig Yoe, a designer and book packager. Yoe recently wrote, "Carl Barks and John Stanley got me jazzed about comics when I was a Tubby-aged kid. When I was an art director for the children's magazine *Bible-in-Life Friends* in the 1970s, I contacted John and offered him a magazine assignment. We struck up a phone friendship when I had to continually ring him up and cajole him into turning in the art. Later, when I moved to New York to work as creative director for The Muppets, I didn't have a clue where to settle. John encouraged me to move near him in Croton-on-Hudson. This proximity drew us even closer."[15]

Stanley wrote to Bob Overstreet, publisher of the *Comic Book Price Guide*, who lived in Cleveland, Tennessee. Overstreet recently recalled, "At a New York comics convention, I bought two original painted covers that were used for Little Lulu coloring books. One was from 1955, and the other one was late 1940s. After I got home, I sent [John Stanley] copies of the artwork for those paintings. It turned out the 1940s cover wasn't his, but the 1950s cover was. And he actually signed a copy of the 1950s cover as confirmation that he did it."[16] Overstreet asked Stanley if he wanted to do a cover for one of the updated annual editions of his *Price Guide*. Stanley agreed: "I would like to do a cover for you. Whenever you're ready I'll send you roughs."[17] While Stanley seems not to have responded to further correspondence from Overstreet at this time, he remained favorably impressed by the publisher. This paved the way for his participation in a comic book convention two years later.

THE STORY OF JOHN STANLEY'S only appearance at a comic con began when Bob Overstreet made a trip to New York to attend the New York Comic Art Convention over the July 4th weekend of 1976. On July 7, as the country was still celebrating the American Bicentennial, Overstreet and comics fan Don Phelps drove from New York City to visit John Stanley at his home in Putnam County, New York.

Don Phelps was best known for his monthly "Sunday Funnies" mini-cons, and as the co-chairman (with Martin Greim and Bob Cosgrove) of Newcon, a large comic book convention in Boston in 1975, patterned after the older, established New York Comic Art conventions. Born in Boston in 1945, Phelps was one of millions of children who read and enjoyed *Little Lulu* in the 1950s. "Bob invited me along, because he knew I was such a fan of Little Lulu. This was in the 1970s, when things were just starting to be known about certain people. Carl Barks was at the forefront, and Stanley was quite a bit behind."[18] Both Overstreet and Phelps were fans of Barks, who had agreed to appear at the upcoming Newcon, scheduled for four months later (October 23–25). If all went well, Phelps planned to invite Stanley to the convention, too.

It was late afternoon by the time Overstreet and Phelps pulled up in front of the Stanley home on Old Albany Post Road. Overstreet recalled, "It was wooded all around his house. You could see all these animals. I think I saw a raccoon in his yard. It was like a Disney story." They were greeted by his wife, Barbara, who welcomed them and told them that John had to work late, but he would be there soon. They were introduced to her sixteen-year-old daughter Lynda and fourteen-year-old son Jim, and entertained by Mrs. Stanley until John arrived, an hour later. He had driven from Fairgate Rule, about ten miles away.

"John rushed in, and apologized for keeping us waiting," Phelps said. "He was wearing overalls and a denim shirt, and his hands were filthy from the silk-screening work. He had to wash up before eating." Phelps immediately sensed tension between John and Barbara. "The tension was palpable. John spoke to her in a cold way. In retrospect, I think he may not

Left: Lynda, Barbara and John Stanley, during Don Phelps and Bob Overstreet's July 1976 visit. **Middle:** Stanley with Bob Overstreet. **Right:** Stanley. **Top:** Posing with Don Phelps. Photos: Bob Overstreet.

had some cover concepts in pencil for *Nancy* comics. He had a complete set of *Choo-Choo Charlie* roughs. And I got a lot of that from him when I was there. He had one Little Lulu page, a complete [finished] piece of original art. I don't know what story it was from. It could have been a title page. He just gave them to me. He didn't want money for them."

The photos taken that evening show no evidence of tension. One has a T-shirt clad Stanley standing before a floor-to-ceiling bookcase where he kept his large personal library. Looking over the titles, Phelps realized that Stanley was an unlikely combination of working class man and literary intellectual. The house itself, according to Phelps, was "a lower middle class type of house. It was an older house. No special attributes to it." Stanley warned his guests that they had a pet snake, and not to be shocked if they saw the reptile slithering around the house. (They never saw it.)

Overstreet recalled, "We hit it off and were having a good time. We talked about Carl Barks and Donald Duck. Stanley said he wished he had been able to do the Donald Duck stories. And Carl Barks also told me, in one of my meetings with him, that he wished that he was able to do the Little Lulu stories. Each of them appreciated each other's strips. We were there for several hours— it lasted and lasted. We really stayed too long. But, you know, Don Phelps is quite a talker." For his part, Phelps said, "I wasn't about to let the opportunity of meeting John go by without gleaning every bit of info I could out of him."

Over the course of the evening, Phelps and Stanley made a strong connection. Phelps, who had a degree in English Literature from the University of Massachusetts, recalled, "He and I, having similar [Irish Catholic] roots, connected right away. After his initial shyness, he warmed up to me during the visit and recognized the fact that our encounter was not a 'fan-boy' idol meeting, but rather out of a respect for his work from a literary level on my part, especially when I mentioned my friend Tom Murray. Tom was a bookstore owner whose graduate degree in children's literature made a solid impression on him. I explained the way John's Lulu work had enthralled Tom as a child, and continued to captivate him to the present day." Having established this rapport, Phelps had the confidence to invite Stanley to the second Newcon. (As a special guest, all his expenses would be paid.) Stanley hemmed and hawed, but finally accepted. It was a perfect end to the meeting.

A few weeks later, Don Phelps also visited Carl Barks in Temecula, California. Barks had canceled his appearance at the 1975 Newcon at the last minute, so Phelps wanted to make sure all was well for Barks's trip east in October. While Phelps was in California, he also visited the Sanrio animation studio and called on Morris Gollub. "Mo Gollub was a director at the studio. I approached him to extend wishes on behalf of John Stanley. Mo dropped his pencil, looked up at me and said, 'John Stanley! God, could we use him at the studio here! One of the greatest story men I've ever known and he's always been the last person to ever talk about his own merits."[19] When Phelps relayed Gollub's offer, Stanley interrupted him mid-sentence to respond, "No interest whatsoever."

having been living with her any more, but had agreed to meet us there to 'keep up appearances.'" They sat down to a meal prepared by Barbara, and after eating, settled into the living room to talk.

Stanley was friendly, but it soon came out that he looked upon his period in comics unfavorably. Overstreet: "He was really bitter about his experience at Western Printing." Phelps: "He told us that his feeling with Western went sour [when] he found out that they had kept fan mail from him, that they were dishonest with him. And there were other reasons, which he didn't care to reveal. He just turned his back on the whole thing. He always seemed to have a deep-rooted disdain for the comic book business." Stanley also said he didn't want to get involved with fandom. Overstreet: "He didn't want to draw Little Lulu any more. He didn't want to be bothered by anybody."

Despite this, when Don Phelps showed him a couple of scripts for *Little Lulu* (obtained from someone who found them in a Western warehouse), Stanley brightened. According to Phelps, "He said, 'Oh, this brings back memories!' and showed it to Lynda, commenting, 'I used to do the cursive lettering,' because he didn't print in his word balloons in the roughs. He used cursive. Then he dug into a closet, and said, 'I have something here that might interest you.' He pulled out the roughs for the first Oona Goosepimple story for *Nancy*." Stanley told Phelps he could keep it. (Actually, it was the script for an unpublished story. Phelps printed its first page in the Newcon 1976 convention booklet.) Overstreet: "He

Opposite: *Nancy* storyboard page that Stanley found in his closet and gave to Don Phelps for the Newcon 1976 program book. **Clockwise from top left:** Barks, Phelps and Stanley; Stanley; with Tom Murray and Phil Seuling, "friends of Newcon."; Harvey Kurtzman and Gil Kane, apparently at the Newcon cocktail party the night before the convention.

Phelps's meeting with Carl and Garé Barks left him feeling confident that they would definitely be making the trip to Boston for Newcon 1976. He wasn't sure that Stanley would actually show up until two or three weeks before the event. Phelps: "He was just not a 'put-me-in-the-spotlight' type of person. My Stanley bio in that Newcon program book was literally written the day before the printer's deadline." That profile by Don Phelps became comics historians' primary source of information about John Stanley in the ensuing years. The photograph that Stanley provided to accompany it—a publicity shot showing Mel Crawford, Dan Noonan, John Stanley and Dan Gormley, standing behind Oskar Lebeck—has been reproduced in many places.

Something else that Stanley gave Phelps for the Newcon booklet was a cartoon Walt Kelly did in the 1940s that poked sly fun at him. They had last seen each other during Stanley's visit with Morris Gollub in 1973. While staying with his old friend, Stanley got together with Kelly, who was in ill health and would pass away on October 18 of that year. According to Gollub, Stanley went to Chuck Jones's animation studio where Kelly was working, and they had (in Gollub's words) "a reconciliation before Kelly

died."[20] Still, despite his great admiration for Kelly's work as a cartoonist, Stanley's dislike of Kelly as a person remained, based on things he witnessed back in the Western days.

NEWCON 1976 WAS HELD at the Hotel 57 Park Plaza in downtown Boston. The guests began arriving on Friday October 23, among them Carl and Garé Barks, Harvey Kurtzman, Gil Kane, Joe Kubert, Dick Giordano and Jim Steranko. A harried Don Phelps had an assistant meet John Stanley and his son at the airport and chauffeur him to the hotel. When Stanley, nattily dressed in a black turtleneck and gray sport coat, entered the lobby of the hotel, Phelps was there to greet him, recalling, "I was happy to see him when he came in. We sat together for a while and chatted. He said that he'd always loved Boston, and that he was happy to be there."

That evening, the convention had a "friends of Newcon" cocktail party, an informal affair with an open bar. All the professionals were invited, as well as other people connected with the industry such as Phil Seuling and photographer E. B. Boatner. Phelps arrived with his mother, an attractive older woman who instantly

More photographs from the pre-convention party: Barks and Stanley together. According to Phelps, "Stanley and Barks were both kind of awkward with each other, which was to be expected."

spied the still-handsome Stanley across the room, and asked Don, "Who's that interesting-looking man over there?" When Phelps introduced her to Stanley, John was charmed by her, and vice versa. "He had these crystal clear blue eyes, stop-in-your-tracks type of eyes," Phelps said. But, when it came to interacting with the other professionals there, Phelps recalled, "[Stanley] was uncomfortable. Stanley and Barks were both kind of awkward with each other, which was to be expected." Camera flashes went off frequently as people posed for photographs here and there. Photos of Stanley at the cocktail party show him with a drink in one hand, and an ever-present cigarette in the other. Carl and Garé Barks received a lot of attention. Boatner made sure to take several photographs of Barks and Stanley together. One of the most frequently reproduced shows them flanking Phelps.

Don Phelps introduced John Stanley to Tom Murray, who was to interview him on his solo panel the next day. Rather than coming from the ranks of comics fandom, Murray came from academia, and held a master's degree in English from Harvard University. He had been an educator, editor and writer, and was then the owner of a children's bookstore in Cambridge, Massachusetts.[21] Phelps: "[Tom] was a huge John Stanley fan. He was particularly fond of the 'little girl' stories Lulu told Alvin. For much of the cocktail party, they were off to the side, talking. Tom had this smile on his face like he was in Heaven. He was in a daze just to be in Stanley's presence, and listening to him."

Tom Murray's academic credentials and his interest in the Lulu stories as children's literature intrigued and impressed

Stanley. Murray recently recalled, "I remember telling him that I knew at least a dozen college professors, including my wife, who had learned to read by reading the *Little Lulu* and *Tubby* comics. I said that they helped shape our orientations toward serious literature, since the best fiction of every type establishes character and makes us ask the question, 'What next?' I was anxious about interviewing Stanley. I had interviewed well-known people before, mainly actors and musicians, but I had always had the benefit of lots of background information before I met them. With Stanley I had only the work, and I hadn't read anywhere near his total output, even on just Lulu and Tubby. Luckily, he was a straightforward and welcoming subject, much like many of the working-class relatives and neighbors I had known as a kid growing up in New York, although obviously much better read."[22] They arranged to meet in the hotel bar before Stanley's panel the next day, to prepare for the event.

TO UNDERSTAND THE SIGNIFICANCE of the John Stanley solo panel at Newcon 1976, on Saturday, October 24, one must keep in mind that it was the closest to an in-depth interview that he ever gave.[23] While all the questions that one would wish to ask could never fit into the fifty minutes allotted, and he was unaccustomed to talking about his time in comics, or speaking before a group, his responses reveal a great deal about his work and his approach to it. Hence, John Stanley fans are fortunate that the comic book legend was interviewed by someone he had come to respect (in the short time they had known each other), and who was able to formulate questions and steer the discussion into areas most likely to elicit a substantive answer. (Many of Stanley's answers and comments at this panel have appeared earlier in this book, on such subjects as meeting Marge Buell, the naming of Lulu and Tubby, and the origin of the Alvin story-time tales.)[24]

Convention co-chairman Martin L. Greim called the room to order, and introduced Tom Murray as "a college administrator, and his specialty is children's literature," who would be the interviewer. Then Greim introduced the other person on the dais: John Stanley. When the applause died down, Murray began, "This is John's first convention, and probably …"

"—his last," Stanley interjected, sotto voice.

"—marks for many of us the surfacing of someone who is very important to us, especially when we first came across his work as children." Murray launched into a somewhat lengthy peroration about what it took to write good literature for children, including a special

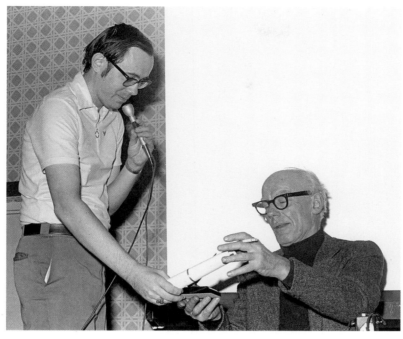

The John Stanley panel was the only time when he was interviewed at length about his career. Convention co-chairman Martin L. Greim gave Stanley a Newcon award at the panel's conclusion, to tumultuous applause. **Bottom right:** Tom Murray, panel moderator, managed to get Stanley to open up a little.

because "when you think of *Treasure Island*, when you think of some of the kind of pulp children's literature that was put out years ago, it had to do frequently with far-off lands and with adventures that were not common, and transported people away from their everyday existence, whereas what you're best known for was within a frame. Your imagination was limited to the world as it was. You didn't do a lot of the Tubby and Lulu stories later on where they'd travel."

Stanley agreed. "It was a tight frame, but I'd like to be absolutely honest. It was easier for me to do that. I'd have to do research if I wanted to send a character out of the neighborhood. I figure you're the same person in your own hometown, in your own backyard, that you are in Alaska, or you name it. You don't change. You carry yourself with you wherever you travel. People's relations with each other, that's all that matters."

Murray asked, "Do you

empathy for them. "Many of us . . . learned how to read on stories like those by John Stanley and Carl Barks. I'd just like to start by asking John . . . about your own sorts of memories, and the things you think contributed to your own thoughts as an artist and as a writer."

Stanley: "A blank." (*Audience titters.*) "At this point, as far as my memories are concerned, it was an average childhood. I don't remember that I was particularly aware as a child in any way. And I sort of grew—who said that?—like Topsy. And that's the way it worked. And as far as insights, I had none. I don't, to this day. I did those stories, and it's a mystery to me how it came about. If someone likes them today . . . [it's like] another guy did them. I didn't do these." There was scattered laughter at the unexpected, blunt self-deprecation of his remarks.

Moderator Murray asked him to name a favorite book when he was growing up. Stanley named *Treasure Island*. "To this day, not a year goes by that I don't read *Treasure Island* again. [Stevenson was] a great master of writing." Murray thought this was interesting,

have any thoughts on the difference between the adult's imagination and the child's imagination?"

Stanley: "The adult imagination is sort of operative. It works. Whereas, a lot of people think that children have more imagination than adults, which is not the truth. You have to be . . . an adult to be able to put things together, to organize material, and to be aware of your readership, how they're going to react to your story. You have to bring them along through the story, from one page to another, which Robert Louis Stevenson [did] to an ultimate degree. I've actually argued this point with a number of people, and they sort of look at me blankly, you know, a curtain comes down. They say 'Children are wonderfully imaginative!' It's not true! I mean, they just go along with things, and they're looking for ideas, and they —well, you never heard of a child writing a first-rate children's book. They can't do it."

When asked where he got his ideas for Little Lulu, Stanley replied, "From within. It always comes from within. Jimmy, my son, never gave me an idea for a story. Not even a good line.

Never! (*Audience laughter.*) It had to come from within myself. I'll give you a line, and you can finish it, I'm sure. When someone asked [Gustave] Flaubert how he knew so much about Madame Bovary, what did he say? He said, 'I *am* Madame Bovary.' Same thing. Little Lulu was *me*. And so was Tubby, and so was everyone else. Little Annie. Everything comes from inside yourself. *Nothing* comes from outside. Really. Nothing imaginative. You don't learn anything [by] observing people. You have to know yourself." He used Charles Dickens as an example. "I don't think [Dickens] spent any great deal of time observing people. At the age of twenty-four he could write about middle-aged men. He could do it with such acuteness. Where did he get it from? He couldn't have gotten it just going around looking in people's faces."

Murray brought up the subject of Tubby's status-seeking and desire for acceptance. Stanley responded, "He was a boy, and a man. Men are that way. You want acceptance, you want to be liked by your family, and you want to —Well, I don't know whether… I wasn't even thinking of these things. I wanted to write an interesting story that would carry a reader from panel to panel to the end."

Murray: "In *Little Lulu*, the dealings with adults are on such a wonderful adversarial level."

Stanley: "Yes, because we all have, I think, to the day we die, and we can live to be 103, we still are annoyed by adults, who presume to know more than we know. (*Audience laughs. A few applaud.*) "We're all children, really. Adults are a pain in the ass, they really are. It's easy to make fun of adults. But they're all we have, you know?"[25] (*Laughter.*) He added some comments about Charles Schulz's *Peanuts*. "No adult has ever been seen in his comic strip. He's smart, because he cut it down to the very essence. It's his ideas that count, whatever they are. They're hard to analyze, but he's great."

When Murray mentioned the stories of truant officer McNabbem chasing Lulu and Tubby, Stanley responded, "This idea of a chase—it recurs. I used it in Nancy and Sluggo in a summer thing." He was referring to the *Nancy and Sluggo Summer Camp* giant from 1960. "Sluggo's next door neighbor [McOnion], a big, heavy guy . . . Sluggo was the bane in his life. He hated him, and they hated each other. It was mutual. And I had more enjoyment doing this, simply because he followed Sluggo all the way up to summer camp, one summer. And he never chased him, actually— he never ran—he just walked slowly after him. And eventually caught up, or came within two or three miles of him, or within sight of him, and then Sluggo would get hysterical and take off, but [McOnion] would calmly walk behind him, and finally, when he cornered him . . . I had more fun, and I did it over and over again, but nobody remembers this! I hate people! (*Laughter.*) The best things I've done, they don't remember. They remember a lot of nonsense in Lulu." (*Laughter.*)

Other topics discussed (briefly) were his work for Dell after the split with Western, such as *Tales from the Tomb* ("it sold like nothing I've ever done"), *Dunc and Loo* ("it came to nothing") and *Thirteen* ("I really bled on those things"). The overall impression

Full spread: Bruce Hamilton, who eventually published the *Little Lulu Library* reprint series, moderated the Stanley-Barks panel at Newcon 1976. Below: Stanley's portion of the Newcon mural that all guest artists were encouraged to decorate. It was about 3' wide and at least 12' long. Photo by Tom Hegeman.

was of a man with a disarming, dry sense of humor who was painfully modest about his work, and about what he had been trying to achieve, which he summed up as the panel was drawing to a close. "I did what I did, and I didn't have it in mind that they should be great or anything else, but just to make somebody read along. And to be interesting."

Murray pointed out, "[In comics] you didn't have the forum to develop any sort of exquisite style." In response, Stanley spoke about the potential of the comic book medium.

"You know, it's possible a comic book writer who's a genius could come along and be a great writer like Shakespeare. [If] somehow he could get through, past editors and whatnot. Theoretically, anyway. It's like somebody painting with a stick dipped in mud, you know? A great artist can do something there that could be recognized as a great piece of work. So far, I don't think there's anything [great] in comics—but yet, it's possible!"[26]

At the end of the panel, Martin Greim stepped up to the podium and gave John Stanley a Newcon award, which prompted a

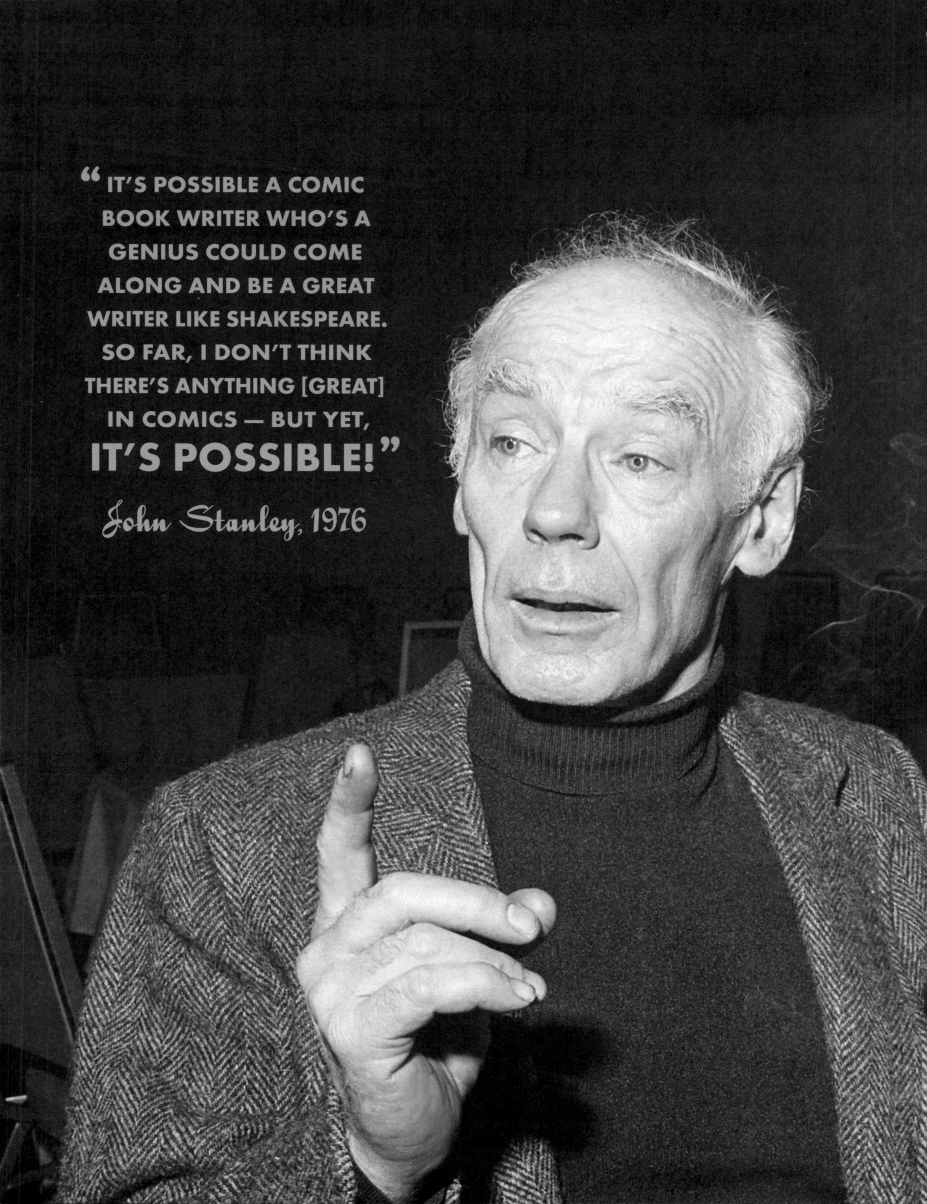

"IT'S POSSIBLE A COMIC BOOK WRITER WHO'S A GENIUS COULD COME ALONG AND BE A GREAT WRITER LIKE SHAKESPEARE. SO FAR, I DON'T THINK THERE'S ANYTHING [GREAT] IN COMICS — BUT YET, IT'S POSSIBLE!"

John Stanley, 1976

Bruce Hamilton and John Stanley.

sustained round of applause. Jim Stanley was in the audience that day. Up to this moment, he hadn't taken the event seriously. The night before, he and a buddy were throwing water balloons off the roof of the hotel. "At that panel, I realized—for the first time—that my dad was 'famous,'" he said later. "He was bemused by the attention fans gave him, but I could see that he'd really achieved something."[27]

He was then shown to a table where he could sign autographs. He drew numerous Little Lulu and Tubby sketches, while chatting with con-goers. Later, he said that he "hadn't put a pencil on a piece of paper for maybe seven or eight years," but that he'd drawn those characters so many times that "I could do it in my sleep."[28] To the comic con mural, which extended the whole length of one wall, he added a sketch of Lulu kicking the side of the boys' clubhouse, with Tubby and Iggy cowering in its doorway. He also sketched Witch Hazel standing nearby.[29]

ON SUNDAY, FANS GATHERED for a panel with both Carl Barks and John Stanley on the dais. Everyone was buzzing about the auction of Barks paintings earlier that day. One of Barks' paintings went for a record-setting price of $6,000. Much of the attention on this panel, moderated by Bruce Hamilton, was on Barks. The

following quotations are from a transcription of the tape by Milo George that appeared in *The Comics Journal*, unless noted.[30]

When Barks was asked about his working methods, he explained, "The way I would start a story was to figure out what I wanted to draw. If I felt I wanted to draw horses, I'd put Donald in a Western type of story, and so on. Then I'd think up a bunch of jokes that would fit the particular locale where I would have the action taking place. When I had a bunch of action gags dreamed up, I'd start locking them together in a synopsis. [Then] I'd start breaking it down into pages and stick in the dialogue. Then I'd start to draw."

Hamilton: "In reading the duck stories, I noticed that you have a punch line at the end of almost every page. Did you plan it that way?"

Barks: "I tried to plan it that way. That's the way we learned to do it at the Disney studios, working on the [animated] shorts. There had to be a little climax just about every few seconds on the screen. That's the way I tried to write the duck stories. At the end of every page, I tried to get something going."

Hamilton turned to Stanley. "John, I'd be interested in knowing the similarities in developing your Little Lulu stories. At the beginning, at least, you were locked into a situation with a little

girl who couldn't get around as much as Carl's ducks could, so how did you approach these problems and what were your similarities and differences?"

Stanley responded: "Surprisingly enough, Carl's method of working is much like mine. I did twelve *Little Lulus* a year, four *Tubbys* and an annual, in addition to other magazines. I wrote scripts for other cartoon characters. I worked much as Carl did, except I made no synopsis. I started from the first panel on the page without having the faintest notion of how it would turn out. And I just hoped for the best, that's all. Generally, it worked out. But [Carl] mentioned something there that really surprises me, because I thought I was unique in this respect." He turned to Carl.

"When you said at the end of every page, you tried to have a little lift there to carry the reader on. I thought that was my thing! (*Laughter.*) It shows that you can kid yourself for twenty or thirty, thirty-five years, and now this is a revelation."[31]

During the panel, he heard how Barks had just broken the $6,000 barrier for a single painting. Stanley quipped, "I'm glad my wife isn't here to hear this." When asked about his post-Lulu work, Stanley mentioned *Tales from the Tomb* ("I . . . had to pay three bucks for it yesterday"), and told how it had been squelched by letters from parent groups. He then made it clear that creating comics was, for him, just a way to make a living. "I did things like *Dunc and Loo*, *Thirteen*, *Ghost Stories* and about fifteen to twenty other characters, and I can't remember a single one of them. That's how important they were to me. *Melvin Monster* is another one —that one had my name on it, I believe. And there were more, but I can't think of them. You just ground them out, and I did the best I could. But I haven't done anything now in about ten years, comics-wise." The panel lasted just thirty-eight minutes, so that Russ Cochran could auction two more Barks paintings afterward.

Carl Barks wasn't doing sketches at the con, although people were always crowded around him for his autograph when they had a chance. He attracted more people than John Stanley, but there was definitely interest in Stanley. According to audience member Harry McCracken, "I remember he seemed a little uncomfortable and surprised by the attention. He did a lot of sketches, including two for me. He asked to borrow my blue ballpoint pen for one of them, a funny drawing of Lulu sticking out her tongue at the group photo of himself and Lebeck in the con program book."[32]

Stanley had fulfilled his obligations as a guest of honor. Don Phelps was particularly delighted with how well Stanley had done, and the way Stanley's appearance at the con had been received. He and Stanley remained friends, and saw each other again in future years. Phelps: "I loved the guy. I was always so impressed with the combination of humility and talent in an individual, perhaps because it is so rare. I've met a lot of talented assholes in my life. The lack of ego displayed by John was so refreshing."

Opposite: John Stanley sketched Lulu for any and all comers at Newcon. He even sketched Lulu razzing the old Western Printing group in a photograph, which appeared in the convention program. Con book sketch courtesy of Harry McCracken. **Above:** John Stanley and unidentified fan.

12

The Long Goodbye

NEWCON 1976 MIGHT HAVE MARKED the beginning of John Stanley taking his place as one of the "gods of comics" on the growing comic book convention circuit. When Phil Seuling asked him to appear at the 1977 New York Comic Art Convention, he agreed, and the announcement went out. Yet, despite a photo spread and article about him in the convention program, Stanley didn't show up.

The existence of fandom had taken him by surprise. While he recognized the sincerity of those who wanted to meet him and know him better, he was a private man who had a difficult time talking about his past in comics because it had ended badly. Don Phelps believes that, in addition to his headaches, depression and alcohol, Stanley also had a problem with anxiety and panic attacks. Phelps later wrote, "I was explaining to him my bouts with occasional panic attacks, and how my symptoms manifested as a racing heart, and so on. He exclaimed that he had experienced the same thing. I got the impression it had been an ongoing problem with him for some time. I still remember the look of surprise on his face when I described my panic attacks. He looked excited and almost relieved at the same time, hearing what he had been experiencing from someone else's lips. That facial reaction is etched in my mind."[1] Stanley never attended another fan gathering except for a small show in Boonton, New Jersey, with Phelps.[2] When the San Diego Comicon gave him its Inkpot Award in 1980, usually done in concert with the recipient's appearance at the convention, Stanley wasn't there to receive it.

At the urging of Phelps, Stanley began doing commissions: "I said, 'John, there are people who would really pay you a high figure for paintings,' and he said, 'No, no, not interested.' I got lots of calls saying 'please try to get him to do a painting for me.' And he finally relented. He did a special one for me, a recreation of the cover of the first Tubby Four Color, 'Captain Yo-Yo.' It had the Tubby logo and the Dell insignia. It was wonderful. He did another

one that was a recreation of one of the Little Lulu Four Colors, one that had all the little figures going around the border. He even put in extra figures. John was wonderfully creative when he wanted to be, but it wasn't often. It was when the mood struck him." Initially, Stanley put a lot of effort into the recreations. Over time (he did between fifteen and twenty, from 1977 to 1992), the quality dropped. "They vary in quality," Phelps said. "Some of them are spot-on, really nice, and others aren't worthy of his talent. He might have been in his cups on those."

He still intended to do the cover for an Overstreet Comic Book Price Guide. In March 1978, three years after agreeing to do it, he wrote:

> Dear Bob,
>
> Sorry for the further delay—your patience with me borders on saintliness. I've sent you a few sketches, one of which I hope you'll be able to do something with—the "girls' lib" thing I like because it's topical. I don't like all the copy on it, the signs, etc. But maybe you can delete or cut some of it. Anyway, if you don't like any of these ideas, let me know and I'll try to dream up a few more.
>
> Sincerely, John Stanley

Overstreet liked the roughs, but he could never get Stanley to finish any of them. When the thirty-fifth edition of the Comic Book Price Guide was published in 1995, it had a Lulu cover, but it was from a painting that had been done on commission, not a piece especially designed for the guide.

While Stanley backed away from further convention appearances, he was usually warm and welcoming to the handful of fans who he considered personal friends, although, when Michael Barrier sent him a copy of A Smithsonian Book of Comic-Book Comics

John Stanley's commissioned paintings vary in quality. **Left:** One of the best is a new version of the cover of *Little Lulu* #23 (May 1950), which was used on the cover of Bob Overstreet's *Comic Book Price Guide* (35th edition, 2005). **Opposite:** Note the detail Stanley put into the borders on his recreations of *Little Lulu* #42 (December 1951) and *Four Color* #31 (December 1946). The images are also more detailed. **Previous spread, left:** One of Stanley's first commissioned paintings after Newcon 1976.

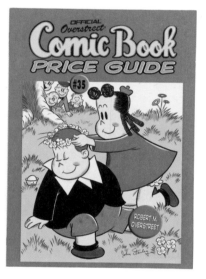

Above: Two John Stanley sketches for possible commissioned paintings, courtesy of Jim Stanley.

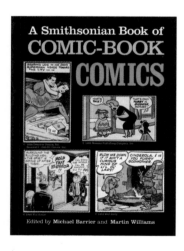

(1981), which reprinted four of his best Little Lulu stories, he didn't thank him for the copy. The book, edited by Barrier and Martin Williams, was a follow-up to *A Smithsonian Book of Newspaper Comics* (1977). Only writer-artist Harvey Kurtzman is represented by as many stories as John Stanley. They are "At the Beach" (*Four Color* #74), "Five Little Babies" (*Little Lulu* #38), "The Little Rich Boy" (*Little Lulu* #40) and "The 'Spider' Spins Again" (*Little Lulu* #81). The book gave his work on Lulu the imprimatur of critical approval and historical importance.

After Newcon and the Barrier-Williams book, Stanley's authorship of the Little Lulu stories became widely known in fan circles. A group of Stanley and Lulu enthusiasts came together in the pages of a new publication called the *Stanley Steamer*. Editor Jonathan ("Jon") A. Merrill of Allentown, Pennsylvania, was a lifelong Little Lulu fan who had a complete collection of the Lulu and Tubby comic books. He worked as a clerical administrator at

AT&T in Morristown, New Jersey. The first issue of the bimonthly fanzine was dated April 1982. the *Stanley Steamer* consisted of shared memoirs of Lulu fans, items of historical research, articles on related collectibles, Lulu trivia and more. One of its major contributors was a teenager named Brad Tenan, who had been a Lulu fan since he was six. It was Tenan who established that much of Lulu's town of Meadowville was based on actual locations in Peekskill, New York, which isn't surprising when one considers that Stanley and his family lived near Peekskill for many years. Other contributors were Michele Maki, Norman Hale, Candace F. Ransom and Jeff Gelb. Stanley himself had little to do with *The Steamer*, although Merrill regularly sent him copies. Then, unexpectedly, the cartoonist sent the page "Snowballs from Heaven," a rough, new Lulu one-pager, which appeared in issue #59.

IN 1983, WESTERN'S *LITTLE LULU* comic book ended its thirty-six year run, a victim of the shrinking newsstand distribution of comic books. New issues dribbled out until, with #268 (published in 1983, with a sixty-cent cover price), it ended. It's fitting, in a way, that the last issue was entirely made up of reprinted stories by John Stanley and Irving Tripp. (Two more issues with new stories drawn by Irving Tripp were completed but not published.)

Just as the comic book died, a new vehicle for Little Lulu was born. In 1983, Bruce Hamilton's Another Rainbow began publishing *The Carl Barks Library*, a series of oversized, hardcover books reprinting Barks's Disney duck stories, mostly in black and white. John Clark, who edited the series, recalled, "I'm probably the one who convinced Bruce that we [Another Rainbow] should do *The Little Lulu Library*. We had come out with the first two or three volumes of the *Carl Barks Library*, and it was doing quite well. Bruce was casting about for some other good project, so I suggested *Little Lulu* to him. He had had some minor contact with *Lulu* in his past, and had bought a couple of John Stanley paintings through Don Phelps, and liked those, but hadn't read many of the Lulu comic books. He said 'let me read a few,' so I took some of my collection over to him, issues that I thought had the best stories. We talked back and forth, and decided to do the *Library*."[3]

Hamilton was already dealing with Western Publishing to procure Photostats of Carl Barks's artwork for *The Carl Barks Library*. He was working with Wally Green, who was in charge of production at Western. It was a simple matter to get the rights from Western to do *The Little Lulu Library*. Jon Merrill suggested to Hamilton that he begin publishing the sets in reverse order, "to encourage customers to keep buying the sets on the way to the much-desired Set 1 with the *Four Color* issues."[4] This also made sense because the early issues had to be traced and re-inked, and that took time. The publisher had a fairly complete set of Photostats except for the first couple of years, which was spotty-to-non-existent. The primary artist on this reconstruction work

was Russ Miller, a local artist in Prescott, Arizona. Also, John Clark did some, as did Gary Leach and Susan Daigle-Leach, who were production artists at Another Rainbow.

Five hundred copies of Volume 6, the first set to be published, had a special bookplate signed by John Stanley and Marjorie Buell. They were each paid $20 per plate, which meant that Stanley received $10,000 for his part. After the plates were signed, relations between Hamilton and Stanley deteriorated. John Clark recalled, "I think Bruce went to Stanley's house to meet with him, because the idea was to get Stanley to draw new covers for the slipcases. Stanley apparently had no interest in it. And I guess Bruce's and Stanley's personalities didn't jibe very well. I don't believe Bruce ever contacted him again after that. Shortly thereafter, we found Irving Tripp who was then retired in Florida, and Tripp ended up doing most of the slipcase covers for us."

Then, after he received the first set of books, Stanley was incensed when Tripp claimed, in his interview ("A Tripp Down Memory Lane"), that he had done the cover of *Little Lulu #1*. On September 12, 1985, Stanley wrote to Hamilton to make it clear that he had done all the *Little Lulu* covers without exception. He ended with, "Perhaps Tripp thinks that all this happened so long ago that most of those concerned are dead or dispersed. *I'm* neither dead nor dispersed. Sincerely, John Stanley."

The coup of *The Little Lulu Library* was its presentation, for the first time, of "The Bogyman," the Little Lulu story rejected by Marge Buell due to its negative portrayal of Lulu. "We didn't think it existed," Clark explained, "and then we acquired

This is number ___24___ of 500 personally signed bookplates for Set VI of The Little Lulu Library.

John Stanley

Marjorie Henderson Buell

These drawings were penciled and inked in 1985 by John Stanley and Marjorie Henderson Buell exclusively for this set of The Little Lulu Library. The signatures on each bookplate are original.

John Stanley and Marjorie Henderson Buell both signed the numbered bookplate included in the 500 sets of the *Little Lulu Library* Volume 6. (The Lulu drawings were done especially for the plate, as well.)

Left: "The Fabulous Treasure of King Tutankhaman." John Stanley's last work for professional publication was this piece for *The Art of Mickey Mouse* (1991) from Hyperion Press, in his best *New Yorker* style, in ink and watercolor (26.7" by 26.7"). Archeologists opening King Tut's tomb find the mummy wearing a Mickey Mouse wristwatch. The job came to Stanley via Craig Yoe, who, along with Janet Morra-Yoe, packaged the book for the Disney-owned publisher. **Right:** Stanley's first concept sketch, sold at auction in 2010. Courtesy of Jim Stanley.

all these Photostats from Western Publishing's archives. Instead of Photostats of the reprint that took its place, they included the Photostats of the Bogyman story! So we thought 'this is a windfall,' really! We've got something that nobody else has seen, ever. Bruce was in fairly close communication with Marge at the time. He got in touch with her, and she still had poor memories of that story, and she still didn't want it published. While she didn't have any say, legally—Western had the say, and they didn't care—Bruce wanted to stay on good terms with Marge. It went back and forth until she reluctantly agreed to give her blessing to the story appearing in *The Little Lulu Library*. But she still didn't like it." For Volume 5, with the story, Bruce wrote a short introduction to the story explaining that Marge didn't approve of it.

In that same volume, Maggie Thompson contributed a piece titled "The Fantastic Mr. Stanley," which talked about the fantasy elements in the Lulu and Tubby stories. Thompson wrote, "When asked what fantasy elements most appealed to him in his own reading, John Stanley told me, 'I really can't say. I don't know what struck me.' However, he added he felt that there were elements of unreality in almost all humorous writers. 'Take comic writers like [Robert] Benchley and [James] Thurber. I enjoy that sort of thing.' He cited Evelyn Waugh as another favorite, and 'today, I enjoy Philip Roth. It's all fantasy. It's very funny, and I love it.' He laughed. 'I love comics, even to this day. I'm ashamed of

myself for buying the *New York Post*. It's strictly junk, but I buy it for the comic strips.'"[5] In 1984, the comics in the *New York Post* were *Agatha Crumm, Mary Worth, Andy Capp, Wizard of Id, Garfield, Dennis the Menace, Momma* and *B.C.*

The Little Lulu Library started out with 8,000 copies of Volume 6, which sold out over a few years. By the time they got to the earliest stories, published in 1992, the print run had been reduced to about 3,000 copies. Some felt that the books should be in color, because the artwork was so simple. At that time, full color wasn't affordable. Clark recalled, "I got wonderful feedback from people at conventions. The kind of publication it was, you didn't get casual buyers. The people who bought it loved Little Lulu, so they would naturally think it was wonderful. A lot of people were grateful that Lulu was back in print in at least *some* form." The redrawn artwork may have hurt sales of the last two volumes. It could never match the artistry of the originals. Clark acknowledged, "Obviously, all of the pages that were recreated—including the ones I did—are inferior to the original Irving Tripp pages. But they are superior to just taking a comic book page and scanning it." Those traced pages function more as a blueprint of those original issues than a reproduction. Nevertheless, taken as a whole, *The Little Lulu Library* served to put John Stanley's work into the hands of thousands of people, many years after he retired from the field.

Above: John Stanley contributed this continuity to Jon Merrill's the *Stanley Steamer*, which ran in the fanzine's penultimate issue (#59, December 1991). "Snowballs from Heaven" shows signs that Stanley's faith in a higher power had been renewed. **Left:** Jim Stanley found this *Little Lulu* piece among his father's papers. It was most likely done in his later years.

Left: John Stanley's Candy McGargoyle page from the Valentine's Day issue of the HoLLywood Eclectern in 1993. Right: Courtesy of Eclectern reader and resident artist Larry Blake, who inked and colored it for a subsequent issue.

JOHN STANLEY WAS SEVENTY years old when *The Little Lulu Library* began. When the last slipcase was printed in 1992, he was seventy-eight, and entering the last year of his life. A decade had passed since he last walked out the door at Fairgate Rule, and over two decades had elapsed since he did his final work in comic books. His last finished work for professional publication was a piece for *The Art of Mickey Mouse* (1991) from Hyperion Press, done in his best *New Yorker* style, which harkened back to his early years working for Kay Kamen. Titled "The Fabulous Treasure of King Tutankhamun," the cartoon shows archeologists opening King Tut's tomb, only to find the mummy wearing a Mickey Mouse wristwatch. The job came to Stanley from Craig Yoe, who, along with Janet Morra-Yoe, packaged the book for the Disney-owned publisher.

Also in 1992, John Stanley received a new fan magazine dedicated to Little Lulu and his other comic book work. Jon Merrill's the *Stanley Steamer* ended with #60 (February 1992). Such was the ongoing interest in Stanley and Little Lulu that longtime fan Ed Buchman immediately launched a successor. He was a retired professor of mathematics whose enduring love of the moppet from Meadowville began when he discovered *Little Lulu* with issue #2 (March–April 1948), when he was almost six. "I contributed to

the *Stanley Steamer*, and when it ceased publication, the inspiration struck me to inaugurate the *HoLLywood Eclectern*. The name was arrived at thusly: 'LL' for Little Lulu, 'Hollywood' as a nod to imagination, 'eclectic' for variety of subject matters, and 'lectern' as a sort of in-joke about my professional life in teaching."[6] Merrill's mailing list for *The Steamer* became the initial mailing list of *The Eclectern*. About 200 readers received the new fanzine several times a year for the next eighteen years. A number of Stanley's sketches for fans would appear in the fanzine. Its readers received a "thank you" from Stanley himself in the Valentine's Day issue in 1993, a new single-page continuity written and drawn especially for them, featuring Miss McGargoyle, much as she looked in the pages of *Melvin Monster*. It was the last of the three one-page continuities created by Stanley for publication in his later years.[7] At seventy-eight, he still "had it." Ed Buchman: "Shortly after [the Miss McGargoyle page was published], Stanley wrote to me again, saying he'd like to send copies of that issue of *The Eclectern* to his son and to his daughter, and so of course I sent him extras for that."[8] He also told Buchman that he intended to do more for the fanzine.

Other fans also stayed in contact with Stanley. In 1993, Brad Tenan phoned him to offer best wishes on his birthday (March 22), and later wrote, "[John] hadn't been out of the house at all since the 'Blizzard of '93' (March 13–14 of that winter). He went on to mention his older sister's then-recent move to a nursing home which was within walking distance of his house. He indicated that although he visited her almost every day, he was enjoying a greater sense of personal freedom to do whatever he wished, whenever he wished."[9] Marian Stanley lived at Sky View Rehab and Health Care center until her passing in October 1997.

Lynda Stanley, who lost her mother to cancer in 1990, became a professional photo retoucher working in Manhattan. Jim Stanley recalled visiting his father from time to time. "We had a lot of good times hanging out in his house in Croton, which is now the house I live in. I would bring over a VCR and we would watch a few movies, have a couple of glasses of wine together, and shoot the breeze about this or that. He loved a good Clint Eastwood movie or a good comedy. One of the last movies I remember bringing over was *Midnight Run*, which he loved until he inevitably fell asleep about seventy-five percent of the way in. He enjoyed listening to George Carlin records with me, because of the bits about the nuns and Catholic school."[10] But, late in his life, his views on spiritual matters changed.

Living alone, perhaps contemplating his mortality, Stanley told Brad Tenan (who was a devout Christian, and asked Stanley about his religious views), "I have rediscovered the Gospel. I became a skeptic [at eighteen]. Who would have ever believed that now I could go on and on—for *hours*—talking about the Book's wonderful message?"[11] It wasn't a return to the orthodoxy of Catholicism. Tenan wrote, "He mentioned that he had been reading many different commentaries about the Gospel, but only those whose authors are not priests or ministers themselves, or who otherwise have any affiliation with religion." He quoted Stanley as saying, "I find their witnesses much more believable."[12] One of the most marked-up books in his collection was *Jesus* by Ch. Guignebert, Professor of the History of Christianity in the Sorbonne (translated from French), published by University Books, New York. He bracketed the quotation, "the Kingdom of God is, of its very nature, a spiritual reality, a force which permeates and can only be grasped by the heart."

Jim Stanley recalled, "His last months before succumbing to esophageal cancer were pretty rough. I think he knew that he was in bad shape, but he was in total denial, as most of us would be. I think he was just terrified of dying in a hospital bed."[13] John Stanley passed away on November 11, 1993, after a protracted battle with the illness. He was buried at the Gates of Heaven Cemetery in Westchester, New York, a Roman Catholic burial site.[14]

STANLEY HAD FALLEN OUT of touch with his friends and fans as he became more ill, leaving them wondering what was going on. He didn't follow up on his promise to contribute more to the *HoLLywood Eclectern*. It wasn't until July 1996 that Brad Tenan was finally able to get in touch with Jim Stanley, and heard about

John Stanley's grandson Adam at the Gates of Heaven Cemetery in 2016. Photo: Jim Stanley.

Left: Jim Stanley, accepting the Bill Finger Award on behalf of his father. Originally an environmental geologist, Jim now works for his own design firm, where he creates 3-D simulations and motion graphics. He married in 1997 and has two children, Isabel and Adam. Photo: Tony Amat © 2016 SDCC, courtesy Comic-Con International: San Diego. **Right:** Jim Stanley with his daughter, Isabel. Photo: Jeff Gelb. **Opposite:** Last page of the *Nancy and Sluggo Summer Camp* (*Dell Giant* #34), 1960.

the passing of his friend and idol. Then, Tenan sent a piece to Ed Buchman titled "John Stanley, A Humble Life," which appeared in *The Eclectern*. It began, "It is with the deepest regret that I announce the passing of the extraordinary comics genius and innovator of Little Lulu comics, Mr. John Stanley." Tenan went on to say that there were no known printed obituaries at either the local or national level, and the funeral services were private.

Although Stanley's passing received little notice at the time, he has posthumously been accorded recognition and awards from the wider comics community. In *The Comics Journal* #210 (February 1999), his Little Lulu tales were included in their list of the "Top 100 Comics of the 20th Century," nestled among the works of Carl Barks, Daniel Clowes, Roy Crane, Robert Crumb and others. (In his personal pantheon, Crumb put Stanley's *Little Lulu* second after E. C. Segar's *Popeye*, and ahead of Harvey Kurtzman's *Mad* and *Humbug*.) Four years later, Stanley was inducted into the Will Eisner Comic Book Hall of Fame, the industry's highest honor.

Stanley's stories were adapted (uncredited) for *The Little Lulu Show* on HBO, broadcast from 1995 to 1999. The undiluted stories of Lulu by Stanley were reprinted in a series of thirty trade paperback books by Dark Horse Comics, from 2005 to 2011, published in the order of original publication. Each book credits Stanley, an important development. Libraries stocked their shelves with these books, and many more were purchased by parents for their children, bringing the adventures of Lulu, Tubby, Gloria, Wilbur and the Boys' club to a new generation of young readers. In addition,

his creations *Thirteen* and *Melvin Monster*, along with many of his Nancy stories, were reprinted from 2009 to 2013 in a series of nine hardcover books by Canadian publisher Drawn & Quarterly. The excellence of his best work ensures that it will endure.

In 2015, Stanley was given the Bill Finger Award for Excellence in Comic Book Writing, an accolade established (as Mark Evanier, chairman of the awards committee, stated), "to recognize writers for a body of work that has not received its rightful reward and/or recognition." Jim Stanley traveled to San Diego in July as a guest of Comic-Con International to accept the award at the annual Will Eisner Awards ceremony. Of his father, he said, "Of course, I regret that he didn't seek help for his personal problems that drove him to abandon his gift, but my overall feeling is that I'm proud to be John Stanley's son and proud of his work and the impact it had on other people. I'm very grateful that people continue to enjoy his work and keep his memory alive."[15]

No one would be more surprised by the accolades and reprintings than Stanley himself. Recognition, beyond what was accorded him by his colleagues, and any form of literary immortality, were the farthest things from his mind when he was creating his Little Lulu stories. As he put it at Newcon, "I did what I did, and I didn't have it in mind that they should be great or anything else, but just to make somebody read along, and to be interesting." For him, creating comics was about nothing more complicated than starting a story with a premise, and then plunging forward, with no idea how the story would end.

Mothers can relax, too...when children read Dell Comics!

When your child buys a Dell comic book, you can be sure it's full of good fun, clean enjoyment . . . and happy adventures.

That's because Dell Comics feature famous characters known to everyone through movies, radio and television, and newspapers. They range from Donald Duck to Little Lulu, from Bugs Bunny to Tarzan — Gene Autry, Roy Rogers and the Lone Ranger.

So it's natural that Dell Comics are favorites by far with children and parents and teachers alike. Over 26,000,000 a month are bought by the most discriminating shoppers in America — your children. And when you see this Dell seal on the cover of a comic magazine, you can rest assured that your child is reading the best there is in comics.

© 1952 • DELL PUBLISHING CO., INC.

GENE AUTRY   MARGE'S LITTLE LULU   LONE RANGER   LOONEY TUNES—MERRIE MELODIES   NEW FUNNIES   RED RYDER   ROY ROGERS   TARZAN   TOM & JERRY   WALT DISNEY COMICS   BUGS BUNNY   CISCO KID   WALT DISNEY'S DONALD DUCK   CARL ANDERSON'S HENRY
HENRY ALDRICH   HOWDY DOODY   LITTLE IODINE   WALT DISNEY'S MICKEY MOUSE   PORKY PIG   TONTO   WOODY WOODPECKER   ANDY PANDA   BOZO   BUCK JONES   GENE AUTRY'S CHAMPION   INDIAN CHIEF   KING OF THE ROYAL MOUNTED   LASSIE   LITTLE BEAVER
LITTLE SCOUTS   POGO POSSUM   POPEYE   REX ALLEN   SERGEANT PRESTON   HI YO SILVER   TOM CORBETT—SPACE CADET   ROY ROGERS' TRIGGER   WILD BILL ELLIOTT   WESTERN ROUNDUP   WOODY WOODPECKER'S   BACK TO SCHOOL   WALT DISNEY'S SILLY SYMPHONIES
GERALD MCBOING BOING   BEANY   ZANE GREY'S COMICS   DOUBLE TROUBLE WITH GOOBER   FLASH GORDON   WALT DISNEY'S LIL BAD WOLF   MARY JANE & SNIFFLES   RHUBARB   ROOTIE KAZOOTIE   TUBBY   FROSTY THE SNOWMAN   WALT DISNEY'S PETER PAN

Acknowledgments

HAVING THE OPPORTUNITY to tell the story of John Stanley's life and work has been a privilege, but doing the research and pulling all the material together was a tremendous challenge. Many people helped with this book, and they have my profound thanks:

Jim Stanley, John's son, was supportive of this project from the start. He provided scans of his father's sketches, ideas for gag cartoons and concepts for possible syndicated strips, as well as numerous family photographs. He sat for a lengthy interview, and patiently answered emails throughout the writing process. The book couldn't have been anything like complete without his participation. (For the record, Jim didn't ask for any changes to the manuscript.)

Frank M. Young, who has studied the work of John Stanley for more than two decades, made all of his resources available and acted as a consultant almost from the beginning of the book. All comic book fans, myself included, are beholden to Frank for his pioneering effort to build a reliable list of Stanley's credits. He doesn't claim his research is perfect, but others who have reviewed it find it persuasive, as does this writer. I recommend his trio of bibliographical books (*John Stanley in the 1940s*, *John Stanley in the 1950s* and *John Stanley in the 1960s*), as well as his book of seven essays, *The Tao of Yow: John Stanley's World*. Frank helped in ways too numerous to mention. In a couple of years of working together, we found that we enjoyed each other's company a great deal and have become friends.

I've dubbed Alan Hutchinson "the Dell man," due to his extensive collection of Dell comics as well as his expertise about the contents and creators of that erstwhile publisher's comic books. All but a few of the scans from Dell comics came from the Hutchinson collection. Obviously, a book with as much artwork as this one was heavily dependent on his contributions.

Barbara Stanley Steggles, John Stanley's niece, provided vital information about John Stanley's family of origin. She patiently answered my many questions in an interview and a number of follow-up emails, and contributed a charming pencil sketch by her uncle.

Michael Barrier helped in many ways. He made his unpublished interview with John Stanley's colleague Morris Gollub available to the author, as well as sending scans from *Mickey Mouse Magazine*, copies of Marjorie Buell's initial contracts with Western Printing (held in the Marge collection at the Schlesinger Library in Cambridge, Massachusetts), photographs and more.

John Stanley's involvement with his fans, after he left comics, proved easier to document than other aspects of his life. For helping to tell this part of his story, I am grateful to E. B. Boatner (for the superb photographs from Newcon 1976, including the one on the front cover, many which have never seen print until now), Leonard (John) Clark, editor of the *Little Lulu Library* from Another Rainbow (for his memories of putting that series together),

Glenn Bray (for artwork, and his early correspondence with John Stanley), Denis Kitchen (for copies of his correspondence to and from John and Barbara Stanley), Thomas Murray, Ph.D. (for his memories of meeting and interviewing John Stanley at Newcon), Bob Overstreet (for his photographs and memories of visiting John Stanley) and Maggie Thompson (who talked with John Stanley in 1974, and wrote several important articles about his work). Special thanks for their help to Jon Merrill of the Stan*ley Steamer* and Ed Buchman of the *HoLLywood Eclectern*. Others who contributed in this area are Aaron Caplan, Bob Cosgrove, Ted Hake, Tom Hegeman and Bradley Tenan, for which they have my thanks.

I want to single out Don Phelps for his part in adding to a multifaceted view of the complex Mr. Stanley. Don was probably the fan who established the deepest rapport with the cartoonist, which was the only reason why Stanley attended Newcon 1976, his single comic-con experience. Had Stanley not appeared on the two panels at that convention, his voice would have been heard much less in this book. I credit my discussions with Don with giving me a better understanding of my subject.

For assistance in other aspects in the book, I want to thank Jim Amash, Joan Appleton, Ben Asen, Jerry Beck, John Benson, Larry Blake, Gary Brown, Lawrence Buell, Sean Clancy, Jamie Colville, Letty Lebeck Edes, Jeff Gelb, Milo George, Michael T. Gilbert, Doris Hagen, William B. Jones Jr., Yvette Kaplan, Tim Lahey, Paul Leiffer, John Lustig, D. Michele Maki, Ph.D, Russ Maheras, Harry McCracken, Lisa McShane, Robert L. Meyer (Helen Meyer's son), Martin O'Hearn, Richard Pini, Gary Sassaman, Bill Spicer, Mike Stoltz, Jenny Swadosh, Tony Tallarico, Roy Thomas, Pete Von Sholly, Hames Ware, John Wells, Kim Weston and Craig Yoe.

I am also grateful to Gary Sassaman, Mike Stoltz and the good people of Comic-Con International: San Diego for permission to use their photograph of Jim Stanley at the Eisner Award ceremony in 2015. Also, I want to acknowledge the invaluable assistance of premier Disney and animation historian Jim Korkis. I heartily recommend his books, including his superlative *Vault of Walt* series.

I would also like to thank the following individuals posthumously: D. J. Arneson, Jean Tamburine Bertolli, Majorie Henderson Buell, L. B. Cole, Vince Davis, Gill Fox, Morris Gollub, Dan Gormley, Margaret Bloy Graham, Bruce Hamilton, Woody Kimbrell, Jack Kirby, Gerald McCann, Dan Noonan, Barbara Tikoitin Stanley, Don Thompson, Irving Tripp, Lloyd White and Bill Williams. Of all my posthumous expressions of gratitude, my most profound naturally go to John Stanley.

Finally, I offer my thanks to my editors Gary Groth and Kristy Valenti, designer Keeli McCarthy, and all the fine people at Fantagraphics Books. This is my sixth book with Fantagraphics. May there be many more."

— Bill Schelly

Opposite: Little Lulu featured prominently in this Dell advertisement from the *Saturday Evening Post* in 1952. Stanley also introduced Woody Woodpecker in comic books and wrote stories featuring Tom Cat (of Tom and Jerry).

Certain items are based on information in "A Little Lulu Chronology" in *The Little Lulu Library* Vol. 1, published by Another Rainbow Publishing, Inc. Important comic books are shown when they appeared on newsstands, typically one or two months before their cover date.

John Stanley is abbreviated "JPS" throughout.

1914

March 22: John Patrick Stanley is born in Harlem, New York City.

1928

September: Approximate date JPS starts high school. He is fourteen.

1932

June: JPS graduates from High School. He receives their Scholarship Award medal (the Saint-Gaudens Medal), given to the graduating student from each New York City high school who completed an elective art course with the greatest distinction.

September 6: JPS begins his first year at the New York School of Art (now called Parsons: The New School for Design).

1934

June: Approximate date JPS ends his second and last year in college. By the fall, he is working at Fleischer Studios as an opaquer, then becomes in-betweener. Stays for about one year.

1935

February: Marjorie Henderson Buell's single-panel *Little Lulu* cartoons begin appearing weekly in the *Saturday Evening Post*, starting with the February 23, 1935 edition. The Lulu panels continue appearing through 1944.

September: Approximate date JPS leaves Fleischer Studio to work for Hal Horne on the *Mickey Mouse Magazine*.

1936

Rand McNally Co. publishes the first Little Lulu book, collecting cartoons from the *Post*.

July: Approximate date JPS moves to Kay Kamen, same month *Mickey Mouse Magazine* is "surrendered" by Horne to Kamen, doing work on Disney-related products, such as the Mickey Mouse watch.

November 26: JPS applies for his Social Security account number. He was on Kamen's staff at the time of this application.

1937

September–December: Attends evening classes at the Art Students League learning lithography. Begins drinking heavily at this time.

1939

First of five more Little Lulu books (reprints of *Post* cartoons) are published by the David McKay company, through 1944.

September 1, 1939: Germany invades Poland.

1940

September 16: The Selective Service Act of 1940 is passed by the 76th US Congress, obligating the twenty-six-year-old JPS to register for the draft.

October 16: JPS registers for the draft in the Bronx.

1941

JPS is rejected for military service due to a history of tuberculosis (minor) and a collapsed lung.

December 7: Japanese attack Pearl Harbor. US formally enters WWII.

1942

JPS turns 28 in March. Last year of freelancing period, doing commercial art and selling cartoons to magazines (no examples have been found).

August: Approximate date JPS meets Oskar Lebeck at Western Printing, and is given two Tom & Jerry stories to draw.

December 1: *Our Gang Comics* #3 (January–February) with first JPS artwork in comic books appears on newsstands (an eight-page *Tom and Jerry* story scripted by Gaylord DuBois). Stanley will draw two more stories from DuBois scripts, then begins doing both script and art.

1943

May: Approximate date *Our Gang* #6 (July–August) with first JPS script in comic books appears, his fourth *Tom and Jerry* story.

June: Approximate date *New Funnies* #79 (September) with first JPS cover appears, featuring Andy Panda. Inside is Stanley's first story (including finished art) for Andy Panda, with origin of Charlie Chicken. He also probably did *Lil' Eight Ball* in the same issue.

December 14: Little Lulu cartoon *Eggs Don't Bounce* is released, the first of a group of eight Lulu cartoons to appear in theaters. Over next four years, a total of twenty-six Little Lulu animated cartoons will be released by Paramount Pictures.

1944

January: Approximate date *New Funnies* #85 (March 1944) with first JPS Woody Woodpecker work (one-pager); first full length Woody story is in *New Funnies* #86.

February: Brother Jimmy Stanley, a lieutenant in the US Air Force, is M.I.A., and is declared dead in July.

October 23: Marjorie Buell signs an agreement with Western Publishing Co., giving them "the right to publish in printed form, in color or in black-and-white, comics magazines or comics [sic] books known as one-shots" starring Little Lulu.

December: Last Lulu panel by Buell appears in the *Saturday Evening Post* for December 30, 1944.

1945

May 15, 1945: Date *Four Color* #74 (June), the first Little Lulu comic book, is published. Story and art by JPS.

May 8: V–E Day.

August 15: V–J Day.

1946

January: Approximate date *Four Color* #97 (February), the second Little Lulu comic book, is published.

October: Approximate date *Animal Comics* #24 (December 1946–January 1947) is published, with *Jigger*, Stanley's first original comic book series. (Ends in *Animal Comics* #30, the book's last issue.)

1947

March: Eight-panel cartoon by Stanley appears in March 15 edition of the *New Yorker*, his only documented sale to the magazine.

July: Approximate date last full-length Woody Woodpecker story by JPS in *Walter Lantz New Funnies* #126 (August 1947) appears; his Woody one-pagers continue through *New Funnies* #131 (January 1948).

November 28: date *Marge's Little Lulu* #1 (January 1948) is published. First issue of Lulu in her own title (thirty-six pages).

1948

June: Approximate date last Tom and Jerry story by JPS in *Our Gang with Tom & Jerry* #50 (September 1948).

November: John and Marian Stanley travel to Europe, visiting Lourdes (France), London and the Stanley family in Ireland.

December: Approximate date *Raggedy Ann and Andy* #32 (January 1949) is published, with *The Hair-Raising Adventures of Peterkin Pottle*, Stanley's second original comic book series. (Ends in *Raggedy Ann and Andy* #38, July 1949). Stanley does covers for these issues, and also begins writing and sometimes drawing the *Raggedy Ann and Andy* feature in #32, continuing through #38.

Moved family to Liebig Street in Riverdale, a higher-class Bronx neighborhood that was also an Irish enclave like Kingsbridge (their former neighborhood).

1949

December: Approximate date *Marge's Little Lulu* goes monthly, with #7 (January), its Christmas issue.

1950

March: Approximate date *Henry Aldrich* #1 is published, with JPS scripts and art by Bill Williams, their first collaboration.

June 5: *Little Lulu* comic strip begins, syndicated by Chicago Tribune-New York News Syndicate. Strip continues to 1969. (JPS has nothing to do with it.)

1951

March: Approximate date *Krazy Kat* #1 (May–June 1951) is published, scripted by JPS.

August: Approximate date *Marge's Little Lulu* #39 (September 1951) is published, with "That Awful Witch Hazel," first official appearance of the character.

December: Marjorie Buell extends the Lulu contract with Western for six more years. Receives an $18,000 signing bonus.

1952

January 29: Date *Four Color* #381 (March) is published, first solo Tubby comic book, with Irving Tripp doing the finished art inside based on JPS storyboards. There would be a total of four "tryout" issues in *Four Color*; then Tubby graduates to his own, self-titled comic book.

June: Approximate date *Marge's Little Lulu* #49 (July 1952) is published, with credits published on the inside front cover. JPS is credited among "Staff writers and illustrators," and as the front cover artist. This is the only time credits were shown in the comic book.

September: Approximate date George E. Brennar, successor to Oskar Lebeck, dies, and is replaced by Matthew H. Murphy.

JPS moves his family to the "big, dark house" at 9 Darby Avenue, Croton-on-Hudson, New York.

1953

January: Approximate date of *Little Lulu Tubby Annual* 1953 (March), first giant Lulu comic book.

May: Approximate date of *Marge's Tubby* #5 (July–September), first issue of Tubby in his own title.

July: Approximate date of *Four Color* #494 (September) with *The Little King* story by JPS.

1954

March: Approximate date of *Marge's Little Lulu* #70 (April 1954), last fifty-two-page issue.

April 22, 1954: Helen Meyer (Vice President of Dell Comics) and Matthew Murphy (editor at Western Printing) defend Dell comics before the Senate Subcommittee to Investigate Juvenile Delinquency in New York City. Murphy utters the familiar phrase "Dell Comics are good comics," which became the company's slogan. (Dell would refuse to submit comic books to the Comics Code Authority.)

1956

Dell publishes the paperback book *This is Little Lulu*, which reprinted a number of Stanley's comic book stories in black and white (and some of Marge's original Lulu panels).

1957

December 19: JPS and Barbara Tikoitin Widmer obtain a marriage license.

December 23: JPS and BTW are married. They set up housekeeping in an apartment at 172 Bleecker Street in Greenwich Village, New York.

1958

June: JPS begins working on Nancy.

November: Approximate month *Nancy* #162 (January) is published, with first JPS stories for the character. Introduction of Oona Goosepimple. He continues at least to #185 (November–December 1961), perhaps longer. (*Nancy and Sluggo* ends with #187, dated March–May 1962.)

December: Lynda Stanley is born.

1959

Early 1959: The Stanleys move from Greenwich Village to Continental Village, upstate. Their new address will be: Old Albany Post Rd, RFD#3, Peekskill, New York.

July 24, 1959: Dell editor Matt Murphy writes to JPS, asking if he has any more Lulu story ideas, although Stanley had previously indicated he did not.

August: Approximate month: *Marge's Little Lulu* #135 (September) is published, the last issue with stories by JPS. Ends his almost fifteen years writing and drawing Little Lulu.

1961

January: Approximate date *New Terrytoons* #4 (March–May 1961) is released, with first Deputy Dawg story by JPS.

March: Approximate date new, nonexclusive comic book contract between Western and Dell is signed, allowing Dell to produce their own in-house comic books.

April: Approximate date Paramount Cartoon Studios Little Lulu cartoon *Alvin's Solo Flight* is released (adapted from story in Dell *Four Color* #165, October 1947).

July: Approximate date of *Around the Block with Dunc and Loo* #1 (October–December) is published, the first original series by JPS of the decade. Art by Bill Williams.

July: Approximate date *Linda Lark Student Nurse* #1 (November 1961–January 1962) is published, with script by JPS. His first "serious" comic book work.

August: Approximate date *Thirteen: "Going on Eighteen"* #1 (November 1961–January 1962) is published, with script by JPS. *Thirteen* would become Stanley's most successful comic book creation. Art in the first two issues by Tony Tallarico; then, through the end of the series, by JPS.

December: Approximate date *Kookie* #1 (February–April 1962) is published. The third original series by JPS launched in a five-month period. Another JPS collaboration with Bill Williams.

1962

January: Approximate date *Nellie the Nurse* (*Four Color* #1304, March–May 1962).

January 1: Paramount Cartoon Studios releases second Lulu cartoon based on JPS story, *Frog's Legs* (adapted from story in *Little Lulu* #21, 1950).

April 16, 1962: James ("Jim") Stanley, son of John and Barbara Stanley, is born in Peekskill, New York.

July: Approximate date *Ghost Stories* #1 (September–November) is published. At least two of the four stories are written by JPS, including "The Monster of Dread End."

August: Approximate date *Tales from the Tomb* (October) is published. All stories written by JPS.

1963

March: Approximate date James Stanley (father of JPS) dies, at eighty-three years old.

June: Approximate date *Clyde Crashcup* #1 (August–October 1963) is published. JPS stories are again finished by Irving Tripp.

Michael Barrier finds that the Catalog of Copyright Entries in the University of Chicago's library credits a "John Stanley" as the author of the Lulu *Four Color* issues. This is the earliest known instance of a fan discovering the man behind Little Lulu. He passes this information along to Don and Maggie Thompson.

1964

June: Approximate date *Thirteen "Going on Eighteen"* #12 (August–October) is published, with the first cover signed by JPS in his career.

1965

February: Approximate date *Melvin Monster* #1 (April–June) is published. JPS created and did the story, art and lettering on this series.

August 11: *Peekskill Evening Star* article/interview is published.

It's Nice to be Little is published (Rand McNally), with art by Jean Tamburine. Reprinted in 1966 and 1967.

1966

The Stanley family move into an apartment in Manhattan at 152 E. 94th Street, New York City.

July: Approximate date *Comic Art* #6 is published, which includes Don and Maggie Thompson's request for the address of JPS, "the cartoonist and, we believe, writer of *Little Lulu*." First known mention of JPS in a comics fanzine.

December 20: Death of Oskar Lebeck, at sixty-three years old.

1967

September: Approximate date when *Thirteen "Going on Eighteen"* #25 (December 1967) is published, the last new comic book by JPS for Dell. (*Thirteen* #26–9 were reprints of #1–4.) The issues of his own creations total 55.

"Bridget and Her Little Brother Newton the Nuisance" for *Wham-O Giant Comic Book*, one page.

1968

No new comic book work by JPS is published this year.

1969

May: *Little Lulu* syndicated comic strip ends.

April: Approximate date *Choo Choo Charlie* (one-shot) is published by Western/Gold Key. Story, art and lettering by JPS.

1970

Summer: Earliest confirmation of JPS working as a silk-screener at Fairgate Rule.

November 5: Date *O. G. Whiz* #1 (February 1971) is published. Last new work by JPS in comic books. The series he created continued for another eight issues by other writers and artists.

1971

March: Glenn Bray receives a letter from JPS (postmarked March 21) in reply to his suggestion (via US mails) that Stanley do recreations of Lulu covers on commission. Earliest known instance of JPS responding to a fan letter. (Michael Barrier and others had written to him earlier, but received no response.)

December 24, 1971: Marjorie Buell retires, selling the rights to Little Lulu to Western Publishing for $99,000 spread over seven years. The comic book is renamed *Little Lulu* with #207 (September 1972).

1973

October: Approximate date JPS visits Morris Gollub in Los Angeles, and "reconciles" with Walt Kelly shortly before Kelly dies (October 18, 1973).

1974

July 1: Denis Kitchen receives self-caricature from JPS, Stanley's first artwork since 1970.

July: Approximate date JPS moves into an old fixer-upper house, per letter to Bob Overstreet dated September 1974.

Maggie Thompson interviews JPS on the telephone, for her article in *Funnyworld*.

1976

July 7: Phelps and Overstreet visit JPS.

October 22: "Friends of Newcon" cocktail party at the hotel, evening before Newcon in Boston. JPS meets Carl Barks.

October 23: Newcon begins. JPS solo panel, moderated by Tom Murray.

Little Lulu #25 (July 1950)

October 24: Newcon Day Two: Carl Barks and JPS panel, moderated by Bruce Hamilton. JPS says much less than Barks.

1978

November: Approximate date Johanna Stanley (mother of JPS) dies, at ninety-five years old.

1981

A Smithsonian Book of Comic-Book Comics by Martin Williams and Michael Barrier includes four Lulu stories by JPS. Barrier receives no "thank you" from JPS for the copy.

Thomas Stanley, John's brother, dies.

1982

April: Jon Merrill's fanzine the *Stanley Steamer* begins, lasting through 1992.

Helen Meyer retires as co-publisher of Dell and consultant to Doubleday.

1983

December 29: *Little Lulu* #268 is published, the last issue (which is entirely made up of reprints of stories by JPS). Two more issues of new material were completed but not published by Whitman. (Publication date per *The Comic Reader* #216.)

1985

Another Rainbow begins publishing *The Little Lulu Library*, a hardbound, eighteen-volume set, collecting the stories from the *Four Color* issues. They begin with Vol. 6 (#68–87). Five hundred sets have a bookplate signed by John Stanley and Marjorie Buell.

1990

Barbara Stanley dies of colon cancer.

1992

The Little Lulu Library ends with Vol. 1, which reprints the *Four Color* issues featuring Little Lulu.

February: Jon Merrill's fanzine the *Stanley Steamer* ceases publication with #60.

Ed Buchman's *HoLLywood Eclectern* begins in the fall of the year, continuing to collect and present data, artwork, photos and other material about JPS and Little Lulu.

1993

May 30: Marjorie Buell dies, at eighty-eight years old, of lymphoma, in Elyria, Ohio, where she was in a retirement home.

November 11: JPS dies of esophageal cancer, at seventy-nine years old.

1996

July: News of John Stanley's passing is announced in the *HoLLywood Electern* #18 by Bradley Tenan.

2004

JPS is inducted into the Will Eisner Hall of Fame.

2005

Little Lulu cover by JPS (a commission) appears on Robert Overstreet's *Comic Book Price Guide* #35.

2015

July: Jim Stanley accepts the Bill Finger Award on behalf of his father at Comic-Con International: San Diego.

Sketch by Stanley, courtesy of Barbara Steggles.

Chapter 1 — City Boy

1   Johanna Stanley was born March 30, 1883. James Stanley was born January 15, 1881.

2   U. S. Census Report, 1920.

3   Author's interview with Barbara Stanley Steggles.

4   Author's interview with James Stanley.

5   Ibid.

6   Bill Spicer and Vince Davis, "Interview with Dan Noonan," *Graphic Story Magazine* #9 (Summer 1968), 13.

7   U. S. Census Report, 1930.

8   Author's interview with Barbara Stanley Steggles.

9   Ibid.

10 This is according to family stories. None of Stanley's juvenile drawings have survived.

11 *The Loom* yearbook, Textile High School, 1932.

12 Jim Amash, "Quality Control, A Conversation with Gill Fox," *Alter Ego* #12 (January 2002), 5, 6.

13 Ibid, 6.

14 Bradley Tenin, "John Stanley, A Humble Life," the *HoLLywood Eclectern* #18 (July 1996), 1.

15 Ibid.

16 The Saint Gaudens Medal was named after the famous sculptor Augustus Saint-Gaudens, a favorite son of the city. Since 1909, the trustees of the School Art League and the New York City Department of Education had joined together to honor New York City public high school students for excellence in visual arts through educational programs, awards and scholarships.

17 *New York School of Fine and Applied Art—Course Catalogue* 1932-1933, http://digitalarchiveslibrary.newschool.edu.

18 Don Phelps, "John Stanley," *1976 Newcon* program, October 1976, 12.

19 John Stanley solo panel, Newcon 1976. Unless otherwise noted, all quotations from this solo panel are from a transcript by the author.

Chapter 2 — Animator and Commercial Artist

1   Milo George, "Carl Barks & John Stanley," 1976 duo panel at Newcon, *The Comics Journal* #250 (February 2003), 159.

2   Jim Amash, "Quality Control, A Conversation with Gill Fox," 7. Fox says he was being paid $17.50 for the same work as Stanley, a few months after Stanley had moved on.

3   *Animated News* ran from December 1934 through April 1937, a total of twenty-nine issues, per Jerry Beck.

4   Animation historian Jim Korkis helped the author explain the various roles Stanley fulfilled at Fleischer Studios.

5   The list, assembled by Jim Korkis, consists of the Color Classics *Time for Love* (released September 6, 1935), *Musical Memories* (November 8, 1935), and *Somewhere in Dreamland*, (January 17, 1936); the Popeye Cartoons *You Gotta Be A Football Hero* (August 31, 1935), *King of the Mardi Gras* (September 27, 1935), the cartoon when the legendary Jack Mercer took over as the voice of Popeye, *The Spinach Overture* (November 11, 1935), and *Vim, Vigor and Vitaliky* (January 3, 1936); the Betty Boop cartoons *Judge for a Day* (September 20, 1935), *Making Stars* (October 18, 1935), *Little Nobody* (December 18, 1935) and *Betty Boop and the Little King* (based on the newspaper comic strip, January 31, 1936). He may also have been an in-betweener on the Betty Boop cartoon featuring Henry, a character some said inspired Marjorie Henderson Buell to create Little Lulu.

6   Jim Korkis, *Animation Anecdotes* (Theme Park Press, 2014). On page 39, Jack Kirby is quoted as saying, "Fleischer animation, like any animation studio, was a factory. It's a factory with long rows of tables. That's what I was doing at Fleischer's. I was sitting at one of those long rows of table with lights underneath. They'd give me this in-between action. I would finish the action on seven sheets of paper."

7   George, "Carl Barks & John Stanley," 159.

8   Phelps, "John Stanley," 12.

9   George, "Carl Barks & John Stanley," 162.

10 Michael Barrier, "Hal Horne's Gag File and the Birth of the Disney Comic Book," www.michaelbarrier.com, March 10, 2012.

11 Dorothy Krumeich, "Stanley Comics Help Quell Furor," *Peekskill Star*, August 11, 1965.

12 Phelps, "John Stanley," 12.

13 Author's interview with Jim Stanley.

14 Phelps, "John Stanley," 12.

15 Dr. Garrett O'Connor, "Breaking the Code of Silence: The Irish and Drink," http://irishamerica.com, February–March, 2012.

16 Author's interview with Barbara Stanley Steggles.

17 Ibid.

18 John Patrick Stanley, application for a Social Security number, Social Security Administration.

19 Author's interview with Barbara Stanley Steggles.

20 Spicer and Davis, "Interview with Dan Noonan," 13.

21 Phelps, "John Stanley," 12. Paraphrasing what Stanley told him in 1976, Phelps wrote that the artist freelanced for one year.

22 George, "Carl Barks & John Stanley," 162.

23 Phelps, "John Stanley," 12.

24 Author's interview with James Stanley.

25 Krumeich, "Stanley Comics Help Quell Furor," August 11, 1965.

Chapter 3 — His True Calling

1   Michael Barrier has pointed out that Lebeck's penchant for fairy tale, nursery rhyme and similarly themed titles "represented an effort by Lebeck, who had written and drawn children's books in the 1930s, to bring to comic books some of the qualities of traditional children's books, especially through rich and rather old-fashioned illustrations." From "Hey Kids! Comics! Walt Kelly Comics!," www.michaelbarrier.com, January 29, 2009.

2   Hames Ware, email to author. Working for Western out of its East Coast office at this time: George Kerr, his assistant L. Bing, Arthur Jameson, Casper Emerson, Harry Parkhurst and others, who were much older and illustrative stylists. Also on hand: Frank Thomas and Ralph Heimdahl.

3   George, "Carl Barks & John Stanley," 159.

4   John Stanley met Oskar Lebeck in August or early September, working backwards from the appearance of his first story in a comic book, which had a January 1943 cover date.

5   Phelps, "John Stanley," 16.

6   George, "Carl Barks & John Stanley," 159.

7   Identification of DuBois as the writer of the early Tom and Jerry scripts is based on page 76 of DuBois's account books. Script identification on the Grand Comics Database site is by David Porta, February 2014.

8   Tuffy's debut in the animated cartoons didn't occur until 1946, when he was renamed Nibbles.

9   Crediting the art on *Tom and Jerry* in *Our Gang* #3 to John Stanley isn't accepted by everyone who has looked at it. It's asserted as Stanley work by Frank M. Young, but historians Michael Barrier and Hames Ware feel that Stanley's artwork began with *Our Gang* #6. In the introduction to his book *John Stanley in the 1940s: A Comics Bibliography* (Deluxe Edition), Young writes, "This illustrated bibliography is the result of several years' exploration, and close scrutiny of dozens of comic magazines edited by Oskar Lebeck for Western Publications, and sold under the Dell imprint from 1943 to 1949. Lebeck's artists seldom signed their work. Yet his best creators left stylistic clues in their efforts. By using known (signed) examples of [Stanley's] highly distinctive lettering and cartooning style as a base, I've attributed many comic book stories to him outright. Themes of his stories, and some oft-used techniques, catchphrases and moods also help to ID his unsigned, work-for-hire efforts. I have studied the work of John Stanley for over twenty years. In that time, I believe I have become familiar with his narrative themes, his characterizations, sound effects [and] moods." In an email to the author, Young elaborated: "I have studied anew the *Tom and Jerry* story in *Our Gang Comics* #3. No disrespect to Mssrs. Barrier and Ware, but there are so many John Stanley tells in the story that I'm convinced it's his work: 1) the lettering compares to his other '40s comics lettering; 2) the expressions of Dinah, the black maid, have that subtlety and carefulness that I associate with Stanley in the '40s; 3) the second panel of page 4—the large 'OW!' and 'SMACK'—are

clearly from his hand; 4) the dancing figures of the mice, in the story's final panel, have a vigor and loose-limbed quality that I see over and over again in Stanley's work. As a maiden effort for a potential employer, it's carefully done. One can see Stanley the artisan, drawing each line with painstaking neatness and clarity. Stanley would, arguably, never draw anything this exact again. It would have been sufficient to impress Lebeck, and assure that Stanley got more work from him."

10 Krumeich, "Stanley Comics Help Quell Furor," August 11, 1965.

11 John Stanley solo panel, Newcon, 1976.

12 Spicer and Davis, "Interview with Dan Noonan," 12.

13 George, "Carl Barks & John Stanley," 159.

14 The Grand Comics Database credits this story to Gaylord DuBois, based on notes in his account books. But, according to Frank M. Young in *John Stanley in the 1940s*: "The records of longtime Western Publications writer Gaylord DuBois . . . include vague references to his having scripted some 1943 Tom and Jerry stories. Alas, his records are often nonspecific, and ask as many questions as they answer."

15 Spicer and Davis, "Interview with Dan Noonan," 13.

16 It depends whether you consider Alvin Jones as John Stanley creation. The basis for Alvin was an undefined toddler in a few of the Marge Little Lulu cartoons in the *Saturday Evening Post*. Buell claimed that she created Alvin. Yet everything we think of about Alvin, the original "rotten kid," including his name, was invented by Stanley. The *Little Lulu* comic book, featuring Alvin, lasted a few more years than *Andy Panda* with Charlie Chicken.

17 Stanley's use of storyboards was similar to the roughs that Harvey Kurtzman used to write his stories for the EC war comic books from 1950 to 1953.

18 John Stanley solo panel, Newcon 1976.

19 Author's interview with Barbara Stanley Steggles.

20 Ibid.

21 Daffy Duck first appeared in *Porky's Duck Hunt*, released on April 17, 1937.

22 Leonard (John) Clark, editor, "The Fantastic Mr. Stanley" by Maggie Thompson, *The Little Lulu Library* Vol. 5 (Arizona: Another Rainbow, 1986), 9.

Chapter 4 — Giving Life to Little Lulu

1 George, "Carl Barks & John Stanley," 159.

2 Leonard (John) Clark, editor, "Life with Lulu, An Interview with Marge" by Bruce Hamilton, *The Little Lulu Library*, Vol. 1 (Arizona: Another Rainbow, 1992), 14.

3 "I wanted a girl . . . seem boorish," is from Kathryn Allamong Jacob, "Little Lulu Lives Here," *Radcliffe Quarterly*, Summer 2006. "The *Post* editorial staff named her . . . carry out an idea," is from Leonard (John) Clark, editor, "Life with Lulu, An Interview With Marge" by Bruce Hamilton, *The Little Lulu Library*, Vol. 1 (Arizona: Another Rainbow, 1992), 14.

4 *Henry* ran in the *Saturday Evening Post* until May 25, 1935.

5 *Merriam-Webster Dictionary*, online: www.merriam-webster.com/dictionary.

6 Leonard (John) Clark, editor, "Marge" by Maggie Thompson, *The Little Lulu Library*, Vol. 6 (Arizona: Another Rainbow, 1985), 643.

7 Contract dated March 15, 1944, between Marjorie Henderson Buell and Western Printing and Lithographing Company Inc. Marge [Marjorie Henderson Buell] papers, 1856–1994, Schlesinger Library, Radcliffe Institute, Harvard University, Cambridge, Massachusetts.

8 Contract dated October 23, 1944, between Marjorie Henderson Buell and Western Printing and Lithographing Company Inc. Marge papers, Schlesinger Library.

9 Phelps, "John Stanley," 12–3.

10 Hames Ware, email to author: "You pose a fascinating question as to which artists at Dell might have been considered for the Little Lulu feature. Artists on [Lebeck's] staff at the time, such as George Kerr, his assistant L. Bing, Arthur Jameson, Casper Emerson, Harry Parkhurst and others were much older and illustrative stylists. Artists like Frank Thomas and Ralph Heimdahl were wonderful but their styles would not have fit either." Another artist who was around at this time was Dan Gormley, who might have been an appropriate choice, except he wasn't a writer.

11 John Stanley solo panel, Newcon, 1976.

12 Barrier, *Funnybooks*, 139. This is the date of publication shown on the card for the copyright registration for Four Color #74 in the Catalog of Copyright Entries. Per Barrier in an email to the author, "I think the May 14, 1945, date

is the closest we can get to knowing when the first issue of Little Lulu was 'really' published, that is, placed on sale."

13 Bradley Tenan, "Marjorie Henderson Buell: A Loving Tribute," the *HoLLywood Eclectern* #4, June 1993.

14 The author acknowledges that there must have been times when Stanley independently came up with an idea similar or even identical to one in the Lulu *Post* panels, or, indeed, in one of the Paramount cartoons. Creative coincidences are more common than most people realize.

15 Maggie Thompson, "Little Ms. Moppet," *Comics Collector* #2 (1984), 68.

16 John Stanley solo panel, Newcon 1976.

17 John Stanley letter to Bruce Hamilton dated September 12, 1985. Regarding the name "Tompkins," it's quite a coincidence that a Tompkins Park exists in Peekskill, New York, the small town that Bradley Tenan discovered was the basis for the town of Meadowville (where Lulu and Tubby lived). Tubby's last name was given as "Trimble" in *Four Color* #164 ("Rainy Day"), and in *Little Lulu* #12 ("Fifty-Fifty Proposition"), the latter issue dated June 1949. The next time his last name was used, it's "Tompkins" in "Guest in the Ghost Hotel" in *Tubby* #7 (January–March 1954), almost five years later. Could it be that Marge Buell had given him "Trimble," not "Tompkins," as he later stated, and that when he forgot it, he picked the first alliterative last name that came to mind? Since, by 1953, Stanley was doing his shopping in Peekskill, with its Tompkins Park, it seems likely that he—not Marge—gave Tubby his permanent last name. Decades later, he may have simply forgotten that he renamed the character. Still, there's no way other than deductive reasoning to think that Stanley's later statements (giving Marge credit for Tompkins) are incorrect.

18 It's odd that Elsie's birthday party is a costume party, although we may be meant to assume her birthday falls on Halloween. Since Buell signed the contract licensing Western to produce Lulu comic books on October 23, 1944, this seems to confirm that Stanley was assigned the feature almost immediately afterward.

19 John Stanley solo panel, Newcon 1976.

20 Bruce Hamilton, "Life with Lulu, An Interview with Marge," 16.

21 John Stanley solo panel, Newcon, 1976.

22 Ibid.

23 John Stanley letter to Bruce Hamilton dated September 12, 1985.

24 In a handwritten letter from John Stanley to Glenn Bray, postmarked March 21, 1971, one can see that his own cursive version of "Little Lulu" looks a lot like the style of that logo. This seems to provide further corroboration that the final Lulu cover logo was based on Stanley's own cursive, but crafted into final form by Ed Marine.

25 With *Little Lulu* #7 through #27, the border was changed to a strip down the left-hand side of the cover. After that, the side strip was dropped, allowing the cover illustration to fill the entirety of each cover.

26 The man running the contest is "Mr. Gormley," named after Dan Gormley, Stanley's artistic collaborator on *Andy Panda* and many other features.

27 Russ Cochran, editor, "Pop-up Feminism at the Back of the Post: Lulu, Hazel and Marge" by R. C. Harvey, *Comic Book Marketplace* #94, 2002, 24.

28 Stanley had already done a Woody Woodpecker story with no dialogue almost a year earlier, in *New Funnies* #102 (August 1945).

29 John Stanley solo panel, Newcon, 1976.

Chapter 5 — Little Lulu: The Classic Years

1 Leonard (John) Clark, editor, "A Tripp Down Memory Lane," interview with Irving Tripp by Bruce Hamilton, *The Little Lulu Library* Vol. 6, 14.

2 George, "Carl Barks & John Stanley," 161.

3 Barrier, *Funnybooks*, 139. Frank M. Young's close study of *Four Color* #115 (and the next four issues of Lulu in *Four Color*) shows that they were lettered by Stanley, apparently in an attempt to keep the look of the feature as consistent as possible as assistants were brought in. But lettering is done on the final illustration boards, causing Young to wonder, "Did Stanley lay out those issues on the boards, as well as letter them? The staging of the drawings is consistent with his other known comics work of the time." Email from Frank M. Young, December 15, 2015.

4 John Stanley letter to Bruce Hamilton dated September 12, 1985.

5 Leonard (John) Clark, editor, "A Tripp Down Memory Lane," *The Little Lulu Library* Vol. 6, 17.

6 Barrier, *Funnybooks,* 270. "Anne DeStefano, who was Oskar Lebeck's secretary throughout the 1940s but by the early 1950s was an editor in Western's New York Office."

7 Jon Merrill, "John Stanley … and Successors," the *Stanley Steamer* #4, 1982, 10.

8 Clark, "A Tripp Down Memory Lane," *The Little Lulu Library* Vol. 6, 16.

9 Michael Barrier, editor, "The Almost Anonymous Mr. Stanley" by Maggie Thompson, *Funnyworld* #16, 1975, 34.

10 Morris Gollub interviewed by Michael Barrier November 2, 1976, unpublished.

11 George, "Carl Barks & John Stanley," 161.

12 John Stanley solo panel, Newcon, 1976.

13 Ibid.

14 Ibid.

15 Ibid.

16 Carl Barks and John Stanley panel at Newcon 1976, transcribed by the author. I was able to listen to the original recording of the panel. In a few cases, my transcription of certain passages differed from that of Milo George, such as this one. (Because I found few appreciable differences between my transcript and that of Milo George in *The Journal,* I've relied on the one in *The Journal.*)

17 John Stanley solo panel, Newcon, 1976.

18 Spicer and Davis, "Interview with Dan Noonan," 13.

19 Barrier, *Funnybooks,* 286.

20 John Stanley solo panel, Newcon, 1976.

21 Mrs. Moppet's name in this story is "Mildred," but Stanley apparently forgot this when he needed to use her first name in subsequent stories. Then he named her "Martha," which became permanent.

22 For the record, when John Stanley had children in real life, they weren't spanked, according to his son Jim Stanley.

23 John Stanley solo panel, Newcon, 1976. Source of both quotations in this paragraph.

24 Ibid.

25 A wealthy Gloria Van Potts is the kidnap victim in "Lulu is Taken for a Ride," *Four Color* #131, but she and Lulu don't know one another. She's prefigured by "Dolly" in "Just a Gigolo" (*Four Color* #158), the same sort of character, probably intended for one-time use.

26 Phelps, "John Stanley," 16.

27 Morris Gollub interviewed by Michael Barrier November 2, 1976, unpublished.

28 Phelps, "John Stanley," 16.

29 Author's interview with Don Phelps.

30 All quotations in this paragraph are from Michael's Barrier's unpublished interview with Morris Gollub, November 2, 1976.

31 Spicer and Davis, "Interview with Dan Noonan," 13.

32 According to Kim Weston, Carl Barks's pay vouchers in 1949 show he received $22 for art and $6.50 for script. So, since Stanley said he was paid Western's "top rate," one can assume he also received $6.50 for each story page. He might have gotten more because of the guidance his layouts gave the artists, but probably not. They would more likely have been considered "script pages."

33 Apart from the $12 page rate for writing in 1958, no information specific to rates paid to John Stanley has been found. The estimates in this paragraph are based on rates paid to Walt Kelly that were found by Michael Barrier in the Pogo Collection at the Billy Ireland Cartoon Library and Museum, Ohio State University, Columbus, Pogo Collection, box 14, folder 3. In records from 1951 and 1952, Kelly's "regular rates" were $32.75 for writing and drawing each comic book page (plus $2.25 if he did his own lettering), and $50 for a front cover, "rates comparable to those paid then to other cartoonists who did not own the properties they worked on," per Barrier. As for bonuses, the Barks pay vouchers indicate that Barks received a bonus of $1,441 in 1948, which he noted was his largest single bonus. However, he apparently received bonuses twice a year, so his total bonus amount for that year might have been twice as much. Since *Little Lulu* didn't sell quite as many copies as *Walt Disney's Comics and Stories* or the Duck issues of *Four Color* in 1948, one can speculate that his bonuses were in the range of $1,000 to $1,500 for an entire year.

34 Per Frank M. Young's John Stanley bibliographies: the total number of pages done by Stanley from the May 1949 issues through the April 1950 issues — work finished in 1949 — was 650, and the total number of covers was 40.

Nevertheless, this figure is a ballpark estimate, and should not be taken as gospel.

35 Leonard (John) Clark, editor, "Marge" by Maggie Thompson, *The Little Lulu Library,* Vol. 6, 644.

Chapter 6 — On the Side

1 Spicer and Davis, "Interview with Dan Noonan," 13.

2 Morris Gollub interviewed by Michael Barrier November 2, 1976, unpublished.

3 Leonard (John) Clark, editor, "The Fantastic Mr. Stanley," by Maggie Thompson, *The Little Lulu Library,* Vol. 5, 10.

4 John Stanley solo panel, Newcon, 1976.

5 Bill Williams (born Alfred O. Williams in either 1917 or 1918) attended the University of Michigan, then moved to California and worked in the animation department of Walt Disney Studios beginning in 1938. In an email to the author, Jim Korkis wrote, "Unfortunately, with the outbreak of World War II, not only were foreign markets closed to the Disney product but the draft took some of Disney's top people and so the planned production schedule (even of theatrical animated shorts) was greatly reduced resulting in many of these newly hired artists leaving or being let go from the studio to seek opportunities elsewhere. He was not there long enough to make an impact." After World War II, Williams relocated to New York City and began working for Johnstone and Cushing, the agency that specialized in doing comic strip-style ads and features for all manner of publications. Before working for Western, he freelanced for Stan Lee at Timely Comics on the features *Lana* and *Little Lana* in titles such as *Annie Oakley* and *Gay Comics.*

6 Rootie Kazootie, the star of the 1950s children's television program *The Rootie Kazootie Club* (1950–1954), was a boy with a magic "kazootie" who wore a baseball cap with an oversized bill. Rootie was a puppet, who interacted with other puppets and the real life host "Big Todd" Russell, as well as other real life actors.

Chapter 7 — Little Lulu in the 1950s

1 Regarding the sales of *Little Lulu,* Helen Meyer, then Vice President of Dell, testified before the U. S. Senate in 1954, "Of the first twenty-five largest selling magazines on newsstands — this includes *Ladies' Home Journal, Saturday Evening Post, Life* and so forth — eleven titles are Dell comics, with *Walt Disney's Donald Duck* the leading newsstand seller. Some of these titles are *Walt Disney's Comics, Warner Bros. Bugs Bunny, Walt Disney's Mickey Mouse, Warner Bros. Looney Tunes and Merrie Melodies, Porky Pig, Walter Lantz Woody Woodpecker, Marge's Little Lulu, MGM's Tom and Jerry.* The newsstand sales range from 950,000 to 1,996,570 on each of the above mentioned titles. I mean newsstands only and I am not including any subscriptions, and we have hundreds of thousands of subscriptions." This testimony before the Senate Sub-Committee on the Judiciary to Investigate Juvenile Delinquency, is at: www.thecomicbooks.com/meyermurphy.html.

2 The *Little Lulu* comic strip continued until May 1969. It was written and drawn by Woody Kimbrell from 1950 to 1964, written by Al Stoffel and drawn by Roger Armstrong from 1964 to 1966, and written by Al Stoffel and Del Connell, with art by Ed Nofziger, in its last years, from 1966 to 1969. (Information derived from the *HoLLywood Eclectern* #12, February 1995.)

3 Nineteen-fifty-one saw the beginning of a ten-issue run of *Little Lulu* with only thirty-six page issues. Dell had scaled back to the slimmer size early that year *except* for its monthlies, but with *Little Lulu* #41 (October 1951), it also lost sixteen pages (roughly two stories) for those ten issues.

4 This was most likely inspired by the Junior G-Man Club and cereal premiums of the 1930s.

5 Leonard (John) Clark, editor, "The Bogyman: Dispossessed," by Bruce Hamilton, *The Little Lulu Library* Vol. 5, 705. Buell's letter to Clark was dated October 30, 1985.

6 Leonard (John) Clark, editor, "A Tripp Down Memory Lane," *The Little Lulu Library* Vol. 6, 16. This is the source of all quotations from Irving Tripp in this chapter.

7 "The Bogyman" was published in the *The Little Lulu Library* V.5, against the objections of Marjorie Buell.

8   Frank M. Young, *John Stanley in the 1950s: A Comics Bibliography*, 2014, 33.

9   Those prototypical Witch Hazel stories were "The Prince in the Pool" (*Little Lulu* #11, May 1949) and "The Dragon Tamer" (*Little Lulu* #25, July 1950).

10   John Stanley solo panel, Newcon, 1976.

11   Possibly coincidentally, the Walt Disney studio's Donald Duck cartoon, *Trick or Treat*, in 1952 also featured a character named Witch Hazel, voiced by June Foray. If Oskar Lebeck or other powers that be at Western Printing noticed the duplication, they took no action, since their relationship with Walt Disney Studios was far more important than a duplication of one of Western's minor characters. Disney also apparently took no action when Chuck Jones, in the animation department at Warner Bros., liked the name in the Disney cartoon so much that he (by his own admission) was inspired to put his own Witch Hazel in the Bugs Bunny short, *Bewitched Bunny* (1954).

12   Barrier, *Funnybooks*, 288.

13   Ibid.

14   Morris Gollub interviewed by Michael Barrier November 2, 1976, unpublished.

15   Ibid.

16   John Stanley solo panel, Newcon, 1976.

17   Phelps, "John Stanley," 16.

18   In 1948, Stanley, along with his parents and older sister, moved from Heath Avenue in Kingsbridge to another Irish enclave in nearby Riverdale (the Bronx). The move seems to have coincided with the retirement of his father from New York Transit, since he turned sixty-five years old on January 15, 1947. Riverdale was a nicer neighborhood, with fewer row houses. The new Stanley home, on Liebig Avenue, was a freestanding, brick structure.

19   Author's interview with Barbara Stanley Steggles.

20   Ibid.

21   Ibid.

22   Michael T. Gilbert, "The Jim Stanley Interview," *Alter Ego* #54, November 2005, 58.

23   Author's interview with Barbara Stanley Steggles.

24   From the author's transcription of the Barks-Stanley panel at Newcon 1976.

25   "A dear friend" from John Stanley letter to Bruce Hamilton dated September 12, 1985.

26   The issues with credits are *New Funnies* #183 (May), #184 (June) and #185 (July). By this time, Stanley was no longer writing for the title.

Chapter 8 — From Lulu to Nancy

1   The slogan "Dell Comics Are Good Comics" first appeared in *Little Lulu* #76 (October 1954), which went into production about the time of the Senate hearings. It was put into Dell's entire output of comic books at about the same time.

2   Thomas Andrae, "The Expurgated Barks," *The Carl Barks Library* (Vol. 2, No. 2). Scottsdale, Arizona, 1984, 522.

3   John Stanley solo panel, Newcon, 1976.

4   Author's interview with Bob Overstreet.

5   Ibid.

6   Barrier, *Funnybooks*, 315.

7   Ibid.

8   Ibid.

9   John Stanley solo panel, Newcon, 1976.

10   Krumeich, "Stanley Comics Help Quell Furor," August 11, 1965.

11   Phelps, "John Stanley," 14.

12   Ibid, 16.

13   A letter from Matt Murphy to John Stanley on July 17, 1958, established his rate at $12 per page. Since Western's page rates were flat through most of the 1950s, he was probably making the same amount when he wrote the Tubby giant, a couple of years earlier.

14   *This is Little Lulu* starts off with several pages of Marge's *Saturday Evening Post* panels (which appear to be somewhat redrawn), and then reprints Stanley stories from 1954 and 1955, such as "Santa Claus in the Park" (*LL* #77), "Bad Dream" (*LL* #83), The Two-Timer" (*LL* #86) and "The Seven-Year Witch" (*LL* #89), and others, including some one-pagers.

15   Author's interview with Jim Stanley.

16   Author's interview with Barbara Stanley Steggles.

17   Author's interview with Jim Stanley.

18   The first book by Zion and Graham, *All Falling Down* (1951), was a runner-up for the Caldecott Medal, presented annually by the American Library Association to the best illustrated book of the year. Another book titled *Really Spring* (1956) was named best illustrated book of 1956 by the *New York Times Book Review*.

19   Krumeich, "Stanley Comics Help Quell Furor," August 11, 1965.

20   Letter from Matthew Murphy to John Stanley dated July 24, 1959. It also refers to Stanley's proposal that Raggedy Ann and Andy be revived. He wrote, "I presented your outlines and art work to Helen [Meyer] on the proposed Raggedy Ann comic and she liked the material but feels we no longer have the same reading age level that used to buy this type of book a few years ago." Letter courtesy of Jim Stanley.

21   John Stanley solo panel, Newcon, 1976.

22   Letter from Matthew Murphy to John Stanley dated September 26, 1958. Courtesy of Jim Stanley.

23   Ibid.

24   John Stanley solo panel, Newcon, 1976.

Chapter 9 — John Stanley and the New Dell

1   John Stanley solo panel, Newcon, 1976.

2   Morris Gollub interviewed by Michael Barrier November 2, 1976, unpublished.

3   Barrier, *Funnybooks*, 331.

4   Leonard (John) Clark, "A Tripp Down Memory Lane," *The Little Lulu Library* Vol. 6, 17.

5   John Stanley solo panel, Newcon, 1976.

6   E. B. Boatner's interview with L. B. Cole, ca. 1979, 1980. From notes, unpublished.

7   Ibid. Cole claimed he had a royalty arrangement with Dell. This has never been substantiated. It's possible he was referring not to royalties, per se, but the promise of year-end bonuses.

8   Jon Merrill, editor, letter from John Stanley dated September 1, 1991, the *Stanley Steamer* #58 (October 1991), 3.

9   John Stanley solo panel, Newcon, 1976.

10   Other titles in the "nurse comics boomlet" are *Nurse Betsy Crane* from Charlton, and *Linda Carter, Student Nurse* from Marvel. Stanley himself would add to it with the humorous Nellie the Nurse in *Four Color* #1304 (March–May 1962), which he wrote and Bill Williams drew. (The cover and some interior pages by Larry Katzman, signed "Kaz," the cartoonist who created the character.) No relation to the Timely comic book *Nellie the Nurse*.

11   All quotations from Tony Tallarico in this chapter are from the author's interview with the artist.

12   John Stanley, the *Stanley Steamer* #58 (October 1991), 3.

13   William B. Jones, Jr., *Classics Illustrated, A Cultural History*, second edition, McFarland Publishing, North Carolina, 2011.

14   Stanley was originally credited as the author of all four stories in *Ghost Stories* #1. He explicitly stated that "I also wrote the first issue of Dell's *Ghost Stories*" in a letter to Bob Overstreet in 1974, and again at Newcon in 1976. However, Martin O'Hearn, considered the closest thing to an authority in identifying uncredited writers by analyzing the stories themselves, only credits him with "The Monster of Dread End" and "The Black Stallion," the last story in the book. He feels "The Werewolf Wasp" and "The Door" don't match John Stanley's storytelling style, and therefore asserts they aren't scripted by Stanley—although he doesn't know who did. It's possible that John Stanley hadn't looked closely at *Ghost Stories* #1 in years, and may not have realized that those stories weren't his. Or, O'Hearn may be mistaken.

15   John Schoenherr passed away in 2010, but his son found his father's work log, which states that the cover of *Tales from the Tomb* (job #226) was assigned on February 7, 1962, and paid for ($200) on April 17, 1962. The cover has often been erroneously credited to Cole, a talented painter of comic book covers in his own right.

16   John Stanley solo panel, Newcon, 1976.

17   Gilbert, "The Jim Stanley Interview," 58.

18   All quotations in this chapter are from Jamie Colville's "Interview with D. J. Arneson," at http://www.collectortimes.com/2010_04/Clubhouse.html.

19   John Stanley solo panel, Newcon, 1976.

20 Seth, introduction, *Thirteen: Going on Eighteen*, The John Stanley Library series, (Montreal: Drawn & Quarterly, 2009).

21 U. S. Senate, Comic Books and Juvenile Delinquency: Interim Report of the Committee on the Judiciary. Washington D.C., March 14, 1955. www.thecomicbooks.com/1954senatetranscripts.html.

Chapter 10 — Leaving "A Young Man's Game"

1   Krumeich, "Stanley Comics Help Quell Furor," August 11, 1965.

2   John Stanley, *It's Nice to be Little* (New York: Rand McNally & Company, 1956).

3   W.F.G., "Have Your Read . . . It's Nice to be Little," review, *The Morning Record*, Meriden, Connecticut, March 22, 1965, 6.

4   John Stanley, *It's Nice to be Little* (New York: Rand McNally & Company, 1956).

5   Krumeich, "Stanley Comics Help Quell Furor," August 11, 1965. What was on television in 1965 that could be considered "rampant mayhem"? The controversial crime drama *The Untouchables* went off the air in 1963. The only show with much violence in the 1964–1965 U. S. television season was *Combat!*, unless one considered *Bonanza* and *Gunsmoke* violent.

6   Ibid.

7   Based on sales statements in the *Thirteen* comic books.

8   Author's interview with Jim Stanley.

9   *Linda Lark* (in its various titles), *Around the Block/Dunc and Loo*, *Kookie*, *Thirteen*, *Melvin Monster*, and *O. G. Whiz*. There were also a handful of minor features he created: *Tramp Doctor*, *Little Petey*, *Judy Junior*, and *Bridget* (*WHAM-O*).

10 Gilbert, "The Jim Stanley Interview," 58.

11 Bradley Tenan, "John Stanley, A Humble Life," the *HoLLywood Eclectern* #18 (July 1996), 1.

12 Gilbert, "The Jim Stanley Interview," 58.

13 Author's interview with Jim Stanley.

14 Ibid.

15 Gilbert, "The Jim Stanley Interview," 59.

16 Barrier, *Funnybooks*, 333.

17 The quotations from Tim Lahey are an amalgam taken from Frank M. Young's Stanley Stories site (http://stanleystories.blogspot.com), additional emails from Lahey to Young, and emails from Lahey to the author.

Chapter 11 — John Stanley and Comics Fandom

1   Michael Barrier, email to author.

2   Don and Maggie Thompson, *Comic Art* #6, 1966, 5.

3   In Don and Maggie Thompson's *A Listing of Dell Special Series Comic Books (and a Few Others)*, the first edition published in March 1968, some issues are credited to certain artists. Names appearing are Carl Barks, Walt Kelly, Jesse Marsh, Charles Schulz and a number of others. Despite the information from Barrier, there's no artist credit for any comic book with Lulu or Tubby. John Stanley's name appears in one place in Don and Maggie's publication, with *Four Color* #1304 which featured *Nellie the Nurse*.

4   Maggie Thompson, "The Almost Anonymous Mr. Stanley," *Funnyworld* #16, 1975, 34.

5   Letter from John Stanley to Glenn Bray, March 21, 1971.

6   Glenn Bray, email to author.

7   John Stanley letter to Denis Kitchen dated December 3, 1972, Columbia University Rare Book & Manuscript Library, Kitchen Sink Press Archive.

8   Denis Kitchen, letter to Stanley dated December 8, 1972, Columbia University Rare Book & Manuscript Library, Kitchen Sink Press Archive.

9   Justin Green, *Bijou Funnies* #5, Kitchen Sink Press, December 1970, 31.

10 George, "Carl Barks & John Stanley," 162.

11 Gilbert, "The Jim Stanley Interview," 59.

12 Ibid, 58.

13 Author's interview with Jim Stanley.

14 Gilbert, "The Jim Stanley Interview," 58.

15 Craig Yoe, email to author.

16 All quotations from Bob Overstreet are from the interview he gave the author.

17 John Stanley letter to Bob Overstreet postmarked September 24, 1974.

18 All quotations from Don Phelps, unless otherwise noted, are from the interview he gave the author (and email follow-ups).

19 Phelps, "John Stanley," 16.

20 Michael Barrier's unpublished interview with Morris Gollub, November 2, 1976. Walt Kelly's ability to produce *Pogo* was hampered by diabetes, which cost him a leg. He managed to continue working into 1973, then passed away on October 18, 1973, at sixty years old.

21 Thomas (Tom) Murray had served as Dean of Continuing Education at Newbury College (Boston), edited books for Doubleday and Porter Sargent Publisher, and had been the Literary and Book Editor of *Boston Review of the Arts*. Through the early 1970s, he contributed articles and reviews to *Broadside* (of Boston), *The Harvard Independent*, and numerous magazines in the Boston area. He subsequently obtained his PhD and is currently a Professor of English and Professional Writing at Fitchburg (Massachusetts) State University.

22 Author's interview with Tom Murray.

23 If John Stanley gave other substantial interviews in his career, they haven't surfaced as of this writing.

24 All of the quotations from the interview are taken from a transcript of the panel made by the author, apparently the first time the tape recording has been transcribed. Only about ten percent of the material had been previously published (in the *HoLLywood Eclectern* #38, Spring 2004), which seems to be from notes taken during the panel rather than from the tape, because of its brevity, and because the wording is often at variance with what was actually said.

25 John Stanley solo panel, Newcon, 1976.

26 Being out of touch, Stanley hadn't seen any of the attempts at graphic novels that had emerged by this time, such as Will Eisner's *A Contract with God*. Or, if he did, he didn't consider Eisner a genius.

27 Author's interview with Jim Stanley.

28 From author's transcription of the Barks-Stanley panel at Newcon, which occurred the following day.

29 The comic con mural was originated by Harvey Kurtzman at the first Newcon. The 1976 mural was a repeat of this idea.

30 George, "Carl Barks and John Stanley," 159–62.

31 From the author's transcription of the Barks-Stanley panel. George had quoted Stanley as saying he would end each page with a "gag" or a "punch line," but on the tape, Stanley uses the word "lift", i.e., a "a little lift there to carry the reader on." This is essentially the same thing, but different enough to note.

32 Author's interview with Harry McCracken.

Chapter 12 — The Long Goodbye

1   All quotations from Don Phelps in this chapter, unless noted otherwise, are from the author's interview (and email follow-ups).

2   In his interview with the author, Phelps recounted driving Stanley to a small convention in Boonton, New Jersey, in 1978 or 1979. The show was organized by Donald Flanagan, and was lightly attended.

3   All quotations from John Clark in this chapter are from an interview he gave the author.

4   Jon Merrill, email to author.

5   Leonard (John) Clark, editor, "The Fantastic Mr. Stanley," by Maggie Thompson, *The Little Lulu Library* Vol. 5, 10.

6   Ed Buchman, email to author.

7   They were "Snowballs from Heaven" in the *Stanley Steamer* #59, a sample page on how he worked which appeared in *The Little Lulu Library* Vol. 15, and the Candy McGargoyle page for the *HoLLywood Eclectern* #3.

8   Frank M. Young, *The Tao of Yow: John Stanley's World* (Washington: Frank M. Young, 2015), 77.

9   Tenan, "John Stanley, A Humble Life," 1.

10 Gilbert, "The Jim Stanley Interview," 59.

11 Tenan, "John Stanley, A Humble Life," 1, 2.

12 Ibid, 2.

13 Gilbert, "The Jim Stanley Interview," 59.

14 Tenan, "John Stanley, A Humble Life," 1.

15 Gilbert, "The Jim Stanley Interview," 60.

Thirteen #13 (November 1964–January 1965)

Dell Giant #34 (1960)

Little Lulu #116 (February 1958)

Raggedy Ann and Andy #37 (June 1949). John Stanley art.

O

Offisa Bull Pupp (character) 80
O.G. Whiz (comic) 135, 171, 177
Oona Goosepimple (character) 106–107, 144, 170
Oswald the Rabbit (character) 33, 36, 71
Our Gang Comics 31–33, 45, 51, 168–169, 173
Overstreet, Bob 101, 143–144, 155, 172, 176–177
Owens, Al 88

P

Parsons 20, 21, 168
Peanuts 7, 55, 126, 148
Peekskill Evening Star 29, 131, 171
Peekskill, New York 29, 60, 90, 104, 124, 131, 142, 158, 170–174
Penthouse Club 65–67
Phelps, Don 21, 28–29, 96, 143, 144, 145, 146, 153, 155, 159, 172, 173, 174, 175, 176, 177
Pogo (strip) 33, 45, 75, 102, 113, 175, 177
Popeye (character) 23, 25, 164, 173

R

Raggedy Ann (character) 33, 75, 77, 102, 169, 176
Ransom, Candace F. 158
"Rocking Horse, The" (story) 64, 68
Rootie Kazootie (character) 78, 80, 175
Rose, Gordon 88
Roth, Phillip 160

S

San Diego Comicon 155, 164, 172
Santa Claus Funnies 81
Santo, Margaret 29
Saturday Evening Post 7, 43, 48, 51, 60, 85, 168–169, 174–176
Schoenherr, John 119, 176
Schulz, Charles 7, 55, 148, 177
Seth (cartoonist) 125, 177
Seuling, Phil 145, 155
Sluggo (character) 106–107, 148, 170
Smith, Lloyd E. 78, 111, 139
Smithsonian Book of Comic Book Comics, A 85
Snow White and the Seven Dwarfs (film) 28
Soglow, Otto 71, 80
spanking 43, 63, 83
Spicer, John 139, 173–175
"'Spider' Spins Again, The" (story) 158
Spiegelman, Art 7
Springer, Frank 119
Stanley, James (father) 2, 13, 28–29, 37, 125, 133, 147, 169
Stanley, James "Jimmy" (brother) 2, 12–14, 28–29, 37, 88, 169
Stanley, James "Jim" (son) 4, 8, 12–13, 15, 28–29, 66, 71–72, 88, 90, 104, 119, 137, 142, 147, 151, 158, 160–161, 163–164, 167, 172–173, 175–177
Stanley, Joanna "Anna" Ahearn 13, 15, 88, 104, 124, 143
Stanley, John
    Animation Career 22–26
    Birth 13
    Commercial Art Career 26–28
    Death 163–164
    Education 13–21
    First Comics Work 31–33
    Leaves Comics Industry 136–137
    Marriage 104–105, 137, 142–143
Stanley, Lynda 104, 131, 143–144, 163, 170
Stanley, Marguerite 13, 28
Stanley, Marian 13, 28, 88, 105, 143, 163, 169
Stanley Steamer (fanzine) 158, 162, 172, 175, 176–177
Stanley, Thomas "Tom" 13, 29, 31–33, 37, 38, 50, 59, 64, 71, 90, 136, 137, 144, 146–147, 168–169, 172–174, 175, 177
Steggles, Barbara Stanley (niece) 8, 13, 28–29, 37, 90, 124, 173–174, 176
Steranko, Jim 145
Stevenson, Robert Louis 14, 18, 147
storyboards 37, 59, 117
Subcommittee to Investigate Juvenile Delinquency 101, 170
summer camp 148
Surprise Books 86

T

Tales from the Tomb (comic book) 10, 99, 118–119, 126, 135, 148, 153, 170, 176
Talk of the Town (column) 71
Tallarico, Tony 116, 117, 119, 120, 170, 176
Tamburine, Jean 131, 171
Tenan, Bradley 137, 158, 162, 163, 172, 174, 177
"Ten Pennies" (story) 88, 98
Textile High School 15, 18, 20, 104, 173
Thirteen "Going on Eighteen" 10, 112, 116–117, 124, 125–127, 132, 133, 135, 139, 148, 153, 164, 170–171, 177
This is Little Lulu 104, 170, 176
Thompson, Don 21, 28–29, 44, 49, 63, 93, 96, 117, 139, 143–146, 153, 155, 159, 169, 171, 173, 175, 177
Thompson, Maggie 40, 77, 139, 143, 160, 171–172, 174–175, 177
Thurber, James 160
Tillie the Toiler (strip) 14
toilet 33

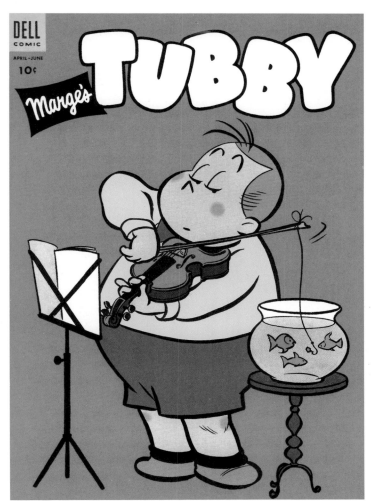

Tubby #8 (Apri –June 1954)

Don Phelps and John Stanley at Newcon 1976. Photo: E. B. Boatner.

BILL SCHELLY has been chronicling and contributing to the fringes of pop culture since the mid-1960s, when he became widely known for his popular comics fanzine *Sense of Wonder*. He began researching the history of comic book fandom in 1991, eventually compiling it in the book *The Golden Age of Comic Fandom* (1995). In 1998, he became Associate Editor of the magazine *Alter Ego*, a post he holds to the present day. His other fandom history books include *Sense of Wonder: A Life in Comic Fandom* (2000) and *Founders of Comic Fandom* (2010).

Schelly has written several biographies of film and comics artists, including movie clown Harry Langdon and comic book scribe Otto Binder. Schelly authored *Man of Rock*, a biography of Joe Kubert (2008). *The Art of Joe Kubert* (2011) and *Weird Horrors and Daring Adventures* (2012) followed, all three published by Fantagraphics, along with his biography *Harvey Kurtzman, The Man Who created Mad and Revolutionized Humor in America*, which won a Will Eisner Award in 2016 for Best Comics-Related Book.